LENTIL UNDERGROUND

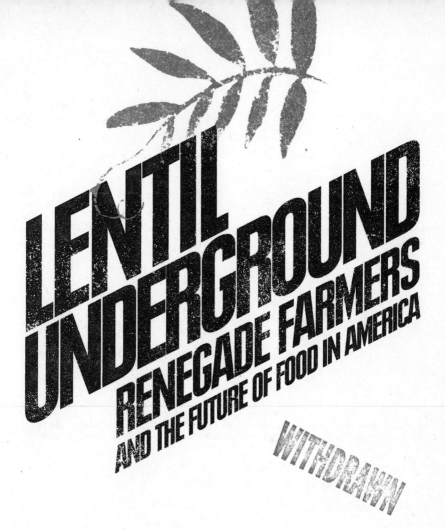

LENTIL UNDERGROUND

RENEGADE FARMERS
AND THE FUTURE OF FOOD IN AMERICA

LIZ CARLISLE

GOTHAM BOOKS

GOTHAM BOOKS

Published by the Penguin Group
Penguin Group (USA) LLC
375 Hudson Street
New York, New York 10014

USA | Canada | UK | Ireland | Australia | New Zealand | India | South Africa | China
penguin.com
A Penguin Random House Company

LIBRARY OF CONGRESS CATALOGING-IN-PUBLICATION DATA
Carlisle, Liz.
Lentil underground : renegade farmers and the future of food in America / Liz Carlisle.
pages cm
Includes bibliographical references.
ISBN 978-1-592-40920-4 (hardcover)
1. Agricultural ecology—United States. 2. Agricultural diversification—United States.
3. Agricultural development projects—United States. 4. Farms, Small—United States.
5. Farm corporations—United States. I. Title.
S589.7.C37 2015
631.5'70973—dc23
2014030229

Printed in the United States of America
1   3   5   7   9   10   8   6   4   2

Set in Clarion MT
Designed by Sabrina Bowers

It is possible that the next Buddha will not take the form of an individual. The next Buddha may take the form of a community, a community practicing understanding and loving kindness, a community practicing mindful living.

—THICH NHAT HANH

CONTENTS

IV

RIPE FOR REVOLUTION

V

HARVEST

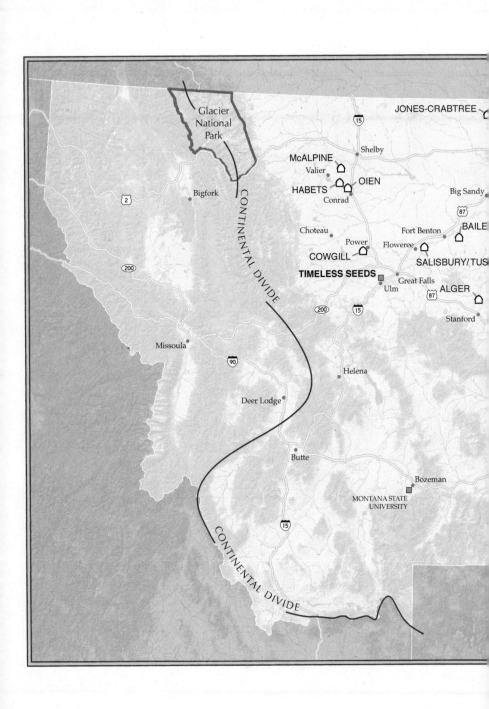

Havre

MANUEL

🛣 2

Malta • LITTLE ROCKIES
MEAT PACKING CO.

Bear Paw
Mountains

🛣 2

BARTA

O'HALLORAN/LOHMULLER

🛣 200

Lewistown

Snowy Mountains

Bull Mountains

SIKORSKI ⌂

🛣 87

Billings •

🛣 90

🛣 90

MONTANA
Places mentioned in *Lentil Underground*

⌂ farms   • towns

AUTHOR'S NOTE

In March of 2008, I filled up my Subaru at the cheapest gas station in Somerville, Massachusetts. Three dollars and twenty-two cents was more than I'd ever paid for a gallon of regular unleaded, even at the height of summer. But I'd scouted the marquees around town, and this was as low as I was going to get. The pump clicked off, and I stuffed the receipt into an envelope in the glove compartment without looking at the total. I knew I couldn't afford it. And gas prices didn't appear to be going down.

Four years into my career as a country singer, I was tired. Exhausted. At first, it had been thrilling to open for LeAnn Rimes and Travis Tritt, to record at Martina McBride's studio in Nashville, and to sing the national anthem at an NFL game. Born and raised in Montana, I'd grown up on country radio, and I loved weaving romantic agrarian lyrics into pretty melodies. When I'd graduated from college, with a new record to sell and a full schedule of shows for the summer, it had seemed like the greatest thing in the world to travel through rural America and tell its story. But now that I'd crisscrossed the country several times in my station wagon, I knew the sobering truth. I'd been lying.

As I listened to the people who came up to chat after my shows, it dawned on me that life in the heartland was not what I'd thought.

Farming had become a grueling industrial occupation, squeezed between the corporations that sold farmers their chemicals and the corporations that bought their grain. To my disappointment, I discovered that most American farmers weren't actually growing food but rather raw ingredients for big food processors. These multinational corporations dictated everything their growers did, from the seeds they planted to the expensive fertilizers and herbicides they needed to grow them. It was a losing game for the farmers, who kept sinking further into debt as their input costs rose and grain prices fell. But the arrangement was great for the corporations, which kept right on dealing chemicals to their captive suppliers of cheap corn, soy, and wheat. Flush with marketing dollars, Big Food was working hard to convince middle America that their folksy branded products were the protectors of the family farm and its wholesome values. I thought about the companies that sponsored my shows and felt a creeping wave of guilt. I'd bought into their phony story hook, line, and sinker—and I was propagating it.

The song I always sang to open my concerts talked about corn popping up in neat rows next to a peaceful river. But in fact, the fertilizer running off America's cornfields had so thoroughly choked the Mississippi watershed with nitrogen that farm towns were subsisting on bottled water, and the Gulf of Mexico was sporting a dead zone the size of Massachusetts. It wasn't as if the flood of fertilizer were helping farmers. All those fossil fuel–based chemicals were sending rural households into bankruptcy, just like gas prices were crushing me. As I drove away from the pump in Somerville, I realized it was time for me to tell the real story of farming, food, and rural America. Maybe I could even help to change it. So in the spring of 2008, I quit the music business. And I joined the lentil underground.

Strictly speaking, I didn't exactly know I was joining the lentil underground when I went to work for US senator Jon Tester in June of 2008. What I knew was that Jon was an organic farmer from a small town in my home state of Montana. He seemed to have some good ideas for fixing the problems with American agriculture, so that farmers could make a good living growing healthy food. And in the process, he was changing the face of national politics. By unseating a three-term Republican incumbent, Jon had handed senate Democrats a razor-thin majority—and a flat-topped populist poster child.

From my first week on the job as Tester's legislative correspondent for agriculture and natural resources, I started getting calls from his equally colorful fellow farmers. They surprised me with deeply considered, homegrown policy proposals, recalling an era of our democracy so distant that I'd long since dismissed it as mythological. Was I on the phone with Franklin? Jefferson? I might as well have been, given how seriously these farmers took their civic duty to tinker, diagram, and reason their way to a better polity. Although I was dubious that I could do anything to shepherd these farmers' unorthodox proposals to the floor of the Senate, I had to admit that my enthusiastic correspondents had some pretty good ideas. Of course, most establishment types thought Jon's buddies were crazy. Strange crops. Messy-looking fields. "Weed farmers," one prominent constituent told me. "They're a bunch of damn weed farmers."

But if these were weed farmers, I gathered, they were remarkably solvent ones. Unlike the other growers who called into the office, these organic farmers weren't complaining about grain prices, because they didn't sell to big corporations, and they were raising a lot more than just grain. They weren't complaining about the cost of chemicals either, because they didn't use them. They'd found a crop that could grow its own fertilizer: lentils.

I got so curious about these farmers and their miraculous lentils that I started calling *them,* peppering them with questions about all the crops in their rotations. But as quickly as I'd gotten excited, I found myself frustrated again. I thought I'd happened onto a simple, technical solution to the crisis in farm country. But instead, my farmer informants kept regaling me with meandering stories that dragged long into my lunch break before I finally cut them off with a polite "Thanks for sharing your thoughts." I was about to give up when one of the farmers leveled with me. "I know you folks out in DC are always looking for a quick fix, and I just want you to know that this isn't it," the farmer said. "But if you'd like to come out and visit, you're always welcome." I hung up the phone, grouchy. I was at work late again, vainly attempting to stay on top of the flood of e-mails about wolves, guns, and abortion. I knew the office wasn't about to send me on a junket to Montana to check out a field of lentils. I was mad at myself for my foolish idealism, mad at myself for wasting time on a dead end.

But as I lay in bed that night, I started thinking more seriously about the farmer's invitation. As he'd warned, this wouldn't be a quick fix. It would take a long time to really understand what these organic growers were up to. I would need to quit my job and focus on this project full-time, probably for several years. I had a lot to learn about ecology, economics, and the real history of the agrarian West—not just the version I'd absorbed from country radio. And yet, maybe it was worth it.

The next evening, I started researching graduate schools, looking for a place where I could get the training I needed and then conduct in-depth field research. It wasn't easy to find a doctoral program with the breadth I was looking for, since most departments focused their students on a highly specialized area of study. But the PhD at UC Berkeley's Geography Department seemed like a good fit. In June of 2009, after thirteen months in DC, I said good-bye to Jon Tester, promising that our next visit would be at his Montana farm. And in August, I moved to Northern California to register for my first semester of classes.

By the summer of 2011, I'd made it far enough into my formal studies to venture out to Montana to meet some farmers. I picked up my parents' station wagon in Missoula, then headed off for a part of the state I'd never been to before—the dry plains just east of the Rocky Mountains. There, in a sleepy little town named Conrad, I found the man I was looking for: Dave Oien.

Dave wasn't the first farmer I'd spoken to when I started working in the Tester office. In fact, I'm not sure I ever talked directly to him at all. But when I asked people to tell me who had convinced them to go organic, the answer always circled back to this little Conrad farm. On these 280 acres—his parents' homestead—Dave had done something truly radical. During the height of the 1980s farm crisis, he'd become the first in his county to plant organic lentils. Back then, Dave had been laughed off as a kook. But now he had more than a dozen other people growing for his small business, Timeless Seeds, which had gotten specialty lentils on the shelves at Whole Foods and on the menus of the nation's finest restaurants.

When I pulled in to the Oien place, I was greeted by an unassuming man in a faded plaid work shirt and jeans. He'd tucked his spectacled eyes under a too-big ball cap, which shaded his face from the sun but also gave the impression that his head was smaller than it was. Slumping a bit as he traversed his garden, the balding farmer curled his six-foot frame toward the landscape, refusing to stand out. He answered my questions politely and factually, as if he were a repairman explaining how he'd fixed my faucet. While Dave played the common yeoman, I settled into my own performance, inspecting his soil as though that was all I was interested in. As I had explained to Dave on the phone, I was here to conduct research for my dissertation about diversified farming systems on the northern Great Plains.

Dave and I talked through each other for several minutes, as I dutifully wrote down his list of crops and the soil amendments he was using. I didn't tell him that I'd been doing my homework on him and his lentils, and that this was more than just a short-term research project. I didn't mention any of the uncanny parallels in our stories. The fact that I was twenty-seven, the same age he'd been when he came back to this farm. The fact that I'd come here on the same road from Missoula that he'd traversed thirty-five years before. The fact that I, too, had been trying to save the world in faraway places before realizing that I needed to start at home. I didn't remind him that I was from Montana myself and that my "research vehicle" was my parents' car.

But of course, my journey had been far longer than the four-hour drive from my parents' house. I'd spent my entire adulthood combing through poetry, policy, and scholarship in search of an agrarian answer to the vexing problems of modern society. I'd consulted authorities of all stripes, from salt-of-the-earth sages in Nashville, to political gurus in Washington, to scientists and food activists in Berkeley. How could we feed the world without destroying it? After several years of searching, I knew there were important answers to this question that I couldn't find in a high-tech lab or a high-powered policy summit, or even in popular local food movements in San Francisco and New York. But those answers might be here in Conrad, if only I could get Dave to talk.

And then he smiled. Without moving his mouth, Dave vaulted his eyebrows into his forehead and opened his eyes so wide they nearly filled the yawning lenses of his glasses. He'd noticed the number four on the far left of my license plate, which every Montanan knows as the code for Missoula. "Did you know Joseph Brown?" he asked me.

Joseph Epes Brown was a legendary figure in my hometown, a professor of religious studies who'd passed away in 2000 after an illustrious but somewhat enigmatic career at the University of Montana. At age twenty-seven, he had traveled the West in an old truck, seeking Lakota elder Black Elk. When Brown finally found the elderly medicine man, in Nebraska, Black Elk was nearly blind, but he greeted his young visitor knowingly. "I've been expecting you," Black Elk told Brown, who would later publish an account of their conversations at the Lakota man's request.

Although I hadn't mentioned it to Dave, I'd read that account. And I knew he had too. One day in the Tester office, curious about this farmer that everyone kept mentioning to me, I'd started digging around for information about Dave and discovered that he had once been a student of Joseph Brown's at the University of Montana. In fact, if I had the dates right, it appeared Dave would've taken Brown's class right before returning to this homestead. As my mind raced to find an answer to Dave's question, my mouth settled for "Yes."

"C'mon in the house," Dave said. "And bring that notebook with you."

LENTIL UNDERGROUND

PROLOGUE

When the summer of 2012 finally scorched its way into the record books as the worst drought since the Dust Bowl, American farmers stopped praying for rain and started filing for insurance payments. Surveying the withered crop across the farm belt, analysts warned that climate change might seriously threaten the American food supply. Local forecasters watched in grim silence as the red zone of federally declared disaster areas swelled to cover 71 percent of the national map. Already squeezed by recession, households across the United States braced for skyrocketing food prices.

Meanwhile, outside a small Montana town on the Missouri River, two dozen vehicles converged on a 3,000-acre farm. Compact hybrids sporting lefty bumper stickers pulled up next to old pickups with gun racks, and PhD engineers enthusiastically greeted college dropouts. From as far north as the Canadian border and as far east as the Dakotas they rolled in, nonchalantly hauling coolers and potluck dishes as if this were just the neighborhood block party.

The occasion was the annual field tour for Timeless Seeds, an organization that, on the surface, appeared to be a modest small business. But what Timeless and its growers were doing out here on the northern plains was nothing short of revolutionary. They'd spent the past three decades quietly but systematically bucking big agriculture, sowing the seeds of a radically different food system. Now they were about to find out whether their experiment was working.

A bit nervous about hosting a field tour just four years into his organic transition, greenhorn Timeless grower Casey Bailey wasn't feeling particularly lucky on this Friday the thirteenth of July. The relentlessly hot weather had thoroughly baked the Baileys, who were scrambling to adjust their harvest calendars and praying their crops would come through. Casey was worried about the looming threat of hail, given the eerie humidity in the air. And as he approached his field of French Green lentils, with more than thirty guests in tow, Casey was embarrassed to discover that the one plant that appeared to love this heat was his "volunteer" stand of sunflowers. Nowhere to be seen on Casey's farm plan, the big yellow flowers had simply blown in from the surrounding area and seeded themselves. Now they were everywhere.

"This is my only field that's bad with weeds," Casey told the crowd staring down at him from a hay-covered wagon. Why did his weed problem have to be such a flamboyant one? Casey brooded. And why hadn't he come out here before the tour and thinned some of this out? Casey's fellow growers tried to put a more positive spin on the increasingly heterogeneous Bailey farm. "It's biodiverse," Doug Crabtree offered in a booming baritone, as his wife nodded. "We've got to stop apologizing," Anna Jones-Crabtree chimed in forcefully, extemporaneously suggesting a mantra: "Mother Nature doesn't monocrop." When Casey failed to look reassured by the Crabtrees' philosophical pronouncements, Timeless CEO David Oien patted his young grower on the back, winking. "You know," Oien said, with the carefree-but-earnest jocularity of a fifties sitcom, "it's not that dirty for an organic lentil crop."

Having farmed in a small Montana town his whole life, sixty-three-year-old Oien could sympathize with Casey's anxiety about planting something so different from what his neighbors were growing. Amber waves of grain were like a religion in this part of the West. Any other plant life was labeled a weed and taken as a sign of some deep character flaw, some profound failure. Here in central Montana, the measure of a man was in plain sight, and it was calculated in bushels per acre. The trouble with all that heroic grain, however, was that it was taking a lot of nutrients and water out of the soil, without giving anything back. Sometimes farmers got away with this rather amazing faith in their land's limitless productivity, and if wheat prices happened to be up, they could even turn a handsome profit. But not in a drought year. Mother Nature was calling foul.

The last time drought had struck the grain belt—in the 1980s—Oien had been a thirtysomething like Casey, worried about how to save his family farm in the face of bad weather and corporate consolidation in the food system. Most people thought the solution was bigger farms, bigger machinery, and more chemicals. That's what Secretary of Agriculture Earl Butz had told farmers like Oien's parents. Get big or get out. Modernize or perish. Watching as their community shrank and their friends died of cancer after too many years manning a spray rig, Orville and Gudrun Oien had begged their son to follow Butz's advice—the "get out" part. Armed with a college degree, Dave could've landed a good job in Seattle or Chicago. But he was too stubborn. He stayed put. He stayed small. And he planted lentils.

When Oien seeded the first organic lentil in his county, it was a radical act. For the past two generations, American farmers like him have had one job: grow more grain. In Iowa and Nebraska, that's corn. On the northern plains, farms specialize in either wheat or barley. All other life-forms stand aside so that farmers can grow one plant, year after year, aiming to fill the bin each August. Every twelve months, bursting seed heads pack the full sum of the farmer's human effort, modern technology, and natural endowments into the original form of stored wealth: grain.

Lentils do exactly the opposite. Instead of mining the soil for nutrients to fuel an impressive harvest, this Robin Hood of the dryland prairie gathers the abundant fertility of the aboveground world—of the air, in fact—and shares it freely beneath the earth's surface. Inside the plant's nodules, bacteria surreptitiously convert atmospheric nitrogen into a community nutrient supply. If wheat is the symbol of rugged individualism, then lentils embody that other agrarian hallmark too often overlooked in the Western mythos: community.

A cheap, healthy source of protein, lentils have been feeding the world since biblical times. They are drought resilient and don't need irrigation. They are also legumes, which means they can convert atmospheric nitrogen into fertilizer. This makes lentils an ideal crop to raise in rotation—since plants grown in the same field the next year can benefit from the boost of leftover fertility. In fact, if farmers grow them as part of a diverse sequence of crops that keep weed pressure at bay, they don't need to use chemicals at all. The plants themselves take care of the functions formerly performed by expensive industrial inputs—just like natural plant communities do in the wilderness.

To young David Oien, it had all seemed so obvious. If family farm agriculture was going to survive, if people were going to take care of the planet and still produce sufficient food, if there was still some sense to be made out of life in rural America—

surely this was the way to do it. But to everyone else in his county, particularly Oien's banker, lentils were anything but obvious. How would he sell them? How would he harvest them? And for that matter, how did he even know they would grow? No one had done this here before, and the agricultural experts at Montana State University were skeptical. Bombarded with dozens of such questions—and dirty looks from his weed-phobic neighbors— Oien realized he was trying to change something much bigger than his parents' 280-acre homestead. He could save his farm, but not alone. To stand up against the entrenched power of the food system's 1 percent, he would need to convince hundreds of other farmers to take the biggest risk of their lives.

A world away from the hippie communes of California and the organic food co-ops of liberal cities, Oien and his nonprofit allies started their sustainable agriculture movement modestly. They set up a series of field trials on their farms, to prove that lentils could grow on the dry northern plains. They built a network of more than 120 Farm Improvement Clubs, to learn how to do it better. Eventually, they crowd-funded a processing plant, passed legislation to make organic certification legal in Montana, and jerry-rigged equipment to clean, plant, and harvest their tiny seeds. But as Oien's wife reminded him, the heady lentil revolutionaries still had to pay their bills. Having built an underground, they needed to set up a front operation.

In 1987, Oien and three of his friends formed a company, Timeless Seeds, to process and market their organic legumes. They started small, peddling fifty-pound bags to whatever farmer friends happened by the Oiens' Quonset hut. Then, in 1994, they diversified into the food market, with a French Green lentil contract for Trader Joe's. Although short-lived, the Trader Joe's contract spurred Dave and his friends to purchase a bona fide processing facility, and within five years, they'd rolled out a full retail line and started working with gourmet restaurants. By 2012, Timeless Seeds had matured into a million-dollar business, and one of its growers was a US senator.

But now that drought had struck again, Timeless and its farmers faced a moment of truth. Oien had won over foodies in the Bay Area and New York with the story of his resilient crop, which was now being touted by renowned chefs. He'd even convinced some die-hard locavores that Montana lentils were a greener choice than conventionally fertilized local produce, given the environmental impacts and shocking greenhouse gas footprint of synthetic nitrogen. It all made sense in theory. Now that theory was about to be tested.

Dismounting from their perch on Casey Bailey's hay wagon, his fellow growers inspected the young man's rapidly drying French Green lentils. Fingering the crackly seedpods, the methodical farmers debated when Casey should pick them up with his combine. Too soon, and he would have a premature crop. But too late, and his lentils would dry up and fall off the stalk—or succumb to the ever-present possibility of a hailstorm. Picturing their own lentils baking in the blistering sun, the stoic farmers sounded the faintest notes of apprehension. They all had several thousand dollars' worth of crops sitting in their parched fields, and they were still a couple of weeks away from squirreling them safely away in their bins. They knew lentils were supposed to be relatively drought resilient, but they couldn't help worrying. Would they make it to harvest?

FERTILE
GROUND

1

HOMECOMING

Overshadowed by the peaks of Glacier National Park, which tower Alps-like on its western horizon, the small farming town of Conrad, Montana, doesn't particularly stand out. Much the opposite, in fact. It's almost as if this modest community on central Montana's dryland plains wants you to know it's not jealous of its ostentatious neighbor. Instead of competing with Glacier's charismatic wilderness, Conrad presents itself as primly unremarkable. Numbered streets hem manicured lawns and uniform rows of wheat and barley into a neat grid, keeping each creature in its place.

Ever since the first homesteaders arrived in Conrad at the dawn of the twentieth century, this tight-knit community on the Rocky Mountain Front has tenaciously maintained the boundary between wilderness and civilization. The mountains of Glacier National Park mark the wild side, where people incur hefty fines for so much as moving a single stone. The windswept agricultural prairie is the controlled side. When people here speak of well-managed farms as "clean," you have the sense that they would be much happier if they could raise wheat in brushed aluminum or stainless steel—anything but the indiscriminately fecund medium of soil.

Engaged in perennial battle with weeds and pests, Conrad's

farmers find themselves stationed at the great divide, not just between the two halves of North America, but between nature and agriculture. Traditionally, that divide has been cast as a bitter conflict, a zero-sum game that pits pristine wilderness against rural livelihoods. Academics refer to this great divide as the "land-sparing" strategy: Places like Glacier are set aside to spare land for nature, supposedly taking people entirely out of the ecological equation. Meanwhile, in places like Conrad, farmers attempt near-total control over uniform fields of grain in order to "feed the world," supposedly taking *nature* completely out of the equation. Across most of middle America, for most of the twentieth century, the conventional wisdom was that this neat partition was the best way to grow enough food to feed humanity without destroying the environment.

Although Conrad was never among the American heartland's most productive communities, the land-sparing strategy seemed to be effective here. When the little farm town's first generation of settlers arrived, during the homestead rush of 1904–18, early researchers at the Montana Agricultural Experiment Station encouraged them to plant a variety of drought-tolerant crops and further diversify their farms with livestock. But railroad baron James Hill had a different idea. In 1909, Hill hosted a Dry Farming Congress to convince farmers that it would be more efficient if they dedicated as much of their land as possible to the crop he happened to be in the business of shipping: wheat. At first, Hill's advice seemed prudent. When farmers plowed up the native prairie and planted wheat, they were able to grow enough food to support their families and earn a good living too. True, a severe drought in 1917 devastated the crop, and 2 million acres ceased production. The Dust Bowl and the Depression sent 11,000 farmers packing and crashed half of Montana's banks. But as modern farming developed, the homesteaders' children regained their confidence, placing their faith in science. They learned to apply synthetic nitrogen fertilizers to increase their yields, and when the herbicide 2,4-D came along in the 1950s, it was a revelation. One pass on the spray rig, and the weeds went away. Liberated from the drudgery of the cultivating tractor, farm families could imagine taking the weekend off and heading up to the lake, or going on vacation in Glacier.

To Conrad's stoic, largely Protestant inhabitants, these mid-century agricultural advances seemed like the work of divine providence, a reward for their pious efforts. It became customary, when passing by a tidy, productive farm, to remark that a good family must live there. Having been blessed with 2,4-D and ammonium nitrate, postwar Conrad appeared to be teeming with such upstanding citizens. In 1950, 70 percent of all the food Montanans ate was grown in state.

But in the early 1980s, as Conrad's second generation of farmers prepared to hand off their homesteads to their own progeny, signs of trouble emerged. Their fields *looked* good, at least early in the season, but the "For Sale" signs popping up amid Conrad's grain were proving a more serious menace than any weed. Behind every bankruptcy was the heartbreaking story of a good farmer undercut by drought or rising fertilizer costs or poor commodity prices. Since they weren't in charge of the markets or the weather, Conrad's farmers tried even harder to control what they could—spraying more herbicides, cultivating more acres. But instead of solving their problems, these efforts just sunk the desperate farmers further into debt. By 1983, US farm foreclosures would reach their highest levels since the Depression. Once again, 2 million acres of Montana farmland went out of production.

Conrad's grain farmers were experiencing the "cost-price

squeeze," one of several problems with industrial agriculture that gradually became apparent over the course of the 1980s. Farmers were paying so much for the sophisticated machinery and chemicals that made their extraordinary sixty-bushel grain possible that they couldn't afford a dry year or a depressed commodity market—the margins were too tight. Meanwhile, the American heartland wasn't just losing people; it was also losing topsoil, at the rate of 3 billion tons a year. Intensive industrial farming methods left soil vulnerable to erosion and severely taxed the fertility of what was left, making it ever more challenging for farmers to keep up. In 1981, Montana watched more soil blow away than any other state in the union. To add insult to injury, the very inputs that were causing problems for Conrad's farms were also causing serious problems for human health and the environment: groundwater pollution, marine dead zones—and alarmingly high rates of cancer. As soil and farm chemicals ran off into the watershed and new superweeds appeared in herbicide-treated fields, Conrad's neat partition between nature and agriculture was thrown into question. Not even Glacier was immune. Climate change, fueled in no small part by the industrial food system, was melting the national park's namesake ice shelves, which were forecast to thaw completely as early as 2030.

For local farmers Orville and Gudrun Oien, Conrad's problems came as a cruel, almost vindictive surprise. Born and raised on nearby homesteads, just ten days and a mile apart, Orville and Gudrun had spent their entire lives with their hands in north-central Montana earth, mixing their labor, as John Locke would say, with the soil. Since buying their own place in 1939, at the tender age of twenty-seven, the Oiens had scrupulously followed federal farm programs and state extension bulletins. They'd planted recommended varieties of grain. They'd applied recommended chemicals. And to supplement the proceeds from their harvest, the industrious pair had managed a small dairy, supplying the Conrad Creamery with fresh milk. With nothing more than this modest 280-acre homestead and their own hard work, the Oiens had raised four children, sent three of them to college, and nearly paid off the farm note. But now, just as they prepared to pass the place on to their kids, all the rules were changing.

It was the summer of 1976, and twenty-seven-year-old David Oien was going back to the land. While his shoulder-length hair meandered out the window toward the Rocky Mountains, the grad school dropout imagined growing his own food, making his own energy, and living in sync with nature. He had read enough about change. He wanted to build it.

Dave's brown Plymouth Savoy was loaded down with the new ideas he had acquired over the past eight years. There were radical political magazines he'd picked up at the University of Chicago, where he had arrived as a wide-eyed college freshman in 1968. On top of those was a copy of *Black Elk Speaks,* the teachings of a Lakota holy man, which Dave had taken to heart when he transferred to the University of Montana to study philosophy and religion. And on top of that was Dave's own vision: the plans he had drawn up for a solar energy collector. Armed with big dreams and some basic carpentry skills, he was ready to transform the world.

Dave wasn't just following some abstract notion of "returning to the land." He was coming home to his family's 280-acre farm— two and a half miles northwest of the Conrad city limits. Like Dave, Conrad had undergone rapid change during the turbulent

1960s and 1970s, and it was barreling headlong into a radically new world. But the future for which Conrad was headed wasn't exactly what Dave and the counterculture had in mind.

When Dave was young, the Oien place still retained some of the trappings of a small, diversified homestead. Commodity grain had been the main event, to be sure, and yet, chickens and carrots and flowers kept the place feeling like home. But in the years since he'd left, Dave's father had followed the dictum of Earl Butz, Richard Nixon's secretary of agriculture, planting "fencerow to fencerow." The Oien place was now one solid stand of malt barley, supported by federal farm programs and controlled with fossil fuel–based chemicals. As Dave tried to envision the place he was returning to, the pile of books in his passenger seat toppled over, depositing Rachel Carson's shocking exposé about chemical pesticides in his lap. Dave knew his dad was using pesticides. He worried that the pond behind his parents' house might have become a version of Carson's *Silent Spring*.

Compared to harrowing Christmastime slogs through snow and ice, the summer season drive to Conrad was a breeze. From the university town of Missoula, Dave could get home in a steady four hours, in just three basic steps: east on Montana 200, up and over Rogers Pass, north on I-15. As the graduate school dropout watched his brief academic life vanish in his rearview mirror, he tried to make sense of his journey. Was he going back or forward?

In Dave's experience, there were two options available to Montana farm kids: come back and inherit the home place or leave for a job in a faraway city. Dave had no interest in taking over his dad's malt barley operation and zero experience with chemical farming. He'd learned nothing about herbicide application or commodity payments, and he didn't want to.

So when he'd graduated from high school in 1968, Dave had gone to the University of Chicago. The farm boy's crash course in urban youth culture had introduced him to a new phrase: "military-industrial complex." Paging through the alternative magazines that were circulating on campus, Dave had put his disenchantment with Conrad in the context of a larger problem. Corporate control—something his hometown Farmers Union chapter was always up in arms about—seemed to be at the root of both the raging Vietnam War and the new chemical-intensive agribusiness. In both cases, wealthy big shots were profiting from death and destruction. To Dave's amazement, the kids in Chicago were dreaming up ways to fight this power. They'd even organized a revolutionary movement: the Weather Underground.

Although Dave had been inspired by his adventure in Chicago, he'd tired of overly cerebral debates and longed to get his hands back in the dirt. For his junior year, he'd transferred to the University of Montana in Missoula, where Rachel Carson and Black Elk had gotten him a little closer to what he was looking for. But Dave was still itching to *do* something. So when he started graduate school at UM in the fall of 1975, the ecological philosophy student ended up spending most of his time engrossed in the handbook from his night-school class: Scott Sproull's alternative energy workshop.

Sproull, a breezy twenty-two-year-old who had learned about methane digesters while working as the night caretaker for the local sewage treatment plant, was just the teacher Dave had been looking for. Devouring Sproull's DIY diagrams and quirky Buckminster Fuller quotes, Dave started to formulate a plan. His final assignment was to build a solar collector and install it somewhere.

His classmates had already started asking around Missoula, look-ing for a sympathetic homeowner who might lend them a roof. But Dave knew just where his collector was headed. Eight years after leaving Conrad, Dave was going home. Unbeknownst to Gudrun and Orville Oien, their farmhouse was about to get one heck of a retrofit.

The Oiens hugged their son, at once happy to see him and con-cerned about how their most free-spirited child would make a life here in Conrad. Even shrewd Orville, a self-trained certified pub-lic accountant who had followed federal commodity program in-centives to a tee, couldn't pencil out a way to make a viable living from this farm anymore. It was too small. The economics of mod-ern agribusiness depended on a massive scale of production, which seemed to be the only way to afford the expensive package of machinery and chemicals necessary to grow the new high-yielding grain varieties. "Get big or get out," Secretary of Agricul-ture Earl Butz had proclaimed. Orville didn't remember anything in that speech about solar collectors.

But instead of worrying about balance sheets and fertilizer prices, Dave was coaxing his sixty-four-year-old father on top of the house, hammer and DIY zine in hand. What the younger Oien had in mind was an extension of the north roof. The addition would create a reflective shed, large enough to accommodate the solar water-heating system he had dreamed up. Orville couldn't argue with the cost savings of the new outfit—250 to 300 dollars a year in fuel oil plus 75 to 100 dollars a year in domestic water heat-ing. So he grabbed some nails and joined his harebrained son.

Day after scorching day, Dave and Orville hammered away,

arousing the curiosity of their neighbors. They built ninety-six square feet of liquid collectors, then installed a battery of 120-gallon water tanks in the basement. Silently sweating through their long-sleeved work shirts, the two men remembered a happy moment they had both let slip out of their memories long ago: Orville making rounds on the tractor while six-year-old Dave sat on his lap, staring up at the hawks.

Working alongside his dad in the blistering sun, Dave could touch all the pieces of his world. Chicago-style community organizing. The wisdom of elders Black Elk, Rachel Carson, and Orville Oien. The satisfaction of literally taking matters into his own hands. Dave had spent the past eight years caught between utopias that needed each other, utopias that kept moving farther apart in their pursuit of a perfect future. For the first time, he could imagine them coming together.

2
AGAINST THE GRAIN

When the Oien family's solar retrofit was completed in 1977, it was the first of its kind in north-central Montana. But it was not the last. Dave lost no time climbing atop his neighbors' roofs, hammer and gospel in hand. He stopped referring to his hometown as Conrad and instead embraced its new identity as "Sun City," energetically assisting a number of solar conversions on the grittier side of the railroad tracks. In 1981, the same year Ronald Reagan took Jimmy Carter's solar panels off the White House, Dave was heralding the arrival of a new renewable energy store in Sun City's downtown. He converted not only the Presbyterian church, but also its pastor, who added 125 square feet of active solar air collectors to his own home. "Ordinary citizens are beginning to generate their own power," Dave wrote boldly in the pages of a nonprofit newsletter, betting 100 dollars against the completion of the Montana Power Company's proposed coal plant. "Small scale hydro and wind electric systems are sprouting up across the country . . . we're at a point in history where we can make a difference, and we'd better do it."

But back on the Oien farm, Dave had to admit, he was still relying on a lot of dirty energy. The farm*house* had shrunk its footprint, but the farm itself was driven by petrochemicals. It was oil that made the fertilizers, oil that made the herbicides, and oil that powered the tractor. If we can have a solar-powered house, Dave said to his dad, why can't we have a solar-powered farm?

Orville had been afraid it might come to that.

It wasn't a good time to experiment with risky new ways of farming, the scrupulous accountant told his son. Margins on a small farm were razor-thin these days, and the Oiens were barely making it as it was. What had kept the operation afloat (and paid for college, Orville gently reminded Dave) was the security of the federal farm program. Uncle Sam paid the Oiens to raise improved barley varieties that required chemical fertilizers and herbicides, like synthetic nitrogen and 2,4-D. The size of that government check was based on the number of acres Orville enrolled and planted as barley ground—his "base acres." If he ripped out the malt barley and seeded something else, Orville explained, he would sacrifice those precious base acres, gambling his livelihood on the whims of both nature and markets. What would the family fall back on if the "solar farm" got hailed out or couldn't sell its crop?

For Dave's dad, sticking with neat rows of high-yielding cereals was about more than just economics. Orville's reputation for tidy fields and sound decisions had been hard-won, earned with decades of stoic labor. The prospect of losing that community respect was almost as distressing to Dave's father as losing the farm. In a small community like Conrad, it didn't make sense to step too far out of line.

Dave didn't care what the neighbors thought. But the philosophy and religious studies major couldn't support himself—let alone his parents—with the modest wages from his summer construction job. So he made a compromise with his dad. The base acres would stay in wheat and barley. But the remaining 15 percent of the property would be reserved for Dave's "oddball" crops. Starting with those two fields, Dave vowed to reorient the farm from oil to sunshine. Slowly but surely, he was determined to cut against the grain.

BROWN GOLD

Dave's idea was to convert the Oiens' fossil fuel–based grain monoculture into a self-supporting diversified farm that ran on manure. Cow manure was a "solar" energy source, because it was the sun that grew the forage crops that fed the cattle. In principle, at least, this solar-powered manure was free, and it could replace the chemical inputs that not only offended Dave's environmental sensibilities, but also got more expensive every time OPEC called an embargo. Manure could replace synthetic fertilizer. Manure—with the help of a methane digester and alcohol fuel still—could replace synthetic fuel. And the combination of cattle and crop diversity could eliminate the need for chemical herbicides. The animals would happily eat most weeds, but unwanted vegetation would have a tough time finding a niche anyway, given the lively mix of plants Dave envisioned.

Dave started by seeding something his dad was familiar with—alfalfa. That was the crop Orville had raised to feed to his own cattle, back when Dave was a kid. In addition to supplying hay, alfalfa also happened to be a good plant to rotate with barley, since it replenished the soil with the very nutrient cereal grains depleted: nitrogen. Maybe they wouldn't need to use so much nitrogen fertilizer if they brought alfalfa back into the rotation, Dave wondered aloud. We'll see, said his straight-faced Norwegian father.

Meanwhile, Orville helped his son construct an "integrated energy system" to convert cow dung into heat and fuel. Supported by a grant from the Montana Department of Natural Resources and Conservation, the Oiens built an 80,000-gallon methane digester, to turn manure into biogas. The idea was that this biogas would heat an alcohol fuel still, which would convert the farm's grain waste into fuel for their trucks and tractors. To capture the heat and carbon dioxide from the alcohol process, the Oiens built a passive solar greenhouse, where they figured they could grow tomatoes and cucumbers for themselves and a few local customers. To further close the loop of the farm's energy system, Dave planned to fertilize his produce with the methane digester's by-product: a crude form of compost.

What Dave was trying to create with all these intersecting projects was central Montana's version of something he had been reading about in the pages of *Mother Jones* and the *Whole Earth Catalog:* an organic farm. In places like California and Oregon, hippies had started planting vegetables on rural communes and in urban community gardens. Some of them had started marketing their produce to kindred spirits, dubbing their products "organic." The principles of this agricultural approach were simple. Organic farms worked with natural processes to grow their food, rather than relying on the off-the-shelf inputs that had become synonymous with modern industrial farming. Organic growers focused less on the size of their crop and more on the health of their soil. They farmed down, rather than up. For children of the sixties like Dave, it was an intuitive concept: ask not what your soil can do for you, but what you can do for your soil.

Of course, Conrad was a world away from those hippie communes, in more ways than one. Dave was 700 miles from the nearest major population center, farming dryland soils in a harsh climate. He couldn't very well start a vegetable truck farm. So instead of copying the systems he'd read about in the magazines, Dave started with the same basic principles and tried to figure out what a Montana organic operation might look like. Working with nature to build his closed-loop solar farm, Dave was finally getting to the question his dad kept pushing him to answer. What would he sell?

THE LAST HURRAH

In 1982, Dave delivered his first package of organic beef to the food cooperative in Bozeman, a college town located half a day's drive south of Conrad in Montana's Gallatin Valley. Officially, there wasn't any such thing as organic beef. The few certifying organizations that had sprouted up—California Certified Organic Farmers (CCOF), Oregon Tilth, Farm Verified Organic—were focused on plants, given that many of their hippie customers were vegetarians anyway. Nobody had bothered to define what organic meant in the context of animals.

But Dave was delighted to explain to his customers how his agricultural system fit the model of organics, and it seemed that in Montana, even hippies ate meat. The Bozeman Community Food Co-op agreed to stock Dave's beef, under his curious brand name, the Last Hurrah. Perhaps Dave was secretly hoping this venture would herald the last hurrah for his dad's malt barley, which he was itching to tear out completely. Or the last hurrah for conventional agriculture and the military-industrial complex. But as it turned out, it was the last hurrah for Dave's organic beef.

In order to slaughter his cattle, Dave had to take them to the

USDA-inspected plant in Choteau, Montana, an hour southwest of his farm. When Dave notified the inspector how he wanted to label the package, he was told it was illegal. The USDA approved only certain language, Dave was informed, and "organic" wasn't allowed. Dave couldn't sell the beef unless he had the USDA stamp. And if he had the USDA stamp, he couldn't have the organic label.

Within a couple of years, the USDA rule was a moot point. The packing plant burned down and was never rebuilt, given that the meat industry was rapidly consolidating. "I guess it turned out to be more like the first hurrah," Dave joked, mocking the naïveté of his initial stab at a Montana organic farm. Building his soil and his agricultural system had been a good start, he realized, but he had been mistaken to think he could be entirely self-sustaining. The closed loop of the "solar farm" would have to be a lot bigger than Dave had originally imagined. If he was serious about creating an alternative to fossil fuel agribusiness, he needed to build a supportive community.

WE'LL HAVE TO DO IT OURSELVES

Dave had stayed in touch with the people who'd been involved in the alternative energy workshops he'd taken in Missoula back in the midseventies, when he'd been flirting with grad school. Many of them—including the workshop's teacher, Scott Sproull—were now members of a nonprofit citizens' group called the Alternative Energy Resources Organization. Dave had joined the AERO Board in 1979, and he'd been more active since the early 1980s, when the group's headquarters had relocated to an old brick building just 150 miles south of Conrad in the state capital of Helena. By that time, Dave wasn't the only AERO member who'd branched out from solar energy to solar farming. A number of the folks he saw at meetings had made the same leap, and they found themselves commiserating about similar frustrations. As it became apparent that AERO was now the meeting ground for Montana's nascent organic farming movement, the group hatched the idea of forming an agriculture-focused task force. The ragtag ensemble of organic farmers held their first get-together in November 1983, midway between Conrad and Helena in the blue-collar town of Great Falls.

AERO's Ag Task Force was a scruffy bunch. These rugged individualists weren't used to serving on committees. But in the course of their valiant struggles to buck the system and become self-sufficient, they had each run up against obstacles they couldn't get around on their own. For Dave it had been the labeling fiasco. For his buddy Jim Barngrover, it was the challenge of finding land, since nobody wanted to lease to a "weed farmer." Several other task force members had another gripe. Their extension agents couldn't give them any advice on biological pest control, so they just kept telling them which chemicals they should spray. It was difficult to get seed, difficult to find markets, difficult to do just about everything.

What brought these people together, however, wasn't their immediate experience of hardship. If all the struggling Montana farmers of the mideighties had been coming to meetings, the task force would have needed to hold them in a football stadium. What set the Ag Task Force apart was their hunch that their problems weren't just about weeds or drought or grain prices. The 1980s weren't a temporary crisis, as the agricultural press had labeled them. Rather, the problems popping up in Montana's farm fields were endemic to Earl Butz's "get big or get out" agriculture. Dave and his comrades saw an opportunity—and an imperative—to change the paradigm.

The task force started a small newsletter, the *Ag Rag,* and began planning the state's first major conference on "sustainable" agriculture. If they could show their extension agents and university researchers that this was a legitimate field of study, that it was of interest to more than just a handful of farmers, maybe they could get some traction. Dave and his buddies purposely scheduled their conference at the state's ag university in Bozeman. Now the experts would have to listen.

By all accounts, the 1984 AERO Sustainable Agriculture Conference was a remarkable success. Two hundred and forty people showed up, from Montana, Wyoming, Idaho, Washington, the Dakotas, and several provinces in Canada. The dean of Montana State University's College of Agriculture accepted AERO's invitation to offer some remarks, and he stuck around to observe the proceedings, bringing several professors and extension agents with him. What they heard was a bracing challenge to traditional research and development.

The keynote speaker for the conference was none other than the leading scholar of agroecology, entomologist Miguel Altieri of the University of California, Berkeley. Altieri had worked with inventive smallholders from up and down the Americas, whose low-input farms mimicked natural systems. The key to such farms, Altieri explained, was to plant a diverse mix of crops that had complementary ecological benefits. In Latin America, for example, farmers used an intercrop of corn, beans, and squash. The beans supplied nitrogen to the soil to feed the corn, so there was no need for chemical fertilizer. In some cases, Altieri went on, people seeded nitrogen-fixing plants and didn't harvest them at all, but tilled them into the soil. This way, he explained, they could fertilize next year's grain crop without using either chemicals *or* animal waste. Planting a fertilizer crop even had a name. Altieri called it a *green* manure.

Eager to see such an approach applied at their own state university, the farmer-organizers of the 1984 conference began bimonthly meetings with Montana State University officials to explore the potential for science and extension relevant to agroecological farming. The answer they got was frustrating. At the beginning of every meeting, the college officials would give the farmers a list of the programs MSU offered that they considered sustainable. But they wouldn't budge on the idea of nitrogen-fixing green manure crops. That was all well and good for Latin America, the academics said, but it wouldn't work in Montana. The seasons were too short and the rain was too scarce. Farmers here should save their limited soil moisture and growing days for their cash crop.

The Ag Task Force members kept going to meetings, but after getting the same answers over and over, they began to lose patience. They planned another conference in early 1987, again drawing more than 200 people. If they could self-organize so effectively, the increasingly brazen farmers started to reckon, they might not need MSU's help after all. When the university representatives presented their standard list of "sustainable" programs one too many times, Dave's buddy Gene May finally laid down the gauntlet. "You know, if you're not going to do what we need you to do," the defiant farmer said, "then we're going to do it ourselves."

GREEN MANURE

Dave Oien was no agronomist, but he had farmed all his life and pored over all the ecological theory he could get his hands on. MSU's flat denials didn't make sense to him. Of course Montana's organic farmers weren't going to use the same plants that Altieri was working with in Berkeley or Mexico. They weren't that simple-minded. But if agroecologists had seen the green manure strategy successfully repeated in ecosystem after ecosystem, there had to be some creature capable of playing that ecological role here in Montana, a biological fertilizer that could survive the harsh, semi-arid climate.

To be a candidate for a green manure crop, a plant had to be able to fix nitrogen. That is, it needed to be able to pull nitrogen out of the air (where it makes up 78 percent of the atmosphere) and pump it into the soil through its roots. Altieri had explained how that worked. Green manure crops hosted symbiotic bacteria in their root systems, and these bacteria could convert atmospheric nitrogen into a form that was usable by plants. This was a similar form of nitrogen, in fact, to the one that farmers were paying for when they bought a bag of fertilizer from their chemical dealer. How about getting it from a plant instead?

This family of fertility-boosting plants—legumes—included several types of beans, forages, and dried peas. Midwestern farmers were already using one of them, soybeans, in rotation with corn. In fact, Dave realized, he had one of these plants growing on his own place. Alfalfa, which he had been raising for cattle feed, was a legume. That was why it had been such a good complement to barley—it reloaded the soil with nitrogen. And a couple of years earlier, Dave recalled, he had hosted another legume on his "odd-ball acres": fava beans. He'd used those for feed too, since they were high in protein. Instead of thinking of these plants as a nutrient source for his cattle, Dave started to see green manures as a means of fertilizing his soil directly, without using livestock as middlemen. He didn't need to go to a USDA-inspected plant to package his beans, so presumably, there would be no problem declaring them organic.

Dave's newly leguminous lens on the world extended beyond the farm. He found himself trolling roadside ditches, looking for drought-hardy plants that could feed his soil. If Dave couldn't identify a legume based on its resemblance to something familiar like alfalfa or fava beans, he dug it up. The telltale sign of nitrogen-fixing plants, as Miguel Altieri had demonstrated, was under-ground. This was where the legumes' symbiotic bacteria lived: in bulbous white nodules at the tips of their roots. Sure enough, Dave discovered with no small satisfaction, there *were* plants growing their own nitrogen here in central Montana, without any irrigation or encouragement from MSU. The "borrow pits" at the edge of the road (so named because the highway department had "borrowed" the soil when digging the roadside ditches) were full of them: milk vetch, purple vetch, yellow blossom sweet clover. They were everywhere. In fact, some of these legumes were already being intentionally planted—the sweet clover was a regular component of pasture mixes.

But Dave wasn't the only one scouting for nodules in the borrow pits. There was another legume renegade on the prowl. A college man. And he thought he'd found the answer.

II

SEEDS OF CHANGE

NEW PLANTS ON THE PRAIRIE

3

MIRACLE PLANT

"Imagine a plant that could eliminate the use of commercial nitrogen fertilizer on millions of cultivated acres," hinted the fall 1984 issue of the *Sun Times,* the Alternative Energy Resources Organization's newsletter. "Imagine a plant that would reduce wind and water erosion on otherwise bare land, and that would help control saline seep. Imagine a plant that would increase soil organic matter, grow like a weed, reseed itself year after year, and dovetail perfectly with the crop-fallow system of farming so evident across the northern Great Plains. In short, imagine a plant that could open the door to a more sustainable agriculture for thousands of farms in the United States and Canada. Sound too good to be true? A futuristic 'miracle plant' of genetic engineering? Hardly. In fact, you probably can find it in your back yard."

"If you can't find it in your own yard, ask your county extension agent," *Sun Times* columnist Dave Oien added cheekily. "He or she will lead you to the Courthouse lawn, where the plant no doubt grows with a vengeance. Just don't mention you're looking for seed. With the possible exception of dandelions, this plant is probably the biggest lawn weed problem in the state."

Dave's miracle plant—black medic—was the semisecret variety trial darling of a rogue agronomist at Montana State University, Jim Sims. While the Ag Task Force was still struggling to make headway with Sims's colleagues, Dave had run into Sims at an experiment station field day. A PhD talking about legumes? Dave marveled. He started pumping his new acquaintance for more details about his research.

Black medic was a relative of alfalfa that was already growing wild in Montana, Jim explained, pulling a handful of textured black seedpods out of his pocket to show Dave. Most farmers had never heard of "medics," Jim continued, because this hardy class of plants was used primarily by Australian ranchers: as a forage crop for livestock. In dry southern Australia, an environment not unlike Montana, ranchers had found that leguminous medics increased the number of livestock they could support on a given pasture. And then they'd had an idea. Since medics seemed to have such a salutary effect, why not follow a few years of medic pasture with a grain crop? Impressed by the Australians' idea, Jim had begun experimenting with some of their medics in his test plots at MSU, to see how much they could increase the fertility of the soil. But to Jim's surprise, all the medics he planted on the research farm were beat out by one he happened to see growing along its edges: *black* medic. This plant, Jim reported, could fix forty to fifty pounds of nitrogen in a growing season, boosting the following year's wheat yields by a whopping 92 percent. And contrary to naysayers' customary objection to green manures, it wasn't a water hog. The hardy legume's shallow roots drew moisture from only the top two feet of the soil surface. Ninety percent of its water needs could be replenished by winter precipitation, so the soil would be ready for grain the next year.

Black medic, it seemed, was the perfect Montana-adapted fertilizer crop. But unfortunately, although farmers hadn't heard of it, their wives recognized it instantly: as the taprooty weed they were forever battling in their yards. Hands on their hips, the female witnesses to Jim Sims's field day performance told him his miracle plant was just plain old trefoil or "black clover." They had enough weed problems as it was, the incredulous farm women protested. They didn't need to go planting them *intentionally*. What was a university man doing, spending taxpayer dollars on such a crackpot scheme?

LEGUME COWBOY

From the second he opened his mouth, it was clear that Dr. James Sims wasn't the typical Montana State University researcher. Raised on a ranch in New Mexico, Jim drew more on the school of hard knocks than on his PhD—and more on field trials than on the tiny plots at the MSU experiment station.

Jim had become intimately familiar with the vicissitudes of Montana, having crisscrossed the state multiple times since moving to Bozeman in 1966. While he was still a graduate student at UC Riverside, the budding soil chemist had been recruited by Montana State to teach the farmers of the northern plains how to apply industrial fertilizers, which was still a relatively new practice. The young professor had been dispatched to the far corners of Big Sky Country to spread the good news of better living through chemistry.

Jim enjoyed the work, but he was convinced there had to be a better way than synthetic nutrients. As a graduate student, he had traveled to Egypt, where his PhD adviser, Dr. Frank T. Bingham, was collaborating with local researchers who worked with legumes. Interested in learning more about nitrogen-fixing plants, Jim had stayed in touch with Bingham, who had managed to find him a grant to attend the World Congress of Soil Science in Adelaide, Australia, in 1968. "That trip," Jim recalled, "converted me to biological systems."

Instead of playing the part of the studious assistant professor, Jim had donned his cowboy hat and talked rancher with the dignitaries in attendance. Most of the legislators and researchers at the congress had their own "stations" (the Aussie term for a diversified livestock and crop operation), and the charming American had managed to score himself a handful of invitations. What he'd witnessed had completely shifted his thinking about how to boost soil fertility back in Montana.

The Australians were using a more efficient strategy than the chemical approach, Jim discovered. After twenty years of experimenting with medics and clovers, the Aussies had developed a system called "ley" (temporary pasture) farming. Under this form of management, legumes were used as both fertilizer and livestock forage, so the soil was continuously regenerated by the agricultural system itself. Sims was astounded by the diverse array of plants the Australians used as soil builders. He returned to Bozeman determined to adapt such an approach to the northern Great Plains.

"I looked about for something I could use for the legume phase that would reseed itself in this environment," Jim recounted, recalling his hunch that most of the Australian legumes probably wouldn't grow as well half a world away. "I was walking about the research farm and there was a bunch of black medic, so I said, well, I could try that. I gathered seed with my hands to get enough to put in the first experiment."

Of course, it wasn't as easy as that. Jim's funding still came from the chemical companies, and his dean and department chair at MSU continued to tell him (as they were telling the Ag Task Force) that the only things that would grow in Montana were wheat and barley. Plus, there was no market for anything else, the authorities insisted. This last argument was a rather circular one, Jim realized—the church of wheat and barley's self-fulfilling prophecy. When he questioned the agricultural marketing experts over in the economics department, they actually told him with a straight face that their models showed low demand for Montana legumes—as if this "low demand" was simply the result of some immutable economic law. And yet, how could anyone demand a product that not only didn't exist, but also had been declared impossible? The hand manipulating the supply side of this equation was anything but invisible.

Once he figured out that MSU's economists didn't have much to offer him, Jim started doing his own research, and he discovered that Montana had supported a profitable pea industry in the 1930s. The pea business had been so lucrative, in fact, that the crop had succumbed to blight because it wasn't being rotated with anything else. When Montana's peas crashed in the late 1940s, the Gallatin Valley Seed Company had moved its operations to Twin Falls, Idaho, inaugurating a sixty-year pea monopoly that Idaho and Washington had swiftly locked in with protective legislation. Jim wasn't fixing to get Montana back into the pea business, but he figured if legumes had grown here before, they could grow here again. Neither the opinions of his colleagues nor the wishes of his funders were going to stop him.

Instead of battling his superiors, Jim went straight to Montana's farmers. It didn't take him long to identify David Oien as a fellow traveler. After meeting Dave at the extension workshop, Jim convinced his new friend to plant a couple of his "oddball acres" with self-seeding legumes. Dave chose a patch of earth right outside his front window, and his first black medic crop went in the ground in the spring of 1983.

Dave started with twenty pounds of medic seed, enough to

plant two acres. He fed the tiny "weed" seeds into a twelve-foot disk drill and let 'er rip. Once again, Dave talked Orville into helping, explaining that this experiment was basically like seeding alfalfa (aka *Medicago sativa*) or sweet clover. Medic was a cousin to those plants, Dave told his dad. It looked similar, they could use the same seeder for it, and besides, a college man from Bozeman was promoting it with *research*. This wasn't just another wild hare dreamed up by Dave's hippie friends in Missoula. Let's see how it grows, Orville said dispassionately from the seat of the tractor, while Dave rode the drill. But Dave couldn't help but be optimistic. It was a perfect mid-May afternoon, and he and his dad were literally planting the seeds of the future together.

What excited Dave most about medic was that it was not just an annual green manure, but the keystone of a long-term cropping system. Dave and his dad would sow the medic this year and let it go to seed. The plant's black seedpods had such thick walls that only about half of the tiny amber seeds would escape in time to germinate this season. The other half would remain in the soil and germinate the next year, along with whatever grain crop the Oiens planted. Dave and Orville's grain would easily canopy out over the low-growing medic, which would obligingly supply nitrogen throughout the season without hogging either sunlight or soil moisture. This farming method—undersowing—was a completely different ball game for cash-grain agriculture. It meant that farmers didn't have to choose between fertilizer crops and grain crops. They could grow them at the same time.

Dave got even more excited when his medic started poking up out of the ground. He had a great stand with good soil cover. It wasn't long, however, before weeds started to creep in, encroaching on the noncompetitive legume. Dave sprung into action, protecting his plants with the tenacity of a first-time parent. Every

three weeks he went out to the fields by himself. He spent long eve-
nings working up and down his two acres, pulling weeds before
they had a chance to spread.

Dave's first year as a black medic farmer yielded 150 pounds of
seed. He wanted to expand his experiment, so he harvested the entire crop and convinced his dad to plant it on ten acres instead of
just two. The Oiens finished season two with more than 650
pounds of the prolific legume. At this point, Dave was running out
of oddball acres, and he didn't want to keep this miracle plant to
himself anyway. He needed to get some friends in on the deal. In
the fall of 1985, Dave managed to convince three AERO buddies to
purchase starter seed from him at 6 dollars a pound: Tom Hastings, Jim Barngrover, and Bud Barta.

A CARPENTER WITH A CONSCIENCE

Bud Barta was the perfect foil for his unconventional crop. The gentle, bearded father of three was muscular, not macho—the kind of
guy you'd hope to have with you if your truck broke down. He credited his father with teaching him the critical skills of life ("farming,
mechanics, and common sense"), to which he appeared to have
added few bells and whistles beyond a bachelors of science in electrical engineering. Although Bud had always earned respectable
grades, he'd been in no particular hurry to go to college, since he'd
enjoyed his post–high school jobs as a carpenter and general con-
tractor. Nor was he particularly eager to hang around academia
after graduation. Neither graduate school nor a high-paying job
with an engineering firm appealed to Bud, who had been just as
happy trimming trees to pay for school as he had been with school
itself. Truthfully, all Bud really wanted was to earn an honest liv-

ing that still left plenty of time for fishing and skiing. So he'd moved back to the 1,200-acre ranch and grain farm where he'd grown up, two and a half hours southeast of Conrad, in Lewistown, Montana.

Bud's quiet workingman's manner matched the character of his hometown. Dubbed Charlie Russell country after the cowboy artist who'd made it famous, Lewistown was a poor-but-proud agricultural hub. People here trusted guys like Bud, who were more doers than talkers. Had he gone straight from trimming trees to managing his parents' farm, Bud might have fit right in with the laconic ways and uniform landscapes of his neighbors. But instead, he'd taken one more handyman job, which had turned out to be quite a bit different from the rest. For the final three years of the heady seventies, Bud had served as the technician for a traveling renewable energy road show.

Living out of a bus with the fourteen other crew members of the New Western Energy Show, Bud Barta had discovered a way of life far removed from his father's simple credo. The troupe—a political take on the old-time medicine show that deployed theater and do-it-yourself demonstrations to "fight the finite energy conspiracy"—left a lasting impression on the humble tradesman. Between performances, the Energy Show often stayed on organic farms, which impressed Bud as a good model for how he might combine his practical skills with his newfound ecological consciousness. By the time he returned to his family's place, Bud had come to believe chemicals were immoral. "They are polluting our water and will have long-lasting effects on future generations," he'd written in the newsletter of the Energy Show's parent organization, the Alternative Energy Resources Organization. "We don't have any right to impose our thoughtlessness on them. I don't want MY kids around chemicals."

But Bud made little progress converting his neighbors (whose property completely surrounded his) or his father (who was leas-

ing it to him). The stubbornly individual son of an equally stubborn agribusinessman, Bud faced the quintessential dilemma of
the second-generation progressive farmer: His father was just as
committed to his own brand of innovation as he was to a low-input
alternative. Bud summed it up matter-of-factly. "My dad was the
first in the county to farm with chemicals; I was the first to farm
without them."

Frustrated, Bud recalled a conversation with one of the organic farmers he'd stayed with during his Energy Show days, a jovial guy his age who had faced similar struggles transitioning his
family operation. I oughta call David Oien, Bud thought. He wasn't
the first. Another AERO acquaintance was already on the phone
with Dave, cooking up a plan to supply hundreds of other farmers
with their "miracle" fertilizer crop.

A MATTER OF LIFE AND DEATH

A philosophically minded thirty-six-year-old with a long face and
an arresting mop of curly hair, Jim Barngrover spoke with a slow,
measured cadence that identified him immediately as a leader.
While Bud's boyish countenance and Dave's ready smile lent a certain exuberance to the nascent green manure scheme, Jim's carefully enunciated tone never strayed too far from solemn. When the
former teacher lectured about this new way of farming, you had the
sense that it was a matter of life and death.

For Jim this was, in fact, the case. While Dave and Bud had
overhauled their farms in anticipation of a crisis, Jim had already
lived the very worst of their fears. As a five-year-old kid growing
up on a sugar beet farm in Worland, Wyoming, Jim had seen his
dad come home sick one day following exposure to the insecticide

parathion. Donald Barngrover never got better. Jim watched in horror while his father gradually succumbed to Parkinson's disease, which forced the Barngrovers to forfeit the family farm. Stoic Donald finally died in 1996, but not before he'd spent forty years wrestling with slow physical and mental degeneration.

Researchers would later confirm the link between Parkinson's and parathion, but Jim didn't wait for the journal articles to come out. Aware that Montana had recently passed a new constitution that promised the right to a "clean and healthful environment," he moved across the state border in 1975 and got involved in anti-pesticide activism and chemical-free farming.

Since Jim no longer had a place of his own, he signed on as a partner in a fledgling biodynamic vegetable and dairy operation in western Montana's Bitterroot Valley, Lifeline Farm. An intellectual center of gravity for Montana's nascent organic movement, Lifeline was a bustling laboratory of new ideas, the bolder the better. So when David Oien started casting about for farmers to grow medic, Jim was game. Now that he had two sons of his own, he was even more passionate about holding Montana to its constitutional promise of a green society.

The third black medic grower for the spring season of 1985 was a second cousin of Dave's, Tom Hastings. Tom and Dave hung out a fair amount anyway, so Tom was up for trying some of this new seed crop that his buddy was so high on. If nothing else, it would get Dave to shut up.

GROWING FARMERS

Nineteen eighty-five was a disastrous drought year. The barley dried up at the Oiens'. Bud Barta's dad had to rely on insurance money. The biodynamic farm where Jim Barngrover was working failed to turn a profit, so Jim went to the state prison in Deer Lodge (to become the garden program director). But the medic that Dave, Bud, Jim, and Tom had planted grew surprisingly well. This was something they should market to their fellow farmers, they decided.

The four men's incipient black medic venture was a new model for an organic farm business in Montana, very different from Dave's original idea of selling pastured beef. Rather than fertilizing the farm with cow manure, Dave and his friends would rely on *green* manures: soil-fertilizing plants. That meant developing a long-term rotation, rather than just annually applying an on-farm input.

If the agronomy of black medic organics differed from that of pastured beef, then Dave's new business model signaled an even more dramatic shift in his thinking. Rather than marketing food to conscientious consumers—with a labeled retail product like his short-lived organic beef—Dave was now proposing to sell soil-building seed. Given all the barriers to reaching organic shoppers—who were concentrated in faraway places like California—why not start with a supply-side strategy: growing organic farmers? Who wouldn't want to ditch chemical fertilizers once they discovered how cheap it was to undersow a fertilizer plant into their crop instead?

Dave called Jim Sims in 1986 to make the pitch. He and his three friends would license the scientist's George black medic variety and sell the seed to other growers. The four partners had even come up with a clever name for the company, which would highlight the perennial character of the product. Unlike annual soil-building crops, which had to be replanted every year, black medic was self-seeding. The new company's name would remind farmers what a miracle this was.

But Dave had told Jim Sims a little bit of a fib. The new venture's name did highlight the perennial character of George black medic. But the origin story of the business and its moniker had another dimension, beyond the straightforward aim to sell farmers on a long view approach to their field operations. When the four founders had gotten together to talk about starting a company, the conversation had stretched long into the evening. Realizing that it was probably getting late, one of the men had asked what time it was. But no one had a watch. Finding their own temporal sensibilities just as nontraditional as their perennial crop, the four friends had stumbled on a name for their enterprise that captured their feeling of both personal and agronomic revolution. At least in the middle of the night, it had seemed that growing black medic constituted a fundamental challenge to the status quo, so deep as to unsettle prevailing Western notions of space and time. "And that," Jim Barngrover says with Aesopian gravitas, "is how we got the name Timeless Seeds."

4

DEEPLY ROOTED

When Dave Oien, Tom Hastings, Bud Barta, and Jim Barngrover officially launched Timeless Seeds in the spring of 1987, they were audacity rich but capital poor. Dave was barely hanging on to his family's farm, where his three-generation household got by on commodity payments, Orville's Social Security check, and local sales of the fresh cucumbers and tomatoes Dave raised in the greenhouse. He and his second cousin Tom had started what sounded like a revenue-generating enterprise: T & D Cleaning. But the "business" was really just a small machine in the Oiens' Quonset hut, a ten-horsepower separator that sorted debris out of their harvest so they could legally sell it direct-to-consumer as seed or grain (if, indeed, they could find any consumers to sell it to). Meanwhile, Bud was still working on an organic transition at his family's homestead in Lewistown, which seemed to be a magnet for hailstorms. And Jim—pleased as he was with his new gig managing organic crop production for a lush 45,000-acre ranch in the foothills of central Montana's Snowy Mountains—still didn't have a place of his own. All in all, it made for a funny elevator speech: four thirtysomethings with unstable income and little business experience, offering weed seeds for sale as organic fertilizer? What farmer was going to take them up on that? The Timeless boys needed to find someone whose notion of value was as unconventional as theirs, someone who was smart enough to get rich but didn't want to. Dave thought he knew a guy who fit that bill: a homesteading college dropout named Russell Salisbury.

JUNKYARD PHILOSOPHER

At the core of every underground is the person whose acquaintance serves as an informal badge of the initiated. Familiar to virtually no one outside the circle, they are known to nearly everyone within it. By now, the legend of Russ Salisbury and his staggering equipment boneyard is almost like the secret handshake of Montana's agricultural resistance. Russ is, you might say, the godfather of the northern plains' organic farming mafia.

If you hang around the right farm tours, it's easy to pick up secondhand tall tales about Russ and his DIY shenanigans. There's the story about the old bale-raising truck he hunted down "way the hell over in Nashua" for 15 dollars, which he spent two days driving home at fifteen miles an hour, only to park it and never use it. That yarn might lead to the revelation that Russ actually *is* using that rusted-out truck: as fencing. He's lined up dozens, probably hundreds (maybe thousands?) of old trailers and vehicles to corral his cattle, because he doesn't like digging postholes. People love to recount the day Russ was banned from the Carter Ferry because he'd sunk it trying to float his herd across the Missouri River. After that, Russ had to drive his cows the long way around in an old yellow school bus he acquired at an auction sale. When the bus tipped over one night, a Good Samaritan pulled over and offered to help, thinking it was full of children. "She gets up right close to those windows and one of them cows bellers out a loud moo," the story goes. "Golly, you shoulda seen that lady jump." Routinely invoked to put people in a good mood, the mythology of Russ Salisbury celebrates a folk hero who is less bulldog and more golden retriever. This folk hero is unfailingly cheerful. Steadfastly loyal. And no matter how persistently the adult humans in his life offer him shiny new toys, he takes the most pleasure in the conspicuously used ones that others find slightly repulsive and inappropriate for polite company.

Secondhand tall tales, however, were not what Dave Oien was after when he first drove out to Russ Salisbury's homestead, a couple of years after a fleeting introduction to its proprietor at AERO's 1984 Sustainable Agriculture Conference. Dave had heard enough stories. Now he wanted to see this place for himself. As a pretext for his visit to Russ's, Dave had ordered a small load of feed barley for the handful of cattle he was fattening at his home farm. But he'd brought along a surprise for his host, too.

From Conrad, Dave figured he could get to the Salisbury place in about an hour and a half. He started out southeast toward Great Falls on I-15, then hung a hard left north on State Highway 87. After twenty miles, Dave saw the sign for Floweree and turned off to the right. Immediately dodging a pothole, he found himself on a sinuous road that wound over and around a series of gentle hills, through the sleepy town of Floweree, then past a few grain bins. From here, things started to look less promising, as signs of civilization gave way to clusters of old, seemingly abandoned farm equipment. Just as Dave started to worry that he might have missed a turn somewhere, he crested a rise and sharply caught his breath. Several hundred feet below, at the base of a steep slope, lay what appeared to be a small village. Hugging a stunning section of the Missouri River, the quaint hamlet sparkled in the midmorning sun. The intense early summer daylight tugged at the contours of the rugged buttes across the riverbank, which were streaked with white rock.

As if it were just as eager to get to Russ's as Dave was, the road rapidly switchbacked its way toward this waterfront Brigadoon, which was flanked with trees. Once Dave was halfway down, he could just make out a large collection of haystacks, carefully piled at the settlement's near edge. As he got closer, he realized that the structures he'd observed from above weren't houses. In fact, he didn't see a single house on the place. Instead, he counted row upon row of old vehicles: trailers, combines, tractors, trucks. There were thousands of them, and most appeared to have been parked there for some time. Dave couldn't begin to guess which of these structures he was meant to pull up to, so he slowed to a crawl and waited for some sort of sign. At that moment, the screen door to one of the trailers opened, and Dave found himself looking up at a bearded, bespectacled man who appeared to share the essential qualities of his yard full of machines: durable, weathered, practical.

Although Dave recognized Russell Salisbury's face, the man standing before him now barely resembled the fidgety farmer who'd politely shaken his hand a couple of years ago, before slinking out of Bozeman's windowless, morbidly fluorescent student union. Here in his element, Russ looked not only a good deal more lively, but also, somehow, larger. The man's bearish arms emerged robustly from his sleeveless T-shirt, more like verbs than nouns. The same was true of Russ's impish eyes, which peeked out from under a well-worn baseball cap. A small, round button just above the left side of the brim declared, "I Love Wind Power."

Russ had grown up on a farm not far from here, he told Dave, inviting his guest inside his home trailer. At age six, he had decided he wanted to be a farmer. And in 1957, as a high school junior tasked with a vo-ag project, he had managed to lease this river bottom, which had been his great-grandfather's homestead. Russ had taken some mechanics courses in college, but he didn't like "paying to learn stuff," so he'd come home and purchased a gas station on IOU. Fixing other people's equipment at the gas station had helped Russ build his skills and his bank account, and he'd rented various pieces of local farm ground while he waited for the opportunity to buy the family place. When the land had come up for sale in 1964, Russ had jumped on it. He'd been raising food here—without chemicals—ever since.

"Up at the college, they said you can't grow wheat unless you treat seed, but I knew better than that," Russ told Dave. "When I ran out of treatment, I'd just keep on seeding, and I couldn't tell where I'd run out." Unconvinced that he needed to use seed treatment, Russ had a similarly skeptical position on herbicides. "I didn't have the money to buy the chemicals, for one thing," Russ explained. "I mean, I could have done it, I could have borrowed it or something, but I didn't want to, and I didn't like putting it on. So if the weeds weren't too bad, I just didn't see them."

Unlike Dave and Bud, Russ hadn't had to transition his place, because it had never been "conventional." Russ followed a different set of conventions. Live simply and live off the land. Don't borrow money, and don't use any inputs. Let the farm limit production, and for God's sake, don't pollute this splendid five miles of Missouri River stream bank with chemicals.

"The land's got its limits on what it can make," Russ told Dave, "so if I have a bad crop, it doesn't really bother me any. We paid the land off and we're not borrowing money on it. When you borrow money maybe you worry about whether the banker's going to come banging on your door. Everybody in the system wants big numbers. It's the biggest numbers, the highest yields—pounds per acre or something. I quit pushing for that a long time ago."

Russ had flatly refused Earl Butz's brand of agribusiness. He didn't trade in the same currency that the new farm economists did, and he was far more oriented to what he sowed than to what he reaped. But as his neighbors expanded, gambled bigger, and planted more grain, Russ had come to believe he must be the only one who was so stubbornly backward. Until, that is, he'd overcome his distaste for college classrooms to attend AERO's 1984 Sustainable Agriculture Conference.

As out of place as he'd felt sitting in a folding chair and staring at a slide show, Russ had been amused to learn from the conference luminaries that his weedy fields were part of a cutting-edge movement, something called "agroecology." And when a farmer from Conrad got up and started talking about growing weeds *on purpose*? Well, Russ figured he might have finally hit on a form of agricultural development he could believe in. "That's why I invited you out here," Russ said to Dave. "I want to hear more about this black medic." Dave looked at Russ like a poker player who'd had his bluff called for the first time. He'd carefully orchestrated this barley deal to surprise Russ with a casual offer of medic seed. But apparently, this had been Russ's plan all along.

In 1986, Russ became the fifth farmer to plant black medic. Both the crop and the business model made sense to the self-taught homesteader, who was accustomed to investing in the long term. He took the lesson of the Australian ley system to heart, integrating livestock so he could plant more of his ground to perennials. Russ's land was, quite literally, a place with deep roots.

But to really appreciate the depth of the burgeoning agricultural underground being cultivated by Dave, Russ, and Timeless, you had to understand its equally deep foundation in its social substrate: a long-standing local tradition of agrarian organizing. To unearth that history, the place to start digging was the shoestring nonprofit that first told Russ he was "organic": the Alternative Energy Resources Organization.

PEOPLE POWER

A "citizens' renewable energy organization" founded in 1974, AERO was the ever-present subtext lurking beneath the story of Timeless Seeds. The New Western Energy Show, for which Bud Barta had served as a technician, had been the nonprofit's flagship project. A few years later, AERO members Dave Oien, Russ Salisbury, and Jim Barngrover had helped launch the organization's Ag Task Force—the same task force that had put on Montana's first major sustainable agriculture conference in 1984. It was AERO's bimonthly *Sun Times* that had published Dave's sustainable agriculture column, "Down on the Farm," in which the legume advocate first touted black medic to his fellow farmers in 1983 under the heading "This Weed Is Good News." Even Scott Sproull—the teacher of the 1976 alternative energy workshop in which Dave had schemed the solar retrofit of his parents' farmhouse—was now an enthusiastic AERO member.

By the time Timeless Seeds opened for business in 1986, the renewable energy nonprofit was well on its way to becoming one of the preeminent voices for alternative farming in the West—and indeed the entire country. AERO was, as the Timeless founders put it, "a clearinghouse of information on sustainable agriculture." While the land grant universities, formal agricultural organizations, and government agencies of the northern Great Plains remained reluctant to embrace ecological approaches to growing food, members of the grassroots group had taken it upon themselves to develop the region's agroecological knowledge base.

Newcomers to the effort—who began showing up to AERO conferences in significant numbers—didn't immediately understand the connection between the organization's agricultural activities and its mission. Why was a renewable energy group so involved in farming? Dave Oien found himself fielding this question so frequently that he'd published a response in his *Sun Times* column:

Why agriculture? Because it is Montana's primary industry, certainly. Because it is a primary energy and resource user. That, too. But the reasoning goes deeper. Agriculture is concerned with ultimate wealth—the ability to provide food and fiber—and it depends in a direct way on natural energy sources—on sun and water and wind, on photosynthesis, on the biology of the soil. Agriculture can be the model for a sane and a safe lifestyle, for an economy that depends on local resources and appropriate technologies, for a close and proper relationship with Nature. Agriculture can be a paradigm for sustainability.

Or, as things stood in Montana in 1986, agriculture could be a paradigm for death and destruction. Aware that statutorily supported economic incentives were working against them, both Dave Oien and Jim Barngrover spent a fair amount of time at the state capitol building in Helena, two hours south of Conrad and a fifty-five-mile drive from Jim's job at the Deer Lodge prison. Determined to knock down the barriers that stood in the way of organic farming, they put on their nicest clothes and scoured the halls of the legislature for like minds.

POLITICAL ROOTS

"I was a slick, highly paid political operative," Jim Barngrover recalls, jokingly reflecting on his history as AERO's official lobbyist. Sporting an unruly Afro and speaking from what appeared to be, quite literally, a soapbox, the gangly young man looked more like a student protester than a power broker. But although Jim didn't *look* like a VIP, he was nonetheless effective. Aided by Dave and the strength of the AERO membership, the volunteer lobbyist made surprising headway with state representatives in Helena.

Thanks to Jim's behind-the-scenes organizing, the Montana legislature passed a joint resolution in 1985, calling on the state university system to establish a program in sustainable agriculture. The nonbinding resolution could have amounted to nothing more than lip service, but AERO made sure the lawmakers put their money where their mouths were. Six years later, Jim and company would successfully carry a bill to fund the first weed ecologist position at the Montana Agricultural Experiment Station. In an earthshaking move, the state university would hire forest ecology PhD Bruce Maxwell—a Peace Corps alum whose first peer-reviewed publication concerned a floral description of native forests in Micronesia—to join the ranks of the "better living through chemistry" good old boys who were typically tasked with advising farmers. That was all yet to come, of course. But in the meantime, AERO celebrated another major political victory.

In addition to the joint resolution on sustainable agriculture research, the 1985 Montana legislature also passed an organic food definition law—the fourth in the country, behind only California, Oregon, and Maine. Even before the ink dried on the bill, Jim and Dave were already putting together a steering committee to write Montana's first organic standards. Dave hadn't forgotten the labeling roadblock he'd hit in his attempt to retail organic beef, and he wanted to make sure Montana's future sustainable farmers had a market. He and Jim became founding board members of the first statewide certifying organization, and they worked hard to foster its strength and grassroots character. Meanwhile, AERO—heavily populated with Timeless farmers—formed the state's original organic growers association in 1987. At each turn, Bud Barta, Tom Hastings, and Russ Salisbury joined the new groups, rapidly building a critical mass that gave the organizations legitimacy and impelling energy.

While it may have seemed to some onlookers that Montana's organic farming movement came out of nowhere (or worse, California), the truth was that it had very deep, local roots. And although the Alternative Energy Resources Organization may have been the place to *start* digging up these roots, you had to keep going to get anywhere near the bottom. Indeed, AERO traced its own origins back to an even older, fiercer citizens' group: the Northern Plains Resource Council.

In 1972, a group of rough-edged cowboys and cowgirls crammed into the living room of a tiny ranch cabin in southeast Montana's Bull Mountains, home to the son of a member of Butch Cassidy's Hole in the Wall Gang. The US Bureau of Reclamation had just released a plan to site twenty-one new coal-fired power plants in Montana, and the ranchers were concerned that such drastic development would destroy their land. Determined to stop the ghastly strip mining, they promised one another they wouldn't let the coal companies buy them out. And to make good on their word, they formed a nonprofit council.

The rancher's group—the Northern Plains Resource Council— proceeded to organize their neighbors. They went from living room to living room, explaining the implications of the proposed mining and urging their neighbors not to sign away their property. When Consolidation Coal started knocking on those same doors, contracts in hand, they were astonished to find landowner after landowner uninterested in their lucrative offers. They were even more astonished when these stubborn ranchers helped convince the Montana state legislature to pass a series of environmental protection statutes. But the most incredible underdog victory came in 1977, when the Northern Plains Resource Council united with like-minded groups across the country to drive a strip-mining regulation bill through the US Congress. In a short five years, Montana's ranch families—led by a particularly resolute group of women—had delivered an unequivocal message: Coal is not the future we want.

When the dust settled and a substantial share of the proposed power plants had been successfully blocked, the niece of one of those forceful women asked a thought-provoking question: If coal is the future we are against, what is the future we are for? This sparky thirty-year-old—Kye Cochran—was one of several countercultural young people whose volunteer labor had supported the crusade of their more traditional agrarian parents, uncles, and aunts. While the Northern Plains Resource Council continued its advocacy against dirty energy (as it does today), several of its fresh-faced volunteers launched a new group, to promote alternative solutions. In another living room—at the roomy Billings Victorian that Kye and her comrades had christened "Bozovilla" (in tribute to a psychedelic political radio theater show)—the Alternative Energy Resources Organization was born.

A proud member of both AERO and NPRC, Russ Salisbury liked reminding people just how far-reaching the roots of Montana's sustainable agriculture movement really were. This "new" approach to farming hadn't begun as a hippie project in the radical sixties and seventies, or as a desperate response to the eighties farm crisis. It had grown out of a deep agrarian heritage, a heritage that underpinned the strip-mining fight, the counterculture, and even Russ himself. Russ didn't quite wear this story on his sleeve, but it was plainly visible on his favorite vest. Denim blue, with a sheepskin lining and collar, it was emblazoned with an orange logo that read "Farmers Union."

LEGISLATION, EDUCATION, COOPERATION

Russ had been a member of the Farmers Union since he was eight. He'd gone to the union's camp every summer and learned its three key principles: legislation, education, and cooperation. Now a local authority on this century-old farmers' organization, Russ thought newcomers to "alternative agriculture" ought to know its story too.

The Farmers Educational Cooperative Union of America was founded in Texas in 1902, as a response to increasing monopoly power in the grain business. The very next year, the group had

formed its first marketing cooperative. From an initial membership of ten, the Farmers Union had rapidly grown in both numbers
and influence, particularly in the grain belt states of Montana, Nebraska, Kansas, and the Dakotas. One grain pool at a time, the
group's members attempted to wrest control of American agriculture back from wealthy corporations. By the early 1940s, the grassroots coalition had established itself as a respected political force,
credited with everything from the cooperative structure of rural
electrification to the institutionalization of the national school
lunch program to the successful campaign for women's suffrage.
As the rural counterpart to the US labor movement, the Farmers
Union sought to organize working people so that they could use
their economic and political power to demand some measure of
control over their own lives.

Unique among American farm organizations, the Farmers
Union had connected the dots between domestic and foreign policies, calling for cooperation among the world's peoples rather
than military and economic competition. Unfortunately, this pre-
scient attention to the disastrous trajectory of globalization had
landed the group in hot water during the cold war, when it was ac-
cused of promoting communism and closely monitored by both
the State Department and the House Un-American Activities
Committee. Although the National Farmers Union never faced
prosecution, its leaders got the message. If they wanted to stay in
business, they'd better soften their critiques of US trade policy
and stick to more traditional agrarian issues. By scaling back its
more ambitious aims, the union had managed to survive the Mc-
Carthy years: but not before its national leadership expelled several outspoken chapters that refused to be silenced.

The Farmers Union had become a bit more staid in recent
years, Russ admitted, but the movement it seeded hadn't slowed

down. The group's populist energy had merely been transplanted to new institutional contexts, where people continued to practice legislation, education, and cooperation in the name of a dignified rural life. "It seemed like AERO became the new Farmers Union," Russ reflected. "They were the new idealistic people thinking and coming up with new ideas."

Still, Russ thought, it was important to remember where so many of the AERO activists' "new" ideas came from. Banding together to stand up to corporate power was something many of them had learned from their parents, whose cooperative ethos and mutual aid had helped them weather both the Depression and World War II. For the substantial and committed membership of that era, the Farmers Union was almost a religion. "My family went to the Methodist church—my folks were always good Methodists—but Farmers Union meant more than Sunday school to me," Russ recalled. "You know, when I think about my upbringing, I can't separate church and my parents and the Farmers Union in my mind."

Russ Salisbury's way of farming was foundational to his character. In truth, it was more a way of life—at once protest and homage, a point of departure and a comforting foothold of continuity. Russ's approach may have cut against the prevailing grain, but it was also true to his heritage in a manner that connected the jocular homesteader to a number of other Montanans. It was no accident that steadfast agrarian populists like Russ were so well represented at AERO conferences and Timeless Seeds field days. For agrarians of his generation, the industrial present was doubly out of step—with both their remembered yesterdays and their intended tomorrows.

Suspended in a late-twentieth-century no-man's-land of corporate greed, people like Dave Oien and Russ Salisbury had to dig underneath the shallow traditions of modern agribusiness, to find

richer soil in which to root their visions for a workable rural society. But they didn't have to dig far. As Russ regaled fresh-faced hippies with his childhood lessons from the Farmers Union, and Dave
roped his dad into planting black medic, unruly young radicals discovered common ground with the stubborn old-timers who'd pre-
ceded them. Together, they defined themselves as a community,
united by a shared inheritance and a shared future that were in-
separable. This was perhaps the true meaning of the name "Timeless Seeds." Plants were their tools, but what these farmers were
really trying to establish was a more stable collective legacy. Instead of focusing on quarterly profits, they poured the lion's share
of their time and energy into building AERO's sustainable agriculture "information clearinghouse," which replaced the logic of trade
secrets with the maxim of sharing what you learned. Legislation.
Education. Cooperation. And, of course, plenty of perspiration.

5
BOOTLEG RESEARCH AND FARMER SCIENCE

December 7, 1988, was a bone-chilling day even for the Judith Basin. The AERO staffers who had organized Montana's first Soil-Building Cropping Systems Conference nervously eyed the too-big-looking stacks of programs they had spent weeks preparing, worrying no one would show. The roads were coated with ice, and the spitting snow made it hard to see more than a few feet ahead. Nonetheless, more than 200 producers and researchers chained up their trucks and drove over to the Yogo Inn in downtown Lewistown. It was the height of the farm crisis, and people were hungry for answers.

The conference promised a stellar lineup of agronomists, crop breeders, microbiologists, and distributors from as far away as Saskatoon, Saskatchewan. David Oien and Bud Barta were on the agenda, and Jim Barngrover was handing out information about Timeless Seeds. But the real attraction was neither the out-of-town hotshots nor the Timeless farmers. Rather, the star of this show was Dave's research partner in his new venture, the chain-smoking soil chemist who had painstakingly bred black medic by propagating seeds collected from wild plants. After twenty-two years of experimentation, Jim Sims was ready to debut this new cropping system, and all eyes were on him. The lone credentialed expert willing to cooperate with Dave and the other sustainable agriculturalists, Jim assured his audience that he knew what they were up against.

"We've got low, erratic precipitation, which is another way of saying drought," the squarely built Sims pronounced, his deep voice spurning theatrics as he got right to the point. "We've got a hot, dry July and August, which is another way of saying drought." Sims ticked off a long list of the other challenges Montana's producers faced: short growing seasons, surprise frosts, harsh winters, isolation from markets. "Add to that nonbeneficial insects, disease and weeds, nutrient deficiencies, few crop species (mostly a monoculture of wheat and barley), the saline seep hazard, the erosion hazard," the folksy scientist continued. "I got tired of trying to list them so I quit."

Sims's assessment wasn't exactly encouraging, but his frankness got farmers' attention. They were sick of hearing about chemical solutions that worked wonders on test plots in the relatively rainy Gallatin Valley, where the state university was located. At least this straight-shooting character appreciated the conditions they were facing out here in farm country.

Sympathetic to farmers' woes, Jim also appreciated the harsh conditions *he* was facing, in the similarly spartan environment of the land grant university system. Public research dollars had dwindled significantly over the past decade, so plant breeders and agronomists had increasingly come to rely on private funding from chemical manufacturers and commodity groups. That wasn't a problem for most of Jim's colleagues, whose research programs were well aligned with the prevailing cash-grain system. But Jim had to invent a clever means of supporting his unorthodox studies.

"We had some grants from the Montana Wheat and Barley Committee for fertilizer research, but not anything else," he recalled, "so we bootlegged research with pulse crops. We satisfied the requirement for working with small grains and fertilizer, but on the side we did a lot of work with cropping systems. The bootleg system; that was really very important."

After a quarter century of bootlegging, Jim was eager to bring his underground research to the forefront and help Montana's farmers address all those challenging conditions he so palpably understood. "We've got to build a cropping system that fits in our environment, in our water resource, in our soil resource, and get around all these problems at the same time," he told the packed audience at the Lewistown conference. The Earl Butz approach to farming, Jim explained, treated soil fertility as a matter of chemistry: a balance of nitrogen, phosphorous, and potassium (NPK) that could be achieved with the correct application of fertilizer. Among the reasons this strategy wasn't working was that soil fertility was also a matter of biology. Soil was alive. Or at least it once had been. By now, industrial agriculture had systematically killed off much of the diverse community of microorganisms in the living fraction of the soil—soil organic matter—which was just as essential to crop health as N, P, or K. To restore the fertility of their land, farmers would need to bring this community back.

This was one of the most underappreciated benefits of crop rotation, Sims continued: Diversity aboveground supported diversity below it, too. When farmers planted legumes after wheat, they weren't just replenishing nitrogen, but cultivating a whole new society underground: symbiotic bacteria, soil-aerating worms, soil-aggregating fungi. It wouldn't happen overnight, Sims cautioned. He had been studying and working on this approach for more than two decades before getting to the point where he was ready to trial black medic on cooperating farms. Even after all that, the black medic system wasn't an out-of-the-box solution. Each producer would need a good ten years to build the soil and adapt a rotation to his or her own place.

Privately, Sims estimated that he'd need twice that much time—twenty years—to change farming practices on any appreciable scale. "Farmers don't just try something on the recommendation of a guy from the university," he said knowingly. But Jim had the sense to stick with a technique he'd used for his chemical fertilizer work: on-farm research. If he wanted to convince farmers that this alternative cropping system really worked, he'd need to host his experiments on their land. That was a pretty big request, though, so the first step was finding a few interested farmers who could convince their fellows to participate. In search of willing cooperators, Sims turned to his partners at Timeless Seeds, who were already busy getting the word out.

SEE FOR YOURSELVES

Six months later and fifteen miles west, the Timeless boys hosted their first major farm tour. By June of 1989, Dave had gotten twenty-six people curious enough about Sims's "miracle" plant to drive out to Bud Barta's place, a 1,200-acre cash-grain operation just outside Lewistown. The crowd was eager to witness medic in action. Nutrients grown by weeds seemed about as realistic as money growing on trees, but with the price of fossil fuel–based nitrogen skyrocketing, these shrewd farmers figured it was worth a day trip to see for themselves. Those who hadn't been to the conference the previous winter had heard through the grapevine about the novel method of undersowing: seeding a nitrogen-building legume at the same time as a cash crop, so as to provide fertilizer free of charge.

Bud ushered the parade of pickups into his front yard, then gathered his guests at the edge of a field that had been planted with wheat the previous year. The typical practice—summer fallow—was to leave such an area bare, so it could store moisture and soil fertility for the following wheat crop. But Bud's field was littered with an irregular smattering of low-growing plants. Sporting trefoil leaves and bright-yellow flowers, the early summer growth was uncannily reminiscent of the invaders his fellow farmers were used to yanking out of their yards. Bud's visitors were surprised. Wouldn't these plants suck up all the nutrients that Bud needed for next year's grain?

"This is black medic," Barta told the crowd, introducing them to the miracle species they'd been hearing about. "It's a legume, like alfalfa, so it fixes nitrogen for my grain crop. But unlike alfalfa, it doesn't suck my soil dry." Barta dug up a medic plant so the crowd could see its nitrogen-fixing nodules and abbreviated root system. "The roots are shallow, because medic doesn't need much water," Barta explained. "In fact, I might end up with *more* moisture for my wheat because the medic keeps the ground covered to limit wind erosion."

"So this is your new rotation crop?" one of the farmers asked. "You plant it in the alternating years instead of summer fallow?" Not exactly, Bud explained.

"See how hard these are?" Bud said, inviting his guests to pinch the dense seed heads of the medic. "Only about half of these will germinate this year. After I harvest those seeds, I can plant winter wheat right into the same field—without tilling the soil. The other fifty percent of the medic will grow up under the wheat, and it will keep releasing nitrogen throughout the season. The wheat will canopy out over top of it, so I won't have any trouble at harvest."

When he'd finished his biology lesson, Bud got to the really juicy part. "As long as I don't till, the medic will reseed itself each year, so I don't have to plant it again. I've drastically reduced my diesel costs, and my fertilizer bill is practically zero." The somewhat private farmer had an understated way of putting things, but everybody in attendance knew what a revolutionary state of affairs they were witnessing. Bud's place was darn near farming itself.

Come back next season, Bud encouraged his visitors, as he and his new business partners wrapped up the tour. The inquisitive tinkerer was just as curious as anyone else to see what would happen next.

TRIAL AND ERROR

Bud Barta's place wasn't just a farm anymore. It was also a research site, lined out in split-block comparisons just like the Oien place. Since nobody but Jim Sims would plant medic on MSU's study plots—which were too small and too well watered to approximate real-world conditions anyway—green manure farmers had to serve as their own scientists and extension agents.

Each year, the Timeless farmers trialed new practices. What happened if they planted their seeds farther apart? Closer together? Deeper? Shallower? Was it better to seed early or late? Alongside their black medic, they added test plots of other legume varieties—Australian medics, Sirius peas, yellow blossom sweet clover. Dave Oien religiously followed research out of Canada, where the university in Saskatoon, Saskatchewan, had hired a legume breeder. Dave drove north across the border to get buckwheat seed, west across the Rocky Mountains to get Austrian winter peas, and up to the little town of Sunburst, Montana, in search of another pea variety called Trapper.

With the help of Jim Sims, the Timeless farmers took notes on the results of their experiments, some of which had now been running for more than five years. But even more important, they invited their neighbors to see for themselves. After that field tour at Bud's place, not a summer went by without at least one Timeless-sponsored demonstration day. The little group's big outreach efforts appeared to be making an impact.

"Organic farming isn't just leaving off chemicals, it's a good management program," one farmer wrote in answer to an AERO survey about the Barta farm tour. "I got to thinking, here I am raising food and spreading poisons on it," another survey read. "It just didn't make sense." A third farmer was even willing to speak to a reporter. "It was just the thing I needed," he told her. "After that conference, I parked my sprayer for the last time." The conferences and field tours were a good start for the new crop, the new company, and the new movement. But if they were going to speed up Jim Sims's twenty-year timetable for changing agriculture on the northern plains, it would take more than one show-and-tell session a year.

LEGUMES ANONYMOUS

Jim Barngrover, now chair of the AERO board, was already thinking one step ahead. Even before he scheduled the field tour at Bud Barta's place, he had applied for a grant to hire a dedicated staffer who could survey the status of sustainable agricultural practices not just on one farm, but across the entire northern Great Plains and Intermountain West. Since no one was officially collecting statistics on organic farmers, nobody could say for sure how many of them there were, what they were doing, or whether it was working. For the most part, organic farmers felt more or less like Dave Oien had when he'd started—alone. So it was quite the shocker when the survey results came back, comprehensively describing a whopping 188 sustainable farms across the region. These farmers were doing all sorts of things—planting green manures, integrating crops and livestock, leaving mulch on their fields at the end of the season—most of which, survey respondents reported, were working pretty well. But the farmers also had research questions— research questions that weren't being addressed by their local universities and extension agents. Frustrated, a lot of them had given up on getting good information from the experts. But the survey hinted that these renegades might be willing to listen to someone else: one another. Although fewer than half of respondents reported working with their county agent, three-fourths cited other farmers as an information source. It was this crucial piece of data that stood out when all the surveys made it back through the mail to their author, Nancy Matheson.

Nancy Matheson had grown up just twenty miles from Dave Oien on a grain farm east of Conrad, and like her neighbor, she was as proud of her roots as she was horrified by their most prominent branches. Although Nancy had gone away to UC Berkeley for college, she'd also come home during the summers to drive a combine, and she'd taken the AERO job partly because it meant she could live in Montana full-time. Although most people tended to look to the countercultural youth of liberal urban enclaves as the most likely leaders for social movements, Nancy found equal potential in the communitarian ethos of her parents and grandparents. In 1990, equipped with the data from her survey, she launched a new AERO program, carefully designed to advance a sweeping vision for sustainable agriculture within a familiar agrarian context.

AERO's new initiative—a network of Farm Improvement Clubs—was based on a series of 1940s-era groups that had been sponsored by extension offices in the Midwest: Corn and beef improvement clubs. Nancy Matheson had become intrigued by these midcentury clubs after hearing about them from a retired soil conservationist who attended an AERO outreach session. She came to believe that it was these homespun farmers' associations—as much as the showy postwar demonstrations put on by various colleges—that had so effectively spread the technology of industrial agriculture throughout rural America. If improvement clubs had ushered in the chemical revolution, Nancy reasoned, maybe they could be repurposed to disseminate the principles and practices of sustainable agriculture. And with the Farm Improvement Club program, AERO's Ag Task Force could make good on the resolution they'd made in the heat of battle with the deans at Montana State University. Farmers could do research themselves.

But Nancy knew such clubs weren't just about the particulars of weed management and drought-tolerant varieties. Like Russ Salisbury, she had grown up in a Farmers Union family, and she'd attended chapter meetings at her country school. Nancy remembered meeting up with her classmates at those meetings, where they'd gathered around the piano and belted out camp songs. Akin to those Farmers Union meetings, Nancy envisioned, Farm Improvement Clubs could provide something their members required more than anything else: community.

Central Montana's sparsely populated plains were lonely enough as it was, and for unconventional farmers, skipping the annual trip to the fertilizer dealer meant losing a friend. Facing the double isolation of rural life and their unorthodox approach, sustainable agriculturalists could find the moral support they really needed at club meetings without ever having to be explicit about it. It was just a bunch of guys talking about drill spacing and seeding schedules.

Nancy's Farm Improvement Club model was simple: AERO offered small grants to groups of four or more producers, up to 800 dollars per club. Each group proposed a project to investigate a common interest or problem related to resource conservation and sustainable production. The Farm Improvement Clubs had to be farmer directed, but they also had to include a technical adviser from either the university or a government agency. This stipulation ostensibly provided farmers with access to expertise and resources, but also served to educate the clubs' technical "advisers" about agroecological practices. At the end of the year, all the clubs gathered to share what they'd learned—and participating farmers frequently offered midseason demonstrations as well. The Timeless farm tours were the prototype for the clubs' field days, which were intentionally not structured as how-to sessions like the experiment stations offered. "These are just farmers who are trying some things and who are willing to let their neighbors come take a closer look," Nancy emphasized.

Beginning in 1990 with six clubs and thirty-three farms and ranches, the program grew to function as a veritable parallel extension service—with the added bonus of slowly bringing along members of the official extension service at the same time. Over the next decade, AERO grants would support more than 120 clubs and 500 participating producers, nearly all of whom were enthusiastically educating their neighbors at field days. By 1994, the USDA was funding AERO to teach its extension agents and soil conservationists about sustainable agriculture. The agency awarded the organization a 91,000-dollar grant to develop and implement training programs across five states.

Not surprisingly, legume rotation and black medic husbandry were the focus of several Farm Improvement Clubs, and Jim Sims appeared repeatedly as a technical adviser. But the roster of AERO-funded farmer science ran the gamut from community gardens to organic marketing to irrigation. Some groups, like the Friends of the Bitterroot Weed Team and the Horse Manure Compost Club, worked on agronomic challenges. Others—like the Echinacea Project and the Fort Belknap Peas and Oats Club—explored experimental crops. The Gumbo Group turned out not to be a foray into southern cuisine but a Choteau-based alliance of legume-alternative trials. They were using plants to improve their local soils, which were so clayey that locals called them gumbo. "If it rains half an inch," Dave Oien wryly remarked, "the roads over there get so muddy you can't drive on them."

The Farm Improvement Club program not only helped Timeless develop their cropping systems, but also dramatically expanded the pool of farmers who were pursuing sustainable agriculture. Skeptics were transformed into advocates, ready to share equipment, swap seed, compare notes, "come out" to their neighbors, and even lobby the legislature if need be. Anybody who still thought this stuff was just for hippies had to face some pretty unlikely looking flower children—like the leader of the Pondera County Alternative Weed Management Club, rancher Tuna McAlpine.

THE LONE RANGER MEETS DR. DOLITTLE

Tuna McAlpine was a former high school wrestler who lived thirty miles northwest of the Oien place, down Bullhead Road in Valier. In the early 1990s, Dave started hearing about this guy who famously "loved knapweed," and he figured he'd found a kindred spirit. But as it turned out, Tuna's reasons for pursuing low-input agriculture were a little different from Dave's. A rock-ribbed libertarian who thought the Republican Party had gotten too soft on guns, Tuna didn't want anybody infringing on his constitutional rights. Not the government, and not Monsanto. Tuna had taken a college degree in modern livestock management and had come home to his family's ranch in 1984 with a suite of chemicals to apply. But the corporate approach to agriculture didn't sit well with him, so he'd converted to the low-input philosophy of Holistic Resource Management and rebelled against everything his professors had taught him. "I'm a stubborn Scotchman," Tuna explained. "I didn't want to suck up to them chemical boys."

Fiercely independent, Tuna made no secret of the fact that he "wasn't much for meetings." Born fighting, as he was fond of saying, the guy wasn't exactly the most likely candidate to facilitate one of Nancy Matheson's moral support groups. But Dave thought the Farm Improvement Club program needed this headstrong rancher, so he submitted an application for a Pondera County Alternative Weed Management Club, with himself as a member and Tuna as the group leader. In the "contact person" field, Dave wrote down his own address, but next to it he wrote a note. "Clay McAlpine will be the contact person . . . he just doesn't know it yet."

Dave knew his long hair and habit of signing documents with a peace sign probably wouldn't appeal to Clay (whose high school buddies had dubbed him Tuna because the five-foot-six-inch wrestler ate so much tuna fish to maintain weight). But the canny founder of Timeless Seeds had another card to play with his neighbor, and it centered on a mutual problem: Pondera County's weed control program. In the form of unsolicited herbicide at the edge of their fields, Dave and Tuna's political grievances collided, with enough force, perhaps, to forge some kind of bond. For Dave, the chemicals at the edge of his organic fields heralded the long arm of the military-industrial complex. Tuna just wanted the freedom to do his own thing on his own land. So when the Farm Improvement Club proposal got funded, and Tuna McAlpine suddenly found himself designated leader of an organization he never knew existed, Dave pitched the group to Tuna as a way to convince the weed crew to leave his property alone. The purpose of the club's meetings, Dave told its somewhat reluctant leader, would be to establish "no-spray zones" for the Pondera County Weed District. In that case, Tuna said, he would be happy to participate. In fact, he'd host. So in June of 1992, ten local farmers showed up at the McAlpine ranch to an astonishingly, almost violently warm welcome.

Two years on from his "epiphany" at a Holistic Resource Management seminar, Tuna was shaping up to become one of Montana's most outspoken organic proselytizers. It was hard to argue with the man's devastating critique of "chemically dependent farming" and "outhouse pork." Everything about Tuna—from the way he stood (legs wide, belly protruding) to the fearlessness with which he rode his four-wheeler around his five-buffalo-jump spread of Rocky Mountain Front—suggested that he was a rough-and-ready man who asked neither help nor permission when pursuing his convictions.

But when Tuna approached his cattle, he revealed another side of himself. Sitting in silence, he would wait and watch for several minutes while his yearlings encircled him. "They're not like humans for social interaction, but they are company," he'd say, almost lovingly. Was this the Lone Ranger or Dr. Dolittle?

At first, Tuna's farm transition had been powered by sheer guts and determination. On the heels of that Holistic Resource Management seminar, he'd lined out a three-part goal for his operation and single-mindedly pursued it, from intensive grazing to direct marketing to organic transition. The classic self-made Montana cowboy, Tuna had of course taken on all these things himself. But attempting to go it alone had humbled him in some surprising ways. For one thing, Tuna wished he'd involved his wife more, rather than assuming he always had to be the macho man. "I guess I've always said, just like my dad did, 'Oh, I'll get it,'" Tuna reflected. "But a guy can't just do everything alone."

Tuna's independent spirit may have been the fire that got him started, but he couldn't sustain the flame by himself. Railing against the establishment had proven exhausting, and, well, lonely. Going organic had alienated him from his own community, Tuna acknowledged, and that was hard: "You don't have common ground with people if you don't farm the same way."

Like dozens of other participants in AERO's farmer science initiative, Tuna found that common ground with his fellow Farm Improvement Club members. The program's winter meetings—when all the clubs got together to share their findings—started to feel like family reunions. No matter what the weather, Tuna got in his pickup and drove to his friends' field tours. Even though he was mainly a livestock man, he planted seed for Dave. People looked forward to the new highlight of Timeless Seeds' annual field tour and barbecue—Tuna's pig roast. The red-blooded rancher also roped a number of new folks into the sustainable agricultural fold, greatly expanding the capacity and appeal of AERO's modern mutual-aid network.

The public face of the Farm Improvement Clubs' camaraderie was just the tip of the iceberg. These people officiated one another's weddings, hunted on one another's land, loaned one another money and equipment, and coalesced into near-telepathic teams at harvesttime. In all these little ways, the improvement clubs turned the peer pressure of small-town life on its head. The same strong social institutions that had stymied change when one person tried to go it alone were effectively recruited to give the emerging movement staying power. The sharp tongues in these little towns cut both ways.

But there was another sense in which rural community made for a double-edged sword. Many people referred to Timeless as a family, and it was an apt metaphor. Belonging to such a strong alliance was supportive but also demanding. Practicing a different form of economy than the one that determined your car payment and your kids' college tuition meant filling the gap with your own sweat, time, and sacrifice. That was hardly ever enough, so these farmers' mutual aid tended to require extra effort from other members of their households too. It wasn't always easy. After all, the undersowers couldn't *just* feed the soil. Somehow they had to feed their families too—and black medic wasn't cutting it.

While Dave was driving all over the state and experimenting with new crops, his wife, Sharon Eisenberg, was supporting their household of six with her accounting business. Timeless Seeds' black medic sales weren't even enough to put food on the table, let alone pay off the farm note, so Dave was still patching together other ventures. There were bedding plants in the greenhouse, sheep on the pasture, and at one point, Dave got the idea that fenugreek might be a good way to make a little extra money.

WHO'S FEEDING THE FARMER?

Looking back on the precarious beginnings of Timeless Seeds, Sharon recently asked Dave to enumerate the full list of microenterprises they'd experimented with, just to keep from losing the farm. "Start at 1980 and go forward," she said tersely. "I'll let the dog out."

After three decades of marriage, Dave and Sharon knew a little something about the difficulty of raising a family while trying to change the world, and they didn't sugarcoat their experience.

"Dave used to have this idea that you can't sell hay off the farm," Sharon said. "Something about how your most precious resource was your organic matter."

"Soil fertility," Dave said, in between bites of pancake. Sunday breakfast was a favorite ritual of Dave's, and this week, he'd tried throwing something new on the griddle: pancakes made from Timeless Seeds' newest crop, a heritage grain called emmer.

"Yes, exactly, you were worried about losing soil fertility," Sharon picked up. "Well, how about some revenue?"

"Yeah, how about losing your money," Dave agreed, chuckling a bit at his naïvely idealistic former self. He and his wife were still in safe territory, but their tone got more serious as they kept talking.

"He spent ungodly amounts of time being gone to meetings," Sharon continued, her voice dropping its pitch with an almost palpable fatigue. "All the other Timeless farmers did the same thing. I guess they needed to be somewhere where they could discuss their ideas with people who would listen—because your fourteen neighbors around here that farm, they're not interested. But the upshot was that he was gone a lot."

"That's true," Dave said, not laughing this time.

"I think I have all the calendars and I could prove it," Sharon pounced, erasing any shadow of doubt.

Dave cracked a smile again. "She keeps records," he teased his exacting chief financial officer, who spent half of each week at her private CPA office and the other half keeping Timeless Seeds' books in order. "It really sucks."

"A lot of the farmers probably wouldn't have gotten to farm, except that they had a wife that had another income," Sharon proceeded, unfazed by her husband's subtle pleas for humor. "That's the toughest part—the toughest part is there was no money in it and the other toughest part is he was gone all the time."

Black medic may have fixed a lot of nitrogen, but it hadn't fixed the problem with agriculture in America—or even Conrad. When AERO published a list of them in 1989, the full tally of Montana's organic farms fit on one page of the *Sun Times*. Little old ladies were still yelling at Jim Sims to stop growing the weed they were trying so hard to keep out of their lawns, while their sons kept right on growing wheat and cursing rising fertilizer prices. Realizing that his sociology had been miles behind his agronomy, Dave changed tactics. Biological wealth was not going to pay the bills. He needed a crop that farmers could use to build their soils—but also sell. As food.

III

TIMELESS
GROWS UP

6

HAVE YOUR SEEDS AND EAT THEM TOO

In 1991, Dave Oien and Tom Hastings drove down to the ag trade show in Great Falls, hoping to sell some of their green manure seeds. The Aggie, as the annual event was affectionately known to locals, was a good marketing opportunity for Timeless. But it was also a chance for Dave to scout out new crops for his experiments. Since Great Falls was the hub of Montana's famed Golden Triangle region, the show drew folks from hundreds of miles away, at least a few of whom were bound to be trying something Dave hadn't heard of yet. One of his favorite people to talk to at these shows was a Canadian farmer named Richard Behnke, who shared Dave's enthusiasm for the alternative agricultural vanguard.

This year, Richard was excited about a legume he had just started growing for the food market: French Green lentils. Like the green manures Timeless was selling, these legumes sponsored their own nitrogen and left some in the soil for next year. But since their seeds were edible, they doubled as a cash crop. You could have your seeds and eat them too.

The market for French Green lentils was significant, Richard reported, and American farmers weren't onto it yet. It might be a great niche for Timeless. Why not expand the business to include "pulse" crops—annual legumes, with seeds you could eat.

Dave hadn't thought of selling an *edible* seed—to consumers. But since the pool of farmers willing to buy green manures didn't seem to be large enough to provide an income, selling food appeared to be a better strategy for staying in business. Lentils could provide a solid bottom line for Timeless Seeds—without sacrificing all the important soil building and movement organizing that was still going on underneath.

It made sense to Dave's cousin Tom Hastings, who went straight back to Conrad and planted French Greens on his place in the spring of 1992. These things are great, Tom reported to Dave. We should plant more. Fantastic, Dave said. Now, how in the heck are we going to sell them? Timeless Seeds was just beginning to get the hang of marketing seed to farmers, who, after all, were mostly their friends. They had no real experience in the food business. When Tom asked where to send his bumper crop, all Dave could think of was the woman who supplied organic produce to Sharon's local buying club, Missoula distributor Sally Brown. Sally's account wasn't nearly big enough to absorb all those lentils, Dave admitted. And then he had an idea.

Back in the early eighties, Sally had told Dave about a trade show in Anaheim, California. She and one of her Montana suppliers had signed up for the natural foods expo, and they'd invited Dave to tag along. The budding organic beef entrepreneur had piled into his friends' station wagon for the twenty-four-hour journey, hoping to learn a thing or two about the natural food business and maybe even drum up some interest in his new product. Although Dave had made some encouraging connections in Anaheim, he'd come home to discover that his organic beef labels wouldn't pass muster with the USDA, so he'd forgotten all about it. But now Dave had a more thoroughly vetted business proposition and a product he knew he could sell. He called Sally, and she told him the show was still happening. What do you think? Dave asked Jim Barngrover. Are you up for a trip to California?

Natural Products Expo West was an eye-opener for the two hayseeds, who had never been to such a big trade show before. When Dave made his first visit to the expo a decade earlier, organics had still been a fringe industry—if, indeed, you could even call it an industry. So Dave was amazed to see what had become of the little health-food event. On the heels of the national panic over Alar (a chemical sprayed on apples to regulate their growth), mainstream consumers were demanding poison-free food like never before. Booth after booth of slick retail products gave notice that organics had arrived—in breakfast cereal, TV dinners, even pet food. And yet, Richard Behnke was right. Nobody had French Green lentils.

Dave and Jim were still poor as church mice. But they resolved to return to Anaheim the following year with a crop to sell. All they had to do was find farmers willing to grow it for them—on an IOU.

THE LENTIL POOL

Dave pulled out his AERO Rolodex and reached deep into his agrarian heritage. Back in the early days of the Farmers Union, he remembered his grandfather telling him, farmers had formed wheat pools as a means of combining their resources and increasing their bargaining power in the marketplace. A form of community capital, the pools allowed cash-poor growers to build a business. Dave didn't see why the same strategy couldn't work for him. How about a lentil pool?

"Here's a crop that's not being grown yet in the United States,"

Dave explained to his Ag Task Force buddies. "There's no guarantee of a crop or a market. But if you plant, we'll help you out. And no matter who else grows for us, we'll always use your crops." Since he didn't have any infrastructure, Dave told the growers they would need to provide their own storage. There would be no legal contract. The pool would collectively determine a fair price for the lentils, and each member would get paid quarterly based on how much they grew.

Dave found seven farmers willing to take the plunge with him: Bud Barta, Tom Hastings, and five other intrepid souls. (Jim Barngrover didn't have his own place, so his stake in the deal was sweat equity.) In the spring of 1993, each pool member planted 40 acres, making 200 in total. Dave figured that would be enough to guarantee a good-size inventory to peddle the following year in Anaheim.

There was a new face in on this lentil pool venture: a third-generation grain farmer from Big Sandy, Montana, named Jon Tester. Tester had joined AERO after reading the proceedings of the 1988 Lewistown conference, which had prompted the young schoolteacher to experiment with longer rotations and new crops. "Fifty acres of lentils built this house," Jon told every visitor to the modest bungalow he had constructed on his great uncle's homestead, explaining that it was a bumper crop of little red legumes that had financed the place. At the time, Timeless was still experimenting with lentils and hadn't started marketing them commercially, so Jon had located an out-of-state buyer, which had since gone under. Eager to find a new market for his prolific legumes, he was glad to hear Timeless was getting into the lentil business, and he took Dave up on the offer to join the pool.

Jon was just two hours east of the Timeless plant, and he liked the idea of good old-fashioned neighborhood organizing. He was thinking of running for the AERO board, and maybe even for the state legislature. With a flattop haircut, a booming voice, and three fingers missing from a boyhood run-in with the meat grinder at his family's custom butcher shop, Jon had prairie populist bona fides. He was just the sort of salt-of-the-earth collaborator Timeless needed to get their new edible seed venture going. "We couldn't do it without the pool," Dave told a reporter. "To build the product, we needed guaranteed production. If one of us got hailed out, we'd still have lentils from the others."

But no one did get hailed out, and ironically, the farmers' good fortune was Dave's biggest problem. When harvesttime rolled around in the fall of 1993, he had tons of French Green lentils on his hands and only so many outbuildings on his 280-acre farm. Where was he going to clean and package all those legumes in time for Natural Products Expo West in the spring?

Orville Oien's "this farm is too small" admonitions echoed in Dave's memory as he drove by the feed mill where he and his dad used to haul barley every week. Pausing the doubting voice in his head, Dave noticed that the mill was not being used. Now, *that* place would hold all these lentils, Dave thought. But given that the other financially oriented folks in this community were just as skeptical about his project as Dave's accountant father had been, who would loan him the money to lease it?

There was no way Timeless Seeds was going to qualify for a conventional bank loan. "They had two questions for me at the bank," Dave recalls. "What is organic? And what is a lentil?" What Dave needed was a renegade financier as different from those buttoned-down loan officers as Jim Sims was from his fellow researchers at MSU. He thought he knew the guy.

Dave went back to the prospectus he'd written up for his meetings with lenders. His goal was ambitious, but simple: Timeless Seeds needed to raise 40,000 dollars in order to move into its first proper facility. There was no use calling anyone who self-identified as an "investor," since bankers had already written this business off as a risky proposition. Luckily for Dave, there was at least one person who thought it was the *bankers* who were the risky proposition. One person who might see the loan officers' thumbs-down as a *good* sign.

For Russ Salisbury, avoiding bankers had paid off. By refusing to practice any form of agriculture that required him to sign on the dotted line, the junkyard philosopher had managed to avoid the farm debt that had piled up all around him. Thanks to his frugal lifestyle, Russ found himself—at the height of the eighties farm crisis—with some resources to spare. It wasn't a lot, but he knew he could make a difference for Timeless. Instead of outright cash, Russ pledged 20,000 dollars' worth of equipment, plus a week's worth of labor to help Dave set it up. Buoyed by Russ's gift, Dave leased the building, sold his 40,000 dollars' worth of shares, and went back to Anaheim in the spring of 1994 ready to hawk some legumes.

Dave and Jim's first trip to California had educated them in some of the niceties of marketing, and they were determined to put their best foot forward this time. In place of the drab bulk bags they'd showed up with the previous year, the Timeless partners carefully arranged a retail-ready display, custom-built by Bud Barta. It was a nifty little exhibit, but Dave didn't expect his lentils to sell themselves. Feeling the weight of his friends' 60,000-dollar vote of confidence, Dave made sure nobody passed the Timeless booth without receiving a great big Montana smile.

Of the 14,000 people who walked by at Expo West 1994, Dave estimated, about 400 actually stopped to look at Timeless Seeds' basket of lentils. The optimistic farmer thought at least a dozen seemed genuinely interested. But after shaking hands and pocketing Dave's card, the prospective buyers disappeared back into the crowd, where the tantalizing propositions of hundreds of other suitors awaited them. Exotic jams, organic face cream, therapeutic tea blends. Taking in the dazzling array of products at the massive trade show, Dave began to wonder if he belonged in this industry. But then, out of the blue, a friend he'd met years earlier called him up with a business proposition.

FAIR EXCHANGE

Ann Sinclair was a seasoned marketer. She had built her career working for Eden Foods, one of the top organic brands on supermarket shelves. But now she was starting her own company, Fair Exchange. She wanted to lead with a soup line called Shari's Bistro. And she wanted to source the lentils from Timeless. Unlike Eden, this wasn't a million-dollar venture. Ann had borrowed the start-up capital from her dad.

Well versed in growing big things from small seeds, Dave and Jim decided they liked Sinclair's vision. Compared to some of the hustles going down in Anaheim, Fair Exchange appeared to offer a much friendlier entrée into the organic industry. In fact, the deal Timeless struck with Ann Sinclair wasn't too far removed from the modus operandi of AERO work parties. "We put up the lentils," Dave later recalled. "Everyone contributed what they had in talent and commodities, and four soups with the new 'Shari's Bistro' label went on the shelves August thirty-first." Just a few months after Expo West 1994, Timeless Seeds had scored its first major customer.

Much like Timeless Seeds' lentil pool, Fair Exchange was based on a cooperative model. Sinclair returned a portion of her proceeds directly to the growers, in "exchange" for everything they contributed. "The growers provide us with their expertise in organic production, consistent quality, and assistance in several key areas of our business," Sinclair professed. "The reality is, the raw ingredient embodies the true wealth of the whole system. In our case, the soil is our fundamental resource base. Without it, we have no business. And without the knowledge of growers who manage the soil, we have no way of tapping that resource wisely and supporting its continued fertility."

"One of the criteria of our product development process is the impact our finished products have on crop rotation on the farm," Sinclair continued. "If we rely heavily on small grains and ignore legumes, which are important to small grain rotation, we undermine our own business growth by ignoring the long-term requirements of the organic farm. The factor of crop rotation can seem limiting at first, but if you build relationships with people in diverse growing regions, and network with the ecological needs of the farm in mind, then this diversity becomes a business strength."

Dave couldn't have found a better champion. Sinclair didn't just want to sell soup—she also wanted to help Timeless rejuvenate Montana soils. And this time, they would actually make money. Five months after the inaugural cans of Shari's Bistro soup hit retail shelves, Timeless received its first dividend check.

It was a surprise to the members of the lentil pool, who hadn't expected any compensation for at least a year. Perhaps this was a viable business after all.

One of those happily surprised farmers was Timeless Seeds' own Bud Barta, who had hit his stride after twelve years as an organic grower. Having built up the fertility on his now fully transitioned farm, Bud had seen his yields steadily climb, and he was starting to get a handle on the weeds too. Bud slotted Fair Exchange–bound French Green lentils into the second year of his four-year rotation, following black medic and before two years of small grains. Bud's preference was to plow down all the black medic—or perhaps another green manure like buckwheat or sweet clover—so as to start off the cycle with a nitrogen-gorged bang. But he reserved the option of harvesting it if seed prices were high, or cutting it for hay if his cattle needed the feed.

The truth was, Bud had to be flexible, because, as exciting as it was to get that first check from Fair Exchange, lentils still weren't paying the bills. In order to support his family, the jack-of-all-trades supplemented his farm work with another gig, Barta Built. The multitalented tradesman enjoyed the challenge of constructing energy-efficient homes for his unsuspecting neighbors. Instead of trying to sell green homes to Republicans, Bud described his handiwork as rustic, affordable, and high quality. No one objected. But Bud wasn't the only Timeless collaborator supporting himself with a side job while he hoped for growth. Fair Exchange had good intentions, but the math just didn't add up.

By the spring of 1995, Timeless Seeds had supplied just 15,000 pounds of lentils for Shari's Bistro soup. The premium they received for their French Greens was tremendous, but the volume wasn't nearly sufficient to support eight families. Without some additional revenue—or at least an evidence-based projection—Timeless and company couldn't stay in business. Unfortunately, health problems were slowing down their champion, Ann Sinclair. The founder of Fair Exchange had to sell her company to deeper-pocketed executives, who changed the brand name, gutted the mission, and eventually shuttered the whole enterprise. Meanwhile, team Timeless had realized they couldn't get by supplying just 15,000 pounds of lentils, so they had entered the belly of the corporate beast as well. With one massive contract.

7
300,000 POUNDS OF LENTILS

Back at the Anaheim trade show in 1994, a woman had stopped by the Timeless booth and picked up a handful of French Green lentils from the bowl on display. "These are beautiful, just like silk," the woman gushed, introducing herself as the buyer for "Trader Joe's." Sounds like a family business out of some little town, Dave thought. So when the buyer told him she wanted at least 300,000 pounds of lentils for her sixty-store chain—for starters—Dave was amazed. And a little dejected. "Sorry, we don't do that," he told the woman, realizing that he was likely passing up the best deal he'd ever been offered. But what could he do? The buyer wanted cute one-pound bags of lentils with her company's label on them—not the dowdy twenty-five-pound sacks that Timeless was supplying for natural-food store bulk bins. Timeless wasn't set up to do that. At least not yet.

Dave, who was used to begging people to give his lentils a chance, was surprised again when the woman persisted, calling him back six weeks later. She asked the astounded farmer to draw up a proposal for an enterprise expansion. Can't you just price out bags, labels, and transportation costs? she asked, as though she were talking about so many widgets. Dave wasn't honestly sure if he could do all those things. But he couldn't say no twice.

Once again, Timeless dug deep into its underground network to support its growth. Russ Salisbury found a bagging machine lying around in his equipment boneyard, fixed it up, and modified it to measure one-pound increments. A friend of Dave's from Conrad thought he could find some people to run the remodeled machine. A key member of the local AERO chapter, Dave's friend was also on the board of Northern Gateway Enterprises, which was looking for steady employment for their developmentally disabled clients. Northern Gateway had a building, and they fronted the money for a sealing machine to go along with Russ's bagger.

The first pound of lentils that Timeless sent to Trader Joe's split open in the mail. So did the second. But Timeless kept trying, and after four months, they'd fine-tuned a package that could withstand the trip to California.

Of course, by now, the little company's back was up against the wall, as they tried to fulfill Trader Joe's gargantuan order. Dave worked fourteen-hour days, supervising three hired hands from six to nine A.M., moving over to Northern Gateway from nine thirty to three thirty, and then pulling two more shifts at night. But even at that unrelenting pace, Dave knew he and his staff couldn't finish the job alone. So he called on everyone he could think of to help out: the families of Northern Gateway employees, the Timeless Seeds board (who came in and put together a few packages after a meeting), even Tom Hastings's sister. All told, nearly thirty people were involved in the effort in some form or another, and before they knew it, the Timeless crew had ramped up production to 2,400 bags a day. In October of 1994, they loaded up a commercial truck with 30,000 packages of lentils—twice the volume they'd sold thus far to Fair Exchange—as a test run for Trader Joe's. By June of 1995, Timeless had sent 395,000 pounds to the California-based grocery chain.

THE RELUCTANT ENTREPRENEUR

It was not easy to keep Timeless true to its mission while cranking out so many bags of lentils, but Dave embraced the opportunity to bring economic development to Conrad. If you wanted to give back, he decided, it helped to have something to give. Now that Timeless had a legitimate processing operation, they could offer jobs to this economically challenged community, even if it was just one or two to start. They could support the nonprofit that provided vocational rehabilitation for north-central Montanans with developmental needs. Dave even bought an ad for the high school yearbook in Dutton, which felt particularly apt. Half an hour out of Conrad, the neighboring town was just a few miles south of Dave's grandparents' first homestead.

"I've lived in Conrad almost all my life," Dave told a bright-eyed intern at AERO, who'd come out to the plant to write an article for the nonprofit's newsletter. "But I didn't become a real part of the community until I started contributing to it economically." Twenty years after moving home, the Timeless CEO's perspective on change had itself changed. He still didn't believe in business as usual. But he was pretty excited about business as *unusual*. If they could make this legume thing really pencil out, Dave realized, he and his friends could have a much bigger impact.

Even consummate activist Jim Barngrover—who had spent countless hours lobbying the legislature—embraced the possibilities of making a difference through the market. Jim had started a small distribution business, Barnstormer's, to supplement his largely volunteer work for Timeless Seeds. He researched his organic and fair trade products carefully, well aware that economic incentives could easily lead such businesses astray from their lofty goals. Selling product without selling out was no mean feat.

But now that they had nitrogen fixation down, this was Timeless Seeds' next big challenge.

CASH COW

The Trader Joe's deal was particularly tricky, because unlike Fair Exchange, the California-based chain wouldn't pay a premium for organic. They didn't care if the lentils Timeless supplied had been sprayed or not. All the farmers in the lentil pool had certified their acreage—in fact, most of them were members of the same Organic Crop Improvement Association chapter. But 300,000 pounds was more lentils than Timeless could scrounge up from their fellow organic growers, or even from conventional growers in Montana. To fill the Trader Joe's order, they'd had to start buying conventional product from across the border in Saskatchewan.

Back when Dave had first planted them in the eighties, lentils had essentially been organic by definition. Herbicide manufacturers in the grain belt had developed their products for use in wheat and barley fields, and the most common formulations killed all broadleaf plants. As every young farmer converting a family place had to patiently explain to their parents, lentils were a broadleaf. If they used chemicals to kill their weeds, they'd kill their crop too. Moreover, broadleaf herbicides could persist in the soil for up to seven years, so there was no question of spot treating a little patch of thistles during a fallow year. In the early 1980s, planting lentils meant parking the sprayer for good.

Ten years on, when Timeless Seeds landed the Trader Joe's contract, there still weren't many nonorganic lentil fields in Montana. But Saskatchewan was a different story. Since the university at Saskatoon had a dedicated pulse-crop breeder, manufacturers north of the border had invested in the development of more targeted chemicals that lentils could withstand. These weren't as toxic as the generalist broadleaf herbicides being used in Montana's wheat fields. But they were a far cry from the "solar farm" Dave had in mind.

Conrad's staunchest organic farmer hadn't intended to get into the business of sourcing and selling chemically fertilized products. But convincing central Montanans to grow organic specialty lentils was slow going, and it occurred to Dave that *conventional* specialty lentils might be the perfect gateway crop. This pitch was simple—here's a niche product that offers a higher return per acre than wheat and doesn't require as much fertilizer. Once Dave had farmers sold on the economic potential of lentils, then he could inform them that their new crop could be grown without *any* chemicals—for an even higher premium.

Of course, the immediate reason Dave needed to buy conventional lentils was to fulfill the Trader Joe's order. Even if that contract wasn't Timeless Seeds' ultimate goal, Dave reasoned, it was a powerful means to that end—probably his best bet of getting more of Montana's farmers out of the commodity trap. That one big deal had made so many things possible. The Conrad processing plant. The first private stock offering. All that equipment from Russ. Had it not been for the lucrative grocery chain opportunity, it was doubtful whether Timeless would have grown their lentil pool to encompass a broader circle of farmers. And without that jump in scale, they wouldn't have been able to offer employment to twelve developmentally disabled baggers.

Dave knew that each piece of his business-cum-movement had to mature apace, in order to keep the whole synergistic system humming along. His heart was on the farm, but he tried to keep his head squarely focused on marketing and infrastructure—to make sure all those lentils would have someplace to go. And yet, adept as he was at inspiring folks to pitch in to help grow his company, Dave was wary of mobilizing the underground on behalf of the market. In truth, he had some nostalgia for the renewable-energy era of AERO, when everything was so much simpler. Back then, his weekends were spent gathering with like-minded people who shared knowledge and labor for free. Like so many of his fellow do-it-yourselfers, Dave had found it fulfilling to come home from a weekend workshop with the tools to immediately make a difference in his own life. It had been easy then: Make your own heat. Collect your own energy. But now that Dave and his friends had made their solar farms into their living and not just their hobby, they were constantly reminded that the economy around them didn't play by the same rules they did. In the murky, somewhat oxymoronic compromise zone known as "green business," the line between selling your product and selling your soul could be hard to draw.

HOLDING THE BAG

In June of 1995 Timeless sent their largest shipment yet to Trader Joe's. As soon as the delivery truck left the Conrad plant, the company's army of packaging staff got right back to work. They never knew when they might get the next call from California, and they wanted to be ready when the truck showed up. But the phone didn't ring. The truck never arrived. Months passed before anyone bothered to tell Dave, but Trader Joe's had dropped the product. Timeless was literally left holding the bag. Thousands of them. Just a few months after what had appeared to be its big break, the company found itself on the verge of bankruptcy.

When the shock abated, Dave began to piece together what had gone wrong. Trader Joe's had asked for ramped-up production in the winter, when their marketing gurus told them people were making lentil soup. Not being farmers, the store's buyers assumed they could instantaneously source some legumes to fill that demand. Once the weather started warming, Trader Joe's customers gave up their soup habit, and the lentils languished on the shelf. So the grocery chain stopped stocking them, figuring they could always pick them up again whenever demand returned. Never mind that this year's crop was already in the ground.

But there had been another problem too, one for which Dave took some responsibility: dental claims. When he'd started calling around Saskatchewan in search of product to fill the Trader Joe's order, Dave had asked for "precleaned" Canadian grade-one lentils, assuming that meant the processor had sorted out all the rocks. Given what a rush he'd been in, Dave hadn't double-checked, and the result was that someone eventually chomped down on Trader Joe's house-brand lentils and broke a tooth on a rock. It turned out that "grade one" meant less than 0.1 percent stones— so theoretically, a pound of French Greens could have ten stones in it and still make the grade! None of the Saskatchewan lentils Timeless sourced were that dirty, but even a single stone in 100,000 pounds was one too many. An embarrassment for Dave (who vowed that Timeless would never again sell lentils they hadn't cleaned themselves), the errant stone had been a liability for his buyer. Since the product didn't seem to be a big hit anyway, Trader Joe's decided not to risk any more phone calls from personal injury lawyers.

The loss of the Trader Joe's contract was devastating. Timeless was committed to purchasing the massive inventory they had asked their farmers to seed, but they had nowhere to sell it. For the past nine months, the company had poured all their time and energy into one customer. They had tailor-made their operation to fulfill one contract, which was now history. "When the product quit working for them, the lights could've gone out," Dave admitted. "But we were totally stubborn."

8

CAVIAR IN THE CATTLE RATION

THE CURIOUS RISE OF THE BLACK BELUGA

Although Timeless Seeds was focused on French Greens, Dave hadn't sacrificed the small part of his own acreage that he reserved for test plots. In between the rows of medics and forage peas was the first lentil Dave ever planted: a tiny black seed developed by the University of Saskatchewan's Indian Head experiment station for use as a green manure, which Jim Sims had started promoting in Montana. Since Dave followed Sims's research so closely, he'd been one of the first American farmers to plant the new variety when it was registered in 1986.

Breeder Al Slinkard hadn't even considered licensing "Indianhead lentil" as a food crop, since the hard seed took so long to cook and its soup "turned an icky grey color." (Slinkard—aka Dr. Lentil—was already semifamous for revitalizing Saskatchewan's agricultural reputation with a gargantuan, bright-green variety called Laird.) But Dave figured a lentil was a lentil, no matter what its official purpose. Indianheads were cheap. They were great for his soil. And since they'd been bred to make nitrogen, they were 24 percent protein. Why not add them to the cattle ration? And for that matter, why not try some himself?

SOMETHING DIFFERENT

In the midst of the Trader Joe's hullaballoo in 1994, Dave had gotten a call from an heirloom bean buyer in Idaho. Lola Weyman had ordered French Green lentils from Timeless, but she wondered if Dave had anything new. She was looking for something different, Lola said. Something nobody else had.

Dave hadn't admitted to any of his neighbors that he was eating his soil-building crop. But Lola seemed like a kindred spirit, so he spilled the beans. "I've got this totally beautiful and unusual black lentil," Dave told her. "It's not released as a food, but it's killed neither me nor the cows nor the pigs nor the sheep." Dave sent a small package of Indianheads off to Lola, then got back to bagging and sealing French Greens.

The following week, Lola called back. "We should call them Black Beluga lentils!" she exclaimed, noting the inky legumes' resemblance to high-end caviar. Dave had never eaten caviar before, but the idea of selling his illicit cattle feed to elite chefs captured his fancy. He knew it was perfectly safe—the Czech peasants who developed the variety had been eating it for centuries before a Russian plant collector showed up to catalog it. But as the lentil cultivar made its way through the international research establishment— from Nikolai Vavilov's seed bank in Leningrad (now Saint Petersburg) to a USDA Plant Introduction Station in Pullman, Washington, to Al Slinkard's lab in Saskatoon, Saskatchewan—it had failed to impress cash-crop breeders, who were looking for big, industrial workhorses like wheat and corn. So for years, the modest lentil had languished in a seed vault, and when Slinkard finally saw fit to release it to commercial farmers, it was as a soil builder. Of course, nobody told the Czech farmers their lentils weren't, officially speaking, food. They'd kept right on raising and eating the little black seeds, especially on New Year's Day, when they were believed to confer good luck. Dave wasn't particularly superstitious, but he fully appreciated another advantage of these lentils, which he suspected wasn't lost on the Czechs either. The standout quality of this variety was that it fixed a lot of nitrogen. That's how it had gotten Al Slinkard's attention—the Canadian breeder had seen all that nitrogen as potential fertilizer for tired wheat fields. But nitrogen could be fuel for human bodies too, which metabolized the key nutrient as protein. When Dave sent his black lentils to the lab for nutrient analysis, he discovered that they contained a whopping 9 grams of protein per half-cup serving, along with copious amounts of fiber, iron, folate, and potassium. No wonder his cattle were so healthy, Dave thought. These lentils were a nutritional powerhouse!

Focused on volume, the industrial breeders of the past half century hadn't stopped to consider that farmers might have *intentionally* selected crop varieties for characteristics other than yield—that, in truth, there might be some wisdom in the old adage "Less is more." But by the mid-1990s, interest in nutrient-dense foods like these forgotten lentils was beginning to resurge among nutritionists and health-conscious eaters. Perhaps, Dave concluded, their time had come. Timeless had stretched its capacity to the max cranking out green lentils for Trader Joe's, but Dave bagged up some black ones himself to send to Lola. Quietly, Black Belugas made their debut in the fall of 1994.

Unlike the Trader Joe's deal, the new variety didn't take off. Lola sold a few packages here and there—to eccentric chefs and specialty food stores—but most people were as skeptical as the breeder had been. A black lentil? Who wanted to eat that? If Trader Joe's had continued to order truckloads of French Greens, Dave probably would have forgotten about his odd little Belugas, which were a tough sell. But when the grocery chain discontinued its order, Dave gave his black lentils another look. With Timeless Seeds on the brink, he and his friends knew they needed to re-align the business with its original values. What could be more fitting than returning to green manure crops—and getting people to eat them!

This time, they decided, they wouldn't look for a big contract from a national distributor. They would develop their own brand, their own packaging, and their own relationships with stores and restaurants. The Timeless boys had long since learned the importance of diversification on the farm. When the Trader Joe's deal collapsed, they realized that diversity was key to the resilience of their business too. Slowly but surely, Timeless built a fan base for Black Belugas, beginning in Montana. They emphasized the added value and unique nutritional benefits of the variety, which, to their knowledge, was higher in protein than any other lentil on the market. Each package bore a Timeless Seeds label and was certified organic. The company cleaned every batch themselves to make sure there were no rocks in the bags.

Dave met personally with as many buyers as he could: Missoula's Good Food Store, Helena's Real Food Market, even the cooperative in Bozeman that had originally sold his organic beef. He asked store managers which regional distributors they liked to work with and started placing Timeless products in independent stores across the Northwest. Although he highlighted Black Belugas, Dave offered his customers other choices too: French Greens, Petite Crimsons, Harvest Golds, Pardinas. Timeless Seeds also supplied non-lentil options from other phases of the crop rotation: split peas, flax, and eventually even barley (albeit an heirloom purple variety). This way, stores could figure out which products their customers liked best—and Timeless had a fallback plan if a particular crop had a bad year. It took six years to build the company back after the Trader Joe's debacle, but by the turn of the millennium, it had emerged stronger than ever. Dave started inviting customers to visit the Conrad headquarters of his growing company, which no longer seemed like such a foolhardy experiment.

LIGHTS, CAMERA, LENTILS

The second person to take Dave up on his offer to visit was Blu Funk, a chef from Bigfork, Montana. A hundred and seventy-three miles and a world away from Conrad, Bigfork drew a mix of tourists headed for nearby Glacier National Park, wealthy summer residents, and local vacationers whose families had maintained waterfront cabins for generations. This little town at the northeast end of Flathead Lake was the apotheosis of big sky chic, and its prime attraction, nestled between upscale art galleries and the Bigfork Summer Playhouse, was Blu Funk's gourmet dining establishment: ShowThyme. Blu knew his customers were buying cowboy paintings by the dozens, and he thought they ought to get a real taste of Montana when they ate at his restaurant. So he started purchasing Black Belugas from Timeless in 1998.

Blu's unique presentation sold ShowThyme's customers on his curious side dish, which brought Dave's lentils out of the soup and onto center stage. ShowThyme's little lentil order steadily increased in volume, and Blu became a loyal Timeless supporter. When he called Dave in 1999 to buy more Belugas, the Timeless CEO could fill out the shipping label from memory. "No, don't ship them," Blu said. "We'll come pick them up."

"Are you sure?" Dave asked. It was a three-hour drive over the

Rocky Mountains, one that people typically made in the other direction. Yep, Blu said, he and his wife, Rose, wanted to see the operation.

Playing show-and-tell with the owners of one of Montana's finest restaurants, Dave registered an unfamiliar feeling: pride. The Conrad plant was still a pretty humble place—more than a little dilapidated. But Blu and Rose were completely taken with it. "I'm going to put Black Belugas on every plate," Blu promised. And he did. Dave's former cattle feed became a star at ShowThyme, where it was served as an accompaniment to every entrée, and Blu's customers started asking him where they could get some lentils of their own.

At the dawn of a new millennium, Timeless Seeds had hit a major turning point. After a decade of valiantly paddling against the prevailing currents of American agriculture, Dave could feel a gathering wind at his back. It was partly that the world had changed since 1986, when Dave and his three buddies started their little black medic business in his Quonset hut. Organic food was now a multibillion-dollar sector of the American economy, and environmentalism wasn't quite the dirty word it had been a generation ago. But if Timeless had benefited from these changes, it had also helped catalyze them. Ten years after everybody told Dave his idea was impossible, he had convincingly proven them wrong, and the evidence was plainly visible in the thousands of acres of lentil fields spread across central Montana. As a result, people who still thought Dave was a little kooky were showing up at his door in increasing numbers, interested in planting some lentils of their own. These weren't the AERO members and solar energy enthusiasts who'd been struggling upriver with Dave all along. This was the mainstream.

Helping his conventional neighbors convert was exciting for Dave, whose vision had always been to transform agriculture on a regional scale, if not a global one. But it was also a departure from Timeless Seeds' kumbaya coalition-building. Conventional growers had different expectations than Dave's buddies did, and most of them had no idea what they were getting themselves into. Dave knew firsthand that farm conversion was an intense process, which unfolded as a series of sweeping changes. First you had to change your mind. Then you had to change your farm. Then you had to change your business and the institutions that served it. And now that you were a weirdo, you either had to change your community or form a new one.

Joining the lentil underground wasn't an easy road, and Dave didn't expect anyone to make the sacrifices he had. So now his challenge was to shorten the learning curve for those who wanted to follow in his footsteps. This was where things stood in 1998, when the last person he would've ever expected showed up at the door of the Timeless plant.

IV

RIPE FOR REVOLUTION

THE MOVEMENT GOES MAINSTREAM

9
THE CONVERT

Three dry years at the turn of the millennium had left barley farmer Jerry Habets desperately searching for answers. Bankrupt, divorced, and about to lose his family's eighty-seven-year-old homestead, Jerry tried the Bible. Then he went to a psychic. And then he went organic.

It wasn't like Jerry had never heard of organic farming. In fact, he had known about David Oien all his life. The Timeless CEO's famously unkempt homestead was just thirteen miles down the road from the Habets place. And since Dave and his cousin Tom were the only farmers in this town of 2,600 people who were intentionally planting weeds in their fields, word got around. Nineteen-year-old Jerry had raised his eyebrows when he'd seen Dave take the Oiens' land out of malt barley. He thought his neighbor was nuts.

And yet, by the turn of the millennium, the mysterious lentil entrepreneur was looking a little less crazy, having managed to get Timeless Seeds products on the shelves at several retailers and in the hands of a rising Montana chef recently featured in *Bon Appétit*. Dave's bumper-sticker odes to sustainable agriculture—"I (heart) Cover Crops" and "Real Farmers Have Green Manure"—no longer seemed quite so countercultural as they had in the late seventies. Back then, organics had been, as Jerry put it, "pretty far out there." But now, "Got Organic?" bumper stickers were commonplace, and Montana even had a statewide trade organization to support the booming industry: the Montana Organic Association. Jerry went to one of the group's conferences and came back convinced that he should convert. That's how he found himself walking in the door of Timeless Seeds, to talk to David Oien about crops.

"FEEDING THE SOIL"

"Jerry Habets is a real success story for Timeless Seeds," Dave told me, as we began to wrap up a late-afternoon interview. My first trip to the Oien place—in 2011—had convinced me that I needed to come back for a longer stint, so I'd returned to Conrad the following summer, packing a voice recorder and a digital camera. Having covered the history of Dave's business, we were now chatting about its current roster of growers, whom Dave was encouraging me to visit. Many of these people were former conventional farmers, Dave told me, and their stories would teach me a thing or two about how difficult it was to change agriculture on just one farm, let alone across an entire region. In order to understand what Timeless had become as the movement went mainstream, Dave told me, I'd need to get in my Subaru and see for myself.

I was reluctant to part company with Dave and Sharon, but I didn't have to drive far. I kicked off my grand tour of lentil farms with a visit to their Conrad neighbor, whose experience epitomized the initial phase of transition. When Jerry Habets had joined the lentil underground, the first change he'd had to make was both the most critical and the most difficult. He'd had to change his mind.

I met up with Jerry on an early May afternoon, just as central Montana's unforgiving sun was reaching its hottest burn of the day. Drought had struck Conrad again—the worst to hit the Great Plains since the Dust Bowl. But this time Jerry was ready. Outfitted with a ball cap to shade his face and a zip-up sweatshirt in case the wind whipped up, he took me on a pickup tour of his farm, pointing out all the things he'd been doing differently since his conversion to "feeding the soil."

"I'd gone bankrupt farming conventionally," Jerry told me, recalling the desperate day when he'd first walked into the Timeless plant. "I didn't have money for chemicals or fertilizers, so that became my transition to organic. I was forced into it financially, but it turned out to be the best thing I ever did. I learned to take care of my soil first, and everything followed from that."

Jerry's relationship to the soil wasn't an abstract philosophy. The dirt his grandfather first plowed up in 1913 made itself at home on the fifty-six-year-old's red, white, and blue plaid work shirt as though it had been woven right into the design. I knew without asking that Jerry had farmed all his life. And that he hadn't majored in philosophy or religious studies, like Dave. In fact, Jerry had spent just one quarter at Montana State before deciding college wasn't for him.

It wasn't hard to see why Jerry had identified himself, for most of his life, as a conventional farmer. Convention was everywhere I looked. We drove by his grandfather's hundred-year-old barn, its roof finally subdued by last year's fiercest storm. Then we passed the hundred-year-old church Jerry had walked to as a boy, which his grandfather and thirteen other families had constructed the first year they'd arrived, even before building their own houses. There were several advantages to being a third-generation farmer, Jerry emphasized, citing his deep connection to this place. Jerry admired his forebears for their hard work and cooperative spirit, and he was proud to carry those traditions forward.

And yet, in recent years, Jerry had also become more cognizant of his ancestors' mistakes. From the day they first busted sod with a moldboard plow, the Habets family and their fellow homesteaders had taken too much from the land, without adequately giving back. When Jerry took on that regenerative work as his own responsibility, he'd run smack into the downside of being a third-generation farmer: It was hard to change course.

Change had certainly left its mark on the Habets place—but it was a particular kind of change. His grandfather's church had closed in 1962, Jerry remarked, pointing to the fields all around it to demonstrate what that church had been replaced with. The Habets family had continued going to Sunday services, in another sanctuary, but in many ways this prairie had converted to the modern religion of the heartland: wheat, barley, and 2,4-D. Prayers for rain were replaced with center-pivot irrigation, and the guarantee of a good crop became a function of chemistry rather than divine providence.

Leo Habets had recognized his son's knack for this clean and controlled way of farming, and he had encouraged Jerry to start leasing some of his own acreage when he was just nineteen. Jerry couldn't resist the pull of the land, but he was a little ashamed to be coming home so quickly from Bozeman, where he'd quit college after just a few months. He wondered if he shouldn't be making something of himself in the wider world rather than staying home to farm. Although he was already bringing in a good crop by his second season, Jerry felt like a yokel compared to his older neighbor David Oien, who lived closer to town and had a college degree. So when Jerry drove by one day and saw a mess of medic in one of the Timeless farmers' plots, he secretly felt a surge of pride. He may have been just a simple farm boy, but he had clean fields.

"THE FARM JUST FEELS BETTER"

"I needed to be humbled," Jerry reflected as we drove past his own weeds, expressing gratitude for the bankruptcy that had forced him to change his ways. Encouraging me to take pictures, he explained just how beneficial wild mustard is for pollinators. In fact, Jerry said, chuckling, the beekeeper he hosted in exchange for honey had been pressing him for his secret. "The bee guy asked me, 'What is that yellow stuff—the bees are all over it,' and I said, 'That's a weed!' The old way of doing things is that when you saw a few weeds out there, you went out and you killed them. But weeds are just as good for the soil or better than what you plant out there."

Now that he, too, was a "weed farmer," his neighbors had started to look at him like he used to look at Dave Oien, Jerry admitted, grinning. "They think I'm crazy; they're wondering what I'm doing. They have no concept that we're actually feeding organisms in the soil with these weeds we're plowing under. Their idea is if there's anything green out there, you're not a very good farmer. But my intention has changed from making money to growing good-quality, healthy food. I think the soil's happier; I really do. The farm just feels better. It's like it knows I'm not going to pillage."

Jerry sighed, pointing out the parched, yellowing barley on the place across the road. Yellow leaves mean nitrogen deficiency and disease, he explained. The adjoining farmer had planted too many barley crops in a row, and his yields had been steadily decreasing as a result. Jerry knew it was no use trying to *tell* his hapless neighbor to change his ways. He'd have to do what Dave Oien had done—patiently build his own organic system and wait for conventional growers to come to him, when they eventually *had* to find out why his crops looked so good in a drought year. To learn this humble way of farming, Jerry explained, you needed to be in the right frame of mind. It was a spiritual process, he told me. "It's almost like you have a shift in your faith and then you understand that the other way wasn't the right way to do it. That's not the way Mother Nature wants things to be done."

A truck approached from the other direction, and Jerry stopped and opened his window to say hello. It was the neighbor, probably the only person Jerry would have seen today if I hadn't been visiting. The affable farmer inquired about Jerry's father's health and told Jerry to congratulate his parents on their sixty-fifth wedding anniversary. These two men knew nearly every detail of each other's lives, a no-nonsense form of intimacy that had been more common around here when there was a farm family for each 280 acres.

"Look, it's not like my neighbors are stupid," Jerry said as we pulled away, as if to explain how he could show so much respect to someone with such yellow barley. "The one over by Dad's told me, 'You know, these chemicals are going to kill us,' but yet he won't go organic. He can't make that leap."

That leap, as Jerry's crop tour underscored, was called organic *conversion* for a reason: Becoming an organic farmer was a radical transformation, as much philosophical as agronomic. For Leo Habets, as for Orville Oien, farming had meant taking decisive action. Success had been measured in quantitative achievements: bushels per acre, percent protein. But Jerry's approach was completely different. Instead of telling me about things he'd done, he'd been telling me about things he'd noticed. Rather than ticking off the usual litany of statistics about northern Montana's ubiquitous annuals (my notebooks were full of "WW" and "SW"—winter wheat and spring wheat), Jerry was sharing some decidedly non-quantitative observations about the perennial drama of life on this increasingly wild farm. I'd been hearing a lot about trees.

"I've got this tree in the backyard that's just greening up now, and that means it's time to plant," Jerry told me as we turned back toward his house. "Most everyone else here's done seeding—their crops are up and starting to suffer for lack of moisture. But the year I converted, I learned to go by what the tree was doing."

The first spring he farmed without chemicals, Jerry explained, he'd gone out to seed at the same time as everyone else. But it had been miserable. His tree—which hadn't quite budded out yet—had been blowing all over the place in the whipping wind. It still felt like winter. So Jerry'd put his seeder back in the shed and waited. His neighbors had dropped subtle and not-so-subtle hints that he should be out working, Jerry recalled, but he'd stuck to his guns and held off for a few weeks. Come August, his patience had been rewarded: While his neighbors' barley had clearly suffered in the hot weather, his had come through okay. Later seeding was better in an organic system, Jerry explained. The crops grew more slowly, and they could hang on, even if there wasn't much moisture. Long stretches without rain were inevitable in this part of the country, and the weather was only getting more forbidding and unpredictable. "We're definitely seeing climate change," Jerry told me. "It used to be you could count on a three-day soaking rain in June; Dad used to call them the June rains. But up until last year we haven't had that, and then it came too early. We haven't had the usual fall frosts."

A SHOCK TO THE SYSTEM

A modest shower finally showed up for Jerry in 2012—on May 24—but there was a downside to the moisture. While the sun was shining, Jerry'd had an excuse to focus on seeding and put off his rainy-day project. But there was no escaping it now. When I pulled into Jerry's driveway for a follow-up interview, I spied him through the window, hunched over his dining room table. "This isn't a very exciting day to visit," he apologized. "I'm doing my organic paperwork."

The pile of certification forms crystallized the challenge of converting. When Jerry took his soil out of chemical management, it had been a shock to his system—and not just in the philosophical sense. After decades of relying on fertilizers and herbicides to kill the weeds, the farm had been ill prepared to do these things for itself—and it showed. Canada thistle had roared back so ferociously that a neighbor had reported the Habets farm as a noxious weed hazard, so Jerry'd been forced to spot treat a number of patches and revoke their organic status.

Those few passes on a spray rig had ushered Jerry into the unenviable purgatory of "split production." Consequently, he now had to separate out nearly sixty individual fields on the maps he prepared for his annual organic inspection. The sprayed sections were classified "T1"—in their first year of a three-year transition back to organic. Next to them were required "buffer" fields that separated "T1" parcels from "organic" ones. Every new crop meant a new field, and Jerry had to meticulously document the cleaning of all his equipment and storage facilities to prove there was no cross-contamination.

On days like this, Jerry was glad to have some like-minded company to help him sort through it all. "Sometimes I forget that there are other organic growers out there," he sighed, staring at a series of figures on his legal pad that refused to add up. "It's like I'm the one guy representing organic farming in this neighborhood. People are watching. It's always on my mind."

DISTRIBUTION DÉJÀ VU

As Timeless Seeds entered the mainstream and the new millennium, its growers weren't the only ones learning their way into the delicate balance between fitting in and standing out. CEO Dave Oien was also evolving his philosophy, as he tried to juggle both ends of the food chain. It wasn't just mainstream growers Dave needed to woo, but also mainstream consumers. Organics was now a multibillion-dollar industry, and the big dreams Dave and Jim had taken with them to their first food show finally appeared to be within reach. But Dave was torn. Did he really want to play with the big boys?

Before Dave could decide whether to reach out to mainstream retailers, they found him. In 2005, he picked up the phone at the Timeless plant, wondering who could be calling from Texas. It was Whole Foods. The Austin-based chain—165 stores and growing—was launching a new Authentic Food Artisan program, and they wanted to include four of Timeless Seeds' specialty crops as featured products. For the second time, Timeless had a shot at a major distribution deal.

Dave mulled the grocery chain's offer. He didn't want a repeat of the Trader Joe's fiasco. He wasn't going to count on this contract, and he didn't expect it to last. But the old processing plant he had purchased more than a decade ago was literally falling down. Had Jerry Habets walked into Timeless for the first time today, Dave admitted, his enthusiastic convert probably would have walked right back out. In order to keep inspiring farm transitions, the business needed a new facility, probably sooner rather than later. Timeless Seeds' ticket into this plant had been Trader Joe's. Perhaps the Whole Foods deal could finance the next one.

Dave decided to accept the national distribution opportunity, but on a few key conditions. The product he sold Whole Foods would be the same thing he sold to Blu Funk and the Good Food Store—organic crops raised by Montana growers like Jerry Habets. The four featured varieties would represent the diversity of these growers' rotations: Black Beluga and French Green lentils from the legume phase, Purple Prairie barley from the grain phase, and golden flax as the representative oilseed. (Oilseeds, as the name implies, are broadleaf plants grown primarily for the oil in their seeds, like sunflowers, canola, or flax.) Timeless would fulfill the new order, but they would continue selling to their other customers too, including the ones who ordered Petite Crimsons or split peas. The character and scope of the business were nonnegotiable.

With a heterogeneous network of collaborators—up and down the food chain—Dave was finally getting a handle on how to run a business like a lentil farm: When in doubt, diversify. Meanwhile, Timeless Seeds' most unexpected grower had taken biodiversity to a whole new level. Back when Dave first seeded black medic, it had been radical to plant two crops at the same time. That's why Jerry Habets had raised his eyebrows at Dave's "messy" fields. But now that Jerry had gotten religion, he'd gone one step messier.

Having had good luck with a two-crop companion planting, he was ready for something even Dave hadn't experimented with: three.

MONTANA MILPA

When I came back to finish my field tour with Jerry Habets, at the height of 2012's scorching summer, the drought was making national news. Like the persistent headlines, the shriveled barley at Jerry's neighbor's suggested that climate change might seriously threaten the future of the American food supply. Jerry actually had a pretty good stand of barley: not too tall yet, but nice and green. He threaded the grain through the calluses of his enormous hands, large even for a man of his six-foot-two stature. Not bad for a dry year, Jerry decided. But it was the buckwheat, whose white blossoms had hummed with bees throughout a scorching June, that he was really excited about.

Much like the medic Dave Oien had raised, Jerry's buckwheat had "volunteered" from the fallen seeds of last year's stand to join his mixed crop of lentils and chickpeas. "It's the best buckwheat I've had in three years and Mother Nature did it," Jerry exclaimed, turning off his truck so I could hear the bees buzzing in the white blossoms. Detecting sufficient excitement in my furious note taking, Jerry took his hands off the steering wheel. "We can get out if you like," he offered.

Only once I crouched down below the canopy of buckwheat did I realize this was probably the only field of its kind in the world. I was completely disoriented amid the tangle of green flourishing beneath the white blossoms, but I immediately noticed two things: It was unbelievably cool down here, and I couldn't see the dirt.

Without speaking, Jerry separated a single individual from the inchoate web of plant matter to help my eyes adjust to the subtleties of the understory. About a third as tall as the buckwheat, this creature seemed far more focused on the bulbous green protrusions at the base of its fernlike leaves than on the pink flowers that appeared, like an afterthought, on only a few of its stems. This, Jerry told me, was a Black Kabuli chickpea, a specialty dry bean available only from Timeless and a handful of other suppliers.

Aside from the novelty factor of its ebony seeds (which made a stunning hummus), the chickpea had other attributes that recommended it to Jerry. First of all, it was drought resilient. Second, it was a legume, so it made its own fertilizer and donated the surplus to the plants that followed it. The problem with the wondrous black bean, however, was that it also appealed to Jerry's neighbors. Not the two-legged ones (who probably had no more idea than I did that it was even out here), but the deer. Last time Jerry'd planted Black Kabulis, the deer had munched his whole crop a week before harvest.

The deer were one reason Jerry'd added a second layer of green under the chickpeas, a low-lying mass I simply could not distinguish into discrete individuals. These Petite Crimson lentils were another of Timeless Seeds' specialty pulse crops, also champion nitrogen fixers that did well without much moisture. Jerry'd tried this crop before too, but a hot spell had burned them up, so he figured the shade of the chickpeas might give them a better shot at survival. When Jerry told me how the Petite Crimsons returned the favor, I chuckled at the thought of a guard lentil. But apparently that was the case: Lentil plants were so unappetizing to deer and ground squirrels that they provided some protection for the Black Kabulis.

Jerry hadn't planned on doing all these things at once. His plan had been to raise just the chickpeas and lentils this year, then plow their nitrogen-rich stalks under after harvest. The lentil/chickpea "stubble" would feed his soil with nitrogen and organic matter, which would in turn support next year's grain crop. This sequential approach to nutrient management—rotation—is how most newly organic farms recover from what Jerry described as not just one, but two traumas. The first trauma had been gradual but devastating: decades of industrial management had slowly depleted the land's organic matter and biological fertility. The second trauma had been more sudden. When Jerry converted to nonchemical management, he had abruptly cut off the source of fertility on which his industrialized farm had come to rely, leaving it somewhat nutrient poor. As tempting as it might be to return to the "band-aid" of fertilizers, Jerry explained, the only real solution to these double traumas was to patiently rebuild the natural fertility of the soil. In general, this meant taking a break from nitrogen-using plants like wheat and barley for one or two seasons during the legume phase of his rotation, which Jerry was more than happy to do. But when the seeds of the previous year's buckwheat spontaneously germinated in the midst of his lentil/chickpea intercrop, Jerry realized his uninvited guest might be on to something.

A solid stand of buckwheat would partially shade the heat-sensitive Petite Crimsons and Black Kabulis, Jerry realized, envisioning a tripartite canopy structure taking shape in his field. The buckwheat would also acidify the soil, which might help convert chemically "locked" forms of soil phosphorous into plant-available versions, much as lentils and chickpeas fix atmospheric nitrogen. Plus, the combination of all three crops would help crowd out the weeds that had dogged Jerry since his conversion.

He didn't know it, but Jerry had stumbled onto an ancient agroecological principle. For centuries, farmers in the Americas had grown three or more plants together to provide complementary nutrients, control pests, and apportion the summer's abundant sunlight to suit each plant's needs. In fact, Miguel Altieri had discussed this system at AERO's 1984 Sustainable Agriculture Conference, using its Mexican name, *milpa*. Jerry's accidental intercrop was a northern cousin to this classic three-sisters combination of corn, beans, and squash. A Montana milpa.

From the looks of the bees humming along in the buckwheat's flowers and the lentil tendrils hooking themselves to its stalks, everybody seemed to be happy with the arrangement. This triple intercrop was an experiment, Jerry admitted to me. He'd never raised *two* other species underneath his canopy crop. He had no idea if they'd all mature at the same time and wasn't sure how he'd separate them from one another if they did. He'd be happy if he just got a buckwheat harvest out of the deal, since the other plants would make a good soil-building plowdown. "But if I time it just right . . . maybe . . ."

Jerry didn't want to jinx himself, but we both knew that yielding three specialty crops off one field would incontrovertibly validate his transition. Now that Jerry had successfully transformed his thinking, he needed to accomplish the same thing for his farm. "I've had to be pretty cautious about it, sort of one field at a time," he told me, "since I started all of this when I was literally bankrupt."

When Timeless Seeds began to take their movement mainstream, their first crop of new growers were people like Jerry, who were worried about losing their land. These distressed farmers were ripe for the first step of conversion—changing their philosophy. But since most of them were buried knee-deep in debt, putting that philosophy into practice was a slow process.

So as Timeless grew, Dave began to court farmers with more secure access to land and capital, who could afford the risk associated with overhauling their field operations. He knew there were several folks in central Montana who had the means to experiment a bit. But since things were working out for them, these more secure growers were also more reluctant to change. To convince his newest recruits to join the lentil underground, Dave had to answer questions he'd never gotten before, very specific questions about net and gross and yield.

That was one of the main reasons why Dave had taken the Whole Foods contract: credibility. With a major national distribution opportunity in hand, Timeless Seeds successfully landed a grant from the state of Montana to conduct a comprehensive feasibility study, in 2005. This helped the company drum up its first commercial financing, from a socially responsible investor west of Missoula called Stranie Ventures (now Good Works Ventures, LLC). The influx of capital allowed Timeless to purchase a much larger, more professional facility just north of Great Falls in Ulm, Montana.

Since he'd already won and lost one major distribution deal, Dave wasn't surprised by the way things unfolded. Business picked up sharply when Timeless products first appeared on the shelves at Whole Foods. The company moved into their expanded facility in October 2006, to great fanfare. Dave started calling around to recruit new growers. And then Whole Foods dropped the Authentic Food Artisan program.

As before, nobody called Dave to tell him the deal was off. But this time, he wasn't caught off guard. Timeless had other customers to sell to, and these days, they were always ready with a plan B in case restaurants went under or distributors declared bankruptcy. Dave had been adamant that all Timeless lentils sold at Whole Foods would bear the company's own label, so disappointed shoppers knew where to find them when they disappeared from the shelves. Dave asked his fans where they'd like Timeless to retail, and they helped him place his lentils and heritage grains in their local grocery stores. Back in 1994, Timeless had needed Trader Joe's. But they'd been more careful this time around, so they didn't need Whole Foods. They had their processing plant, they had their loan, and they had all their numbers crunched into a neat and tidy feasibility study. Thus equipped, Dave was ready to recruit a new breed of Timeless grower.

Not long after Whole Foods lost interest in "authentic food artisans," Dave started talking to a young guy who had just come home to his family's conventional wheat operation, 78 miles east of Conrad in Fort Benton. Having traveled extensively and managed a community garden, Casey Bailey had already changed his mind. Now he was ready to change his farm.

10

THE KEVIN BACON OF CENTRAL MONTANA

Two hours out of Conrad and just across the Missouri River, I arrived at the second stop on my tour of Timeless growers. This was my first visit to Casey Bailey's place, which for four generations had been admired as one of the most carefully managed grain farms in the region. Casey could have made a good living by following in his dad's footsteps. But instead, the thirty-two-year-old had done something audacious. He'd gone organic.

When I arrived at the Baileys' on that sunny May morning, the first thing I saw was an enormous angular spider crawling slowly but precisely behind Casey's tractor. Hundreds of skinny black legs were gliding just below the surface of the soil, synchronized by a fire-engine-red body. As Casey approached the end of the row, the steel spider's exotic brand name became visible from the dirt road. The Baileys' neighbors slowed down as they passed my Subaru, peering across the tidy buffer strip and twisting their tongues on the machine's unpronounceable script lettering: "Einböck."

"This is the tined weeder," Casey explained, whisking me into a don't-blink tour of his operation. "I bought it from Austria. It can weed in between the spelt, right in between the rows." What was spelt? I wondered. The bubbly long-distance runner was talking so fast that I worried even my digital recorder wouldn't keep up. Apparently, this was the pace of learning on this farm: as you go. Rather than try to stop Casey's high-speed train of thought, I made a note and figured we'd get around to the spelt sooner or later.

"I think it's a real art to do it well," Casey continued, bringing me back to the in-crop weeder. "It beats the plants up, scores the heck out of them with fourteen-inch-long tines, but as scary as that seems, it doesn't kill the crop. You just have to go like heck and not look back." Casey was going like heck all right, but I couldn't understand why he was in such a hurry. The Baileys weren't rich, but unlike Jerry Habets, Casey hadn't made the leap to organics under financial duress. So who was Casey trying to keep up with? "I'm racing the weeds," Casey explained, groaning. After a decade of chemical management, the Bailey farm was habituated, and Casey's organic transition had sent his soil into an agricultural version of withdrawal.

FARM REHAB

Casey himself had already been enthusiastic about the idea of organic agriculture when he grew his first lentil field for Timeless in 2009. But he knew his *farm* would probably take a little longer to kick its reliance on chemicals, so he'd tried to wean it off fertilizers and herbicides one field at a time. Still, the Baileys' strung-out soil continued to battle thistles, and Casey's neighbors were starting to drop hints. He needed to figure out new ways to kill the unwanted plants popping up in his crop—and quickly.

The tined weeder's spidery legs removed shallow-rooted weeds without ripping out his crop, Casey told me, and he could also use the machine to fine-tune soil moisture levels. As long as he didn't

drive *too* fast, it seemed to work. "It actually looks like it stimu-
lates the plants," Casey reported hopefully. "I noticed that the
places where I used it, the crop was two or three inches taller."

But as Casey dug into these surface-level questions about
weeds, he discovered that they cut deeper than he originally imagined. Unwanted plants, he learned, were a sign of unbalanced
soils. In order to control them, he needed to develop carefully
planned rotations, so that nutrient users like grain alternated
with nutrient producers like lentils. If he could fill the ecological
niches on his farm with harvestable plants, he wouldn't attract so
many uninvited ones. This was a completely new take on agriculture for the born-and-raised conventional farmer, who had always
lined out his field operation one crop at a time and kept everything
fastidiously separate. Now he had to think hard about how his
plants could work together.

After considering several crops that might complement his
nitrogen-fixing lentils, Casey had decided to plant nitrogen-feeding
spelt, a heritage grain that had recently become popular with
gluten-sensitive consumers. Finding markets for his new crops was
key for Casey, who had to prove his ecological approach could support a secure livelihood, the way his dad's conventional grain operation always had. As the fourth-generation manager of a respected
family farm, Casey had to explain to his family and neighbors why
he was doing things differently. Because driving a funny-looking,
foreign-sounding weeding machine straight through your crop
was really, really different.

The typical technique in Fort Benton—or anywhere else in
rural America, for that matter—is to cultivate *before* you sow. Tilling the ground in advance of planting is an age-old strategy. Tem-
porarily clearing the weeds out of the way gives the crop a head
start, and if your seedlings grow fast enough, they can monopo-

lize the sunlight and shade out any unwanted growth below. Or, I should say, preseason tillage *used* to be the typical technique. Far from chasing arcane weeding machines across the Atlantic, Casey's neighbors have long since parked their John Deere plows and Massey Ferguson cultivators in the shed. These days, American grain growers abolish their weeds with one expeditious pass on the sprayer—and then they go to the lake. Just a day's drive east of here, in fact, commences the geographic signature of the Midwest: mile upon mile of identical corn and soy plants, genetically altered to resist herbicides. Since their crops are impervious to their chemicals, farmers in Nebraska and Indiana can apply weed killers as liberally as the law allows. It's a simple, one-shot solution.

Fort Benton's primary agricultural product—wheat—hasn't yet followed the genetically modified path of the heartland's corn and soy, but it seems only a matter of time. For everyone in this neighborhood but Casey, tillage is fast fading into a mere metaphor, a quaint children's-book notion of what Old MacDonald does on the farm. It felt "revolutionary" and "crazy" when he dusted the cobwebs off his dad's old plow for the first time in decades, Casey admitted. But if he was going to farm the Bailey place organically, he'd need to embrace the challenge of weed management—and the extra effort and continual troubleshooting that came with it. The holy grail, Casey told me, getting back to the discussion about rotations, was to establish such a perfectly balanced plant community on his farm that he could prevent weed problems rather than treat them. He was convinced that the best weed-management strategies were subtle and biological: choosing the right plants to rotate (alfalfa was key), timing his seeding just right, spacing his rows a little closer together. By paying attention to little things that helped his crops thrive, Casey hoped to minimize the amount of time and fossil fuel he spent making passes on the tractor. But as he tweaked and tinkered his way toward that long-term vision, Casey had to do something about the weeds that were growing on his farm now. He took a "lesser evil" approach to this dilemma, balancing the pros and cons of tillage and chemicals. In this case, Casey felt, careful tillage was more in line with "how nature works."

The colossal steel spider sitting in Casey's spelt may have been more in line with nature, but it was a glaring about-face from local culture. Like most kids taking up their parents' profession, Casey wanted nothing more than to lie low as he experimented with his own way of doing things. But the highly visible process of organic conversion had forced him to explain himself. "My neighbors were like, what are you doing over there?" Casey recalled, laughing. The bright-red tined weeder had blown his cover.

FOOTLOOSE IN FORT BENTON

Cultivation—weeding mechanically rather than chemically—is the single practice that most starkly distances organic farmers like Casey from the familiar rhythms that characterize their central Montana communities. Casey and his fellow tillage farmers run on a different schedule, with different machinery, different inputs, and an entirely different philosophy. These organic growers not only face an ever-adapting cast of wily weeds (which have evolved into impressively resilient beings in the face of the neighbors' herbicides). They also have to contend with the farm industry that has congealed around grain monocultures and chemically driven "zero tillage" farming, which is rapidly becoming the mainstream management strategy on these erosion-prone Great Plains. This double whammy of social and ecological challenges means that those on the diversified, organic path have had to cultivate their friendships and their problem-solving capacities as carefully as they till their fields.

"What we need, you know, is a good pest management app," Casey said to me, whipping out his smartphone to take note of what appeared to be poor germination in his safflower. Casey had been talking about the app idea with other Timeless growers, but in the meantime, he was busy putting the "social" in social media—synching his phone and his laptop, updating his Facebook page, and nonchalantly moving millions of bits of information around the world in his search for the proper cultivator or the secret to eradicating field bindweed. Just four years after Bob Bailey let his son experiment with organics on a fifty-acre plot, the ambitious youngster had already joined the board of the Montana Organic Association and become one of Timeless Seeds' key growers. Casey's fledgling venture was a veritable Kevin Bacon of Montana's sustainable farming community, except that you didn't have to trace anywhere near six degrees of separation.

In the course of diversifying his farm, Casey seemed to have met everyone. Amaltheia Dairy's Nate Brown had sold Casey four pigs, which had permanently altered the olfactory character of Casey's Volkswagen Jetta on the trip home from Bozeman. A quirky independent breeder from Big Timber, Dave Christensen, had supplied Casey with the seed for his first planting of open-pollinated corn. When I asked about the robust grass across from his lentils, Casey had to say the name twice, to make sure I caught the pronunciation. This Kamut (Kuh-MOOT) was contracted to Bob Quinn, a Big Sandy farmer who had become famous for developing and trademarking the popular ancient grain.

Though Casey's connections appeared far-flung, I noted a common thread. I'd seen that open-pollinated corn before, I realized—

on a visit to the Timeless plant in Ulm. Another farmer—Ole Norgaard—had launched a small business to package the corn into corn bread and pancake mixes, and since he didn't have sufficient electrical power on his farm to operate his milling machinery, he'd parked his mill at Dave's facility. Big Sandy farmer Bob Quinn didn't need any help from Timeless, having made millions on Kamut. But Quinn's most recent venture hinted that he might have been talking with Dave too. The safflower Casey and I were standing in was bound for Quinn's Oil Barn, an on-farm fuel venture uncannily reminiscent of the integrated energy scheme that had long ago transformed the Oien homestead into the talk of Conrad. Sure enough, I found out, when Bob had begun considering a transition to organics back in the eighties, he'd spoken at length with Dave, who had helped recruit the now famous Big Sandy entrepreneur into the Farm Improvement Club program.

The latest in a long line of organic farmers whom Dave had inspired, Casey planned to sell about a third of his harvest to his mentor. I wasn't surprised that Casey's French Green lentils were headed for Timeless at the end of the season, but I was interested to learn that Dave had also tapped Casey to experiment with emmer, one of three heritage wheats gaining popularity in high-end restaurants under their collective Italian common name "farro" (along with spelt and einkorn). Since he had a committed buyer for these two premium crops, Casey had the freedom to experiment with other things too: millet, mustard, and grass-fed cattle.

Casey's catholic appetite for projects matched his similarly ecumenical enthusiasm for information and people. A former music major at the University of Montana, Casey had also taken courses in religion (at Westmont College in Santa Barbara), urban studies (in San Francisco), and liberation theology (in Guatemala). The sole Timeless farmer who had been to both a major Occupy protest and countercultural mecca Esalen, Casey had started an intentional community in Missoula while he was in college there. When he'd come home to farm, Casey had brought all these experiences with him, to the bewilderment of Fort Benton. One of his musical buddies from college visited every summer to help with harvest, Casey told me, grinning mischievously. "One year, we were playing 'Confirmation,' you know, the Charlie Parker tune. We got so we had it down, and then a rancher came by because he thought it was a dying cow."

Singing arias in the tractor cab and practicing yoga in the field, Casey upended nearly every stereotype about men in rural America. He was more than happy to cook while his girlfriend, Kelsey, took care of outdoor chores. In fact, Casey *liked* baking his own bread from the Kamut and spelt he raised. He also stocked organic soap in his tidy bathroom and enjoyed the aesthetic pleasures of watching his diverse fields bloom: "farming for colors." Among those colors were purple—the hue of his specialty barley— and pink, the shade Casey had semi-accidentally painted his barn. Although he swore the color had looked different on the paint can, Casey liked seeing the look on people's faces when he playfully nicknamed his business Pink Barn Organics. The athletic farmer was already notorious as the only man in town sporting Red Ants Pants—designer workwear made by a Montana company with a flair for the burlesque and a mission to flatter its (mostly female) customers' curves.

Unabashedly himself, Casey clearly relished the opportunity to introduce little bits of difference to this traditional farm country. And yet, his posture toward his neighbors was fundamentally respectful and humble. Casey felt his fellow farmers—from Fort

Benton to Guatemala, organic community gardens to conventional family farms—were all fighting the same problem, and that they needed to work together to solve it. At the heart of that problem, Casey believed, was disconnection from the earth. Even if they hadn't been physically removed from their land, he observed, farmers around the world were experiencing a spiritual separation, as their jobs and landscapes became just as industrial as any city. "Monoculture, monoculture, monoculture," Casey lamented. "It's kind of like the rural person's concrete—mind-numbing."

Casey wasn't convinced that organic advocates or political progressives had all the antidotes for this oppressive monotony, nor did he think his conventional neighbors on the east side of the Missouri had it all wrong. Western Montanans might think things were all flat and predictable out here, he teased me, but there were plenty of colorful twists and turns around these labyrinthine gullies and craggy river breaks. "Life isn't black-and-white," Casey told me adamantly, "and neither are any of our particular situations."

"IT'S HARD TO GO COLD TURKEY"

For example, what we were about to do next was the very thing Casey'd been trying to avoid by using the tined weeder and all those synergistic crops. We were gonna spray.

"Can you follow me in the Ford?" Casey asked, handing me the keys to a beat-up brown truck with a container of 2,4-D in the bed. "I need to take this stuff out to my dad." I nodded, and Casey hopped into the cab of a small tractor-trailer, which appeared to have been a furniture van in a previous lifetime. His own load included a mammoth tank of water, a medley of herbicides, and the hookup for refilling the sprayer that Bob Bailey was currently running on the family's conventional acreage.

"It's hard to go cold turkey with this organic stuff," Casey explained. "I'm in both worlds. Timeless and Dave's vision, that's where my heart is, but today I'm doing the very opposite of organic. I'm out here with these bandages of spray and fertilizer until I can figure out how to make this organic thing work."

Making it work, I gathered, meant confronting the dilemma that had vexed Montana's organic farmers from the beginning: weed control. Montana actually lost organic acreage in 2012, and when the statewide organic association asked the dropout farmers why they gave up, they fielded a litany of one-word responses: bindweed, knapweed, cheatgrass, kochia. Insects and disease aren't much of a problem in this neck of the treeless plains, because Montana is so cold and dry that even the bugs and the fungal pathogens have packed their bags for California or the Pacific Northwest. Given the short seasons and long dry spells, the creatures that survive out here are the hardiest people and the hardiest plants: stubborn farmers and stubborn weeds.

Central Montana's two most intransigent communities engage in a constant tussle with each other, and it's a delicate dance. When organic farmers cultivate to control their weeds, they also expose and disturb their soils, so they need to be careful not to sacrifice too much moisture, organic matter, or underground biodiversity. Excessive tillage has beat up the farm ground around here, so extension agents and conservation bureaucrats often encourage farmers to stop plowing and just use chemicals instead. But even in the face of state-of-the-art herbicides, the weeds here never really go away. In fact, a number of Timeless growers have noticed that their families' weed problems actually multiplied during the previous generation, when their parents started using chemicals.

Rather than attacking his weeds with shock-and-awe poisons, Casey approached weed control as an attempt to win a lasting peace, or at least a détente. I came to appreciate why a lentil farmer might benefit from a background in community organizing and religious studies, as Casey described his approach to fostering co-existence among his human and nonhuman neighbors. Since neither the neighbors nor the weeds were going away anytime soon, Casey explained, he did his best to get to know them better. He was particularly keen to enroll the wisdom of the old-timers around him, aware that their detailed knowledge of this place and its history would help him establish a successful organic system.

It hadn't taken Casey very long to figure out that property lines mean nothing to plants. Thanks to the constant movement of wind, water, and soil, both his crops and his weeds were engaged in an incessant biological conversation with all other botanical life in the vicinity. Sooner or later, Casey would have to deal with his neighbors' chemically adapted weeds, because their seeds would blow over to his place. And if they planted GMO alfalfa, Casey would be vulnerable to pollen drift—when the breeze decided to send that new genetic material to establish itself in Casey's fields, whether he liked it or not. Given that organics couldn't realistically get anywhere going it alone, Casey made a point to reach out. Starting with his dad.

DOING THE MATH

Bob Bailey warmed the crisp air with an ear-to-ear smile, still toiling cheerfully away at age sixty-eight. While Bob loaded his spray rig with the three herbicides in the tractor-trailer, his son laid out the logic of the chemical approach. "We just put in seven thousand dollars," Casey computed in awe. "Seven two-and-a-half-gallon jugs at a thousand dollars each. It pencils out to spend that kind of money fighting weeds—isn't that crazy?" I nodded in agreement. It was a lot of money, all right, but Casey did the math for me.

"Compare this sprayer—with a hundred-and-twenty-foot boom, going twelve miles an hour—to organic plowing—a fifty-foot plow, going six miles an hour. With the organic method, you cover three hundred acres a day; with this outfit, fourteen hundred and forty acres day. Killing weeds this way costs less per acre, because glyphosate and fuel cost less than pulling a plow running diesel."

Casey shuttled the 2,4-D over to his dad, then turned back to me. "So if we could start oilseed pressing and running *that* for fuel instead of diesel, that would feel so good. It would feel like freedom." Aha. Now I knew why Casey was so excited about the safflower he was growing for Bob Quinn's Oil Barn. Thirty years after the methane digester and alcohol fuel still had gone up at the Oien place, Quinn had developed another concept for a solar farm. Farmers like Casey would grow safflower, press it into oil at the Oil Barn, rent it to local restaurants as frying oil, and then pick it up and use it to fuel their tractors. A maverick experiment station breeder from Sidney, Montana—a modern-day Jim Sims—had spent thirty-eight years developing the high-oleic safflower that would burn clean in both human bodies and diesel engines. Casey had been one of the first to sign on for the pilot project.

Bob Bailey squinted in the blinding sun to read the time on his cell phone, admitting to me that he'd been learning—slowly—how to text. The elder Bailey was open to his son's new ideas, and he had been listening to Casey's proposals as intently as I had. "I've never done it this other way," Bob told me, "but Casey's helping me learn. You can get an equilibrium going and things take care of each other. With conventional farming, you might spray something out, and it would make something else worse." Although Bob could see the biological wisdom of Casey's approach to farming, however, he was painfully aware of the math his son had just rattled off. Spraying herbicide did indeed pencil out, and so long as Bob Bailey stuck with this prevailing calculus, there would be a chemical company and an equipment dealer behind him.

Stumped by a seemingly insoluble math problem, Casey had begun to conclude that his weeds were the least of his difficulties. He was eager to change his farm, but there was only so much he could do from the seat of his tractor, or even his elegant Austrian cultivator. Like most folks in Fort Benton, Casey had always observed the unspoken rule of "Live and let live," focusing on his own operation and staying out of his neighbors' affairs. But as he talked to his dad, Casey came to understand that the actions of everybody around him—from his loan officer to his fellow farmers to his insurance agent—were shaping his choices. If he wanted to do things differently, Casey needed to think beyond his own enterprise to the ones that were connected to it. In order to change his farm, he'd have to stick his nose in other people's business.

This was the third stage of conversion, both for Timeless growers and for the company itself: becoming increasingly sophisticated about the rest of the food system, beyond the farm gate. Where could they get financing? Proper equipment? Could they find a seed-cleaning facility that saw organics as an opportunity rather than just a risk of weed contamination? Right about the time Casey began growing for Timeless, Dave started talking business with two other farmers who were eager to work out some answers to these questions. Doug Crabtree and Anna Jones-

Crabtree needed to figure these things out quickly, because they were starting the most ambitiously diverse farm in Montana— from scratch. Dave was surprised that two midcareer professionals in Helena had bought farmland 250 miles northeast of their house, just shy of the Canadian border. But the Timeless CEO had to admire the Crabtrees' dedication. Back in the eighties, Dave recalled, his AERO buddy's fateful stand against Montana State University had initiated a DIY fervor on dozens of Montana farms. But Doug and Anna were taking that same attitude to their equipment dealer and their banker. Unwilling to let such institutions constrain their vision, the Crabtrees took a three-step approach to every enterprise necessary to their field operation. Infiltrate. Innovate. And if need be, duplicate. If the farm industry wouldn't do what they needed, Doug and Anna resolved, farmers would have to team up and do it themselves.

A fair indication of the lengths to which the Crabtrees were willing to go in order to responsibly steward a patch of land was the sheer duration of the drive required to get there. From the couple's home in Helena, it was a three-hour trip to Havre, the town referenced in their farm's formal address. From there, the journey continued *another* forty-five minutes north, passing perpetual fields of conventional grain that seemed to stretch forever.

This was the point at which, on my first visit to the Crabtrees' farm, I instinctively pulled out my phone to make sure I was still on the right track. And then I had to laugh at myself. Where exactly did I think I was going to get a cell signal from? Heaven? More out of inertia than faith, I kept going, hoping for some sort of landmark. And then, just before the Canadian border, the uniform landscape erupted into a succession of distinct, multicolored strips. Here it was, the only organic farm for miles around, home to a good portion of Timeless Seeds' Black Beluga lentils.

Looking for all the world like a garden that had somehow fallen into a magnifying glass and emerged as a 1,280-acre farmstead, the Crabtrees' operation was the most labor-intensive I'd seen yet. So I was astonished to learn that Doug and Anna both had full-time office jobs. They were raising more than a dozen crops— on the weekend.

11

A PhD WITH A DIRTY SECRET

It was the fifth official day of summer in Hill County, and Doug Crabtree and Anna Jones-Crabtree's crops were beginning to reach ankle height. Doug and Anna were pleased to see that all sixteen of them appeared to have established reasonably well, including the Black Beluga lentils, which had started sporting nitrogen-fixing nodules a couple of weeks ago. Four seasons into farming this 1,280-acre spread, the Crabtrees were still working hard to improve the soil. They weren't there yet, but the nutrient base they'd built up was beginning to bear fruit. Or rather, it was giving forth a cornucopia of grains, legumes, and oilseeds. "Nodules, little baby nodules!" Anna crowed excitedly, as the Crabtrees scouted their lentil crop. "That is the most magical thing in the world," Doug agreed.

Closer to Canada than it is to the nearest town, the Crabtrees' dizzyingly diverse farm is cold, windy, and smack-dab in the middle of nowhere. Aside from a few conventional farming neighbors, the only thing around is an abandoned air force base. The shadow of the spooky surveillance radar station doesn't look like the most auspicious place to launch a bold model for the future of dryland farming. But fortysomethings Doug and Anna have a track record of assiduously avoiding easy roads. Sometimes, the Crabtrees have found themselves navigating life's potholes out of necessity. If Doug's family farm hadn't gone bankrupt in the eighties, he might still be tending one of the largest cash-grain operations in Ohio. On the other hand, he might not. The main reason Doug and Anna are out here seeding the north forty appears to be their sheer stubbornness. Headstrong even for Montana, the Crabtrees share an unflinching commitment to the gold standard of green living.

Unlike cautiously politic Casey Bailey, I quickly learned, Doug and Anna made no apologies about sticking their noses in other people's business. In her off-farm life, Anna was a sustainable operations director for a federal agency, and she wasn't afraid to tell managers to change their procurement policies or power down their computers over the weekend. Doug was a veteran organic inspector who had observed and evaluated hundreds of farms and processing facilities throughout the northern plains—candidly.

In fact, it was Doug's job that had put Dave Oien on the Crabtrees' radar. As director of the state of Montana's organic certification program, Doug had been among the first to learn that Timeless Seeds had moved into a new facility in Ulm and was seeking new growers. He and Anna had been talking for years about buying a farm, and they could envision how it might come together—diverse rotations, high-value specialty crops, ecological management. Unfortunately, the farm the Crabtrees saw in their mind's eye was sort of like the maddeningly elusive picture on top of a puzzle box—upon opening the box, they'd had difficulty finding the right pieces to construct their intended whole. The right land. The right financing. The right markets. Trying to find all these pieces at once was a daunting proposition, and it didn't help to be organic. But the expansion of Timeless Seeds—a local company that actually wanted to buy the stuff the Crabtrees wanted to grow—was like that key corner piece that made it seem feasible to assemble the rest of the jumble into a workable picture. The Crabtrees took an epic road trip, scouting available land as far north as Alberta and as far east as North Dakota. At long last, in 2009, they closed on two sections of land, twenty-four miles north of Havre. Doug and Anna named their new place Vilicus Farms, after the Latin word for farmer, or rather the *other* Latin word for farmer. Most Latin textbooks used *agricola,* which translated to English as "one who labors on the land," Doug explained. But he and Anna preferred *vilicus,* which more nearly described their notion of a farmer: One who *belonged* to the land and was honor bound to care for it.

THE 250-MILE COMMUTE

Sporting Carhartt jeans and two layers of fleece, Anna admired the subtle early-season stirrings of her austere surroundings. Waxing poetic over the smallest signs of life in her sleepy-looking field, she noted a ladybug clinging to a delicate blossom. "Isn't it beautiful here?" she exclaimed.

I had to laugh. Getting out in nature on the weekends is the big prize for professionals like Anna who land plum jobs in the heart of Big Sky Country. But for reasons her officemates still struggled to fathom, Anna had skipped over the world-class wilderness available just minutes from her desk in Helena and instead invested her upper-middle-class income in the opportunity to drive 250 miles every weekend to "farm camp." While her friends enjoyed lakeside cabins and mountain ski chalets, Anna delighted in the musty rental where she and Doug had spent all their free time for the past four years. Tall and confident, Anna juggled a farm, a full-time job, and a very active presence on the Timeless Seeds board.

When she'd joined the Timeless board in 2010, Anna had pushed Dave to think beyond the farm to the food system. Could the company improve the sustainability of its products at other points in their life cycle? Where were the bottlenecks in the operation? Could Timeless eliminate them by bringing more capacity in-house? Anna celebrated when the business finally got its first state-of-the-art color sorter in January 2012, thanks to a particularly supportive distributor who financed it. There was a definite whiz-bang factor to this gadget, which used an electric eye to identify off-color lentils and sort them out of the batch with a mighty puff of compressed air. But the color sorter was also an essential component of the Timeless production chain. The truth was, when farmers delivered their Black Belugas to the plant in Ulm, they weren't all black. Inevitably, some portion of the lentils had split open, revealing their yellow insides—and there was almost always some errant wheat and barley in the batch as well. The chefs who were popularizing Timeless Seeds' nitrogen-rich legumes as haute cuisine were paying for black lentils, not yellow ones, and they were unlikely to appreciate it if their order contained complimentary wheat and barley seed. So, before shipping its product out to customers, Timeless had to sort out any lentils that weren't picture-perfect—and anything that wasn't a lentil.

At first, the company had struggled along with the only machines they could afford—a leased color sorter from Costa Rica and a used model they bought from a friend in Canada—both of which were in constant need of repair. Then they'd gotten a lucky break: A nearby grain plant had installed its own 500,000-dollar color sorter and agreed to work in Timeless product on a fee-for-service basis. But there, to Anna's consternation, the lentils had languished—sometimes for months. Since the Timeless color-sorting order was such a minor part of the larger processor's business, it was not a priority, which meant Dave's entire inventory rested on when—and whether—things at the other facility happened to be slow. So it was a huge relief to both Anna and Dave when Timeless installed a machine of its own, one that actually worked. Now that Timeless had its own color sorter, they could separate Black Belugas from cracked Belugas themselves, whenever they needed to. It seemed like a trivial victory, but with every added measure of self-determination, the lentil underground gained more ability to focus on its mission.

Pulling apart leaves and digging up roots, Anna herded three spirited Jack Russell terriers, matching the nervy dogs' unflagging energy with her running narrative of observations. The lentil scout's long blond hair was pulled back in braids, and she was wearing work gloves so she could use every spare moment to pull a few weeds. Accustomed to making things happen, Anna epitomized the expression "hands-on." Sure, she could earn a comfortable living sitting behind a desk churning out spreadsheets, but she'd rather be driving a tractor and running a grease gun.

Doug Crabtree was even more in love with this place than his wife was. Having spent two decades on other people's farms—as a tenant, researcher, and organic inspector—he was overjoyed to be tilling ground of his very own. "Overjoyed" was probably a better adjective for Anna than it was for Doug, who spoke in a deliberate Ohio drawl (if, indeed, there is such a thing). The stockier, more staid Crabtree didn't wear his excitement on his sleeve to quite the extent that his wife did. But the intensity of Anna's running commentary was reflected in her husband's piercing gaze. Together, they made an imposing duo.

The Crabtrees' color-coded field maps and detailed rotation spreadsheet hinted at Doug's day job: organic certification program manager for the Montana Department of Agriculture. In 1999, a first-term state senator from Big Sandy named Jon Tester had carried a bill to create a state-administered certification program, and Doug had been hired to build and manage it. The veteran organic inspector's first day in his new Helena office had been a bit of a culture shock—not so much for Doug as for his colleagues. At first, they'd felt right at home with the midwestern farm product, who'd seemed like a regular steak-and-gravy kind of guy. But when the staff hit the break room at noon, Doug had whipped out a meal unlike anything they'd ever seen, full of dubious vegetables and exotic spices. "Nobody steals my lunch, because they don't know what it is," Doug told me. "They ask, though, because it smells so good." A decade later, Doug's colleagues still weren't sure what to think of his lunch, but they had to respect his management acumen. Having seen the good, the bad, and the ugly of agricultural record keeping, Doug clearly took pride in Vilicus Farms' tidy, precise system.

According to the Crabtrees' map, their farm was divided into sixty-eight strips, separated by pollinator plantings that provided habitat for native bees. Each strip had been seeded according to its cropping history and soil conditions, with the typical sequence proceeding from spring grain to green manure to fall grain to oilseed to edible legume. Since Vilicus Farms averaged a minuscule

11.47 inches of annual precipitation, the Crabtrees' primary goal with this rotation was to build soil organic matter to better hold precious water. Replenishing nutrients and organic matter came in a close second, hence all the legumes and green manures (preferably less thirsty varieties). As I'd discovered when trying to make cell phone calls from the Crabtrees' fields, it was quite windy north of Havre, so the crop sequence also served to reduce erosion. Finally, cycling through so many species kept the bugs and the weeds from getting too comfortable. Doug and Anna rattled off several more reasons why it was agronomically advisable to seed this or that crop—saline seep, songbirds, soil carbon—but that was all gravy.

For the 2012 season, the Crabtrees were using sixteen different plants to accomplish this series of lofty objectives, but they'd selected this year's planting from a staggering twenty-four-crop repertoire identified in their rotation plan. As the document acknowledged, the future of any one of the Crabtrees' strips could shift according to an ever-fluctuating cast of variables: nitrogen levels, weed pressure, rainfall—and, of course, markets.

POWDERED FLAX AND PROCESSING PEAS

At ten thirty P.M., a Honda hybrid with TIMELSS plates rolled into farm camp. It was Dave Oien—a bit later than expected, but bearing a carton of organic eggs and a fresh batch of granola. Timeless Seeds' CEO had made the two-and-a-half-hour drive from Conrad to conduct the first field visit of the 2012 season and negotiate contracts for the three crops he was buying from Vilicus Farms: emmer, flax, and Black Beluga lentils. Although Anna, Doug, and Dave unanimously voted to save the business conversations for morning, they couldn't resist launching into a discussion over a late-night snack. The impassioned exchange crystallized the tensions of transitioning from underground movement to aboveground enterprise.

Dave had just returned from a trade show in China, and he was excited about a potential Asian buyer for one of his pulse crops. "I think the pea deal might work out," he told the Crabtrees, cheerfully.

"What are they using them for?" queried Anna, who always seemed to have a question.

"They're processing them for nutritional supplements," Dave responded.

"Is that really the answer? Processing? Is that sustainable?" Anna's voice quickened and amplified with each word.

But Dave had a question of his own. "What are you eating?" Timeless Seeds' CEO asked his most tenacious board member.

"Potato chips," Anna admitted.

"That's reality," Dave continued. "Processed food. Ninety percent of the products that we sold to Taiwan—your flax being one of them—were powdered."

It was near midnight, but Anna could not go gently into the dark realities of the global food system. With a principled resolve that must have reminded Dave of his own forty-three-year-old self, she shot him a look that said, "I didn't give up my weekends and my life savings to sell powdered flax to Taiwan." If sufficient local markets for whole foods weren't readily available, then Anna was determined to create them. She was partnering with a young nutrition professor from Montana State, who had already hatched plans to host a series of three workshops for Montana chefs about the health benefits and culinary potential of organic lentils. Meanwhile, Anna and Doug had worked so hard to develop a relationship with their most supportive chef that the woman had given the

Crabtrees the first piece of furniture for their new farmhouse: a baking table. Even farm-to-table wasn't good enough for the Crabtrees. They were so deep into reciprocal relationships with their buyers that they were literally bringing the table back to the farm.

I thought Dave might roll his eyes at Doug and Anna's direct-market evangelism, having been there and done that. But he welcomed Anna's energy, glad that someone other than himself was taking on the lentil underground's grunt work. Still, Dave hoped to shield this younger version of himself from burnout. "Don't you get tired sometimes?" he asked Anna, with a knowing smile. Anna didn't hesitate. "You do what you gotta do to live your dream," she replied. In this case, what Anna had to do was go to bed, since it was past midnight and the trio had already scheduled a six thirty A.M. contract negotiation. By the time the boys rolled out of bed on Monday morning, Anna had already fired up three burners, infusing farm camp with the smell of garlic and the sizzle of cast-iron skillets.

"CAN'T WE JUST DO A SCHEDULE?"

While Dave munched on a veggie scramble, Doug and Anna laid out the terms they wanted to see in their contract. At a minimum, they wanted to get paid on time for their crop—or count on a guaranteed interest payment if Timeless was behind. Similarly, Doug and Anna hoped to establish a contractually stipulated storage fee that would kick in if Dave missed their agreed-on date for crop delivery. Ideally, the Crabtrees wanted to see the Timeless plant run on a predetermined calendar, so they could plan ahead. "Can't we just do a schedule?" Anna asked. "Say, this is when all the Belugas come in, pick your month?"

Doug and Anna's ultimate goal, however, was to get paid based on the number of acres they seeded rather than the pounds of harvested crop they delivered. Although this way of paying farmers was a radically new proposition for wholesale buyers, Anna and Doug pointed out that direct-market consumers had been doing this for decades—through community supported agriculture. Increasingly popular with the local food crowd, CSAs were essentially farm subscriptions, in which the subscriber paid up front for a season of produce and received weekly boxes of whatever the farmer was able to successfully harvest. If individual consumers could afford to share risk with farmers in this way, Doug and Anna reasoned, surely wholesalers and processors could too. The Crabtrees had already negotiated one such contract for their durum wheat—with an organic pasta company. Now they were hoping to do the same for their lentils.

"Frankly, Timeless Seeds is a big reason we decided to do this and do it here in Montana," Doug told Dave. "We want to see Timeless grow and succeed."

"But we need a more clear road map and plan," Anna added, tag-teaming. "Maybe it's just the engineer in me."

CREATIVE CAPITAL

Dave liked the idea of buffering his growers from the layered uncertainties of (1) farming (2) specialty (3) organic crops. But the problem was, Timeless Seeds didn't have enough of a buffer from those uncertainties itself. Because Dave and his three farmer partners had launched the company at a time when organic food was not considered a legitimate business model in Montana, they'd never properly capitalized. Since none of them had money and banks wouldn't lend to them, they couldn't set up Timeless Seeds as a formal cooperative, even though they were sharing time, money, and equipment. So the Timeless boys had chartered the business as a Montana C Corporation and raised money from friends who'd chosen more lucrative occupations. Those friends—mostly AERO members—had become shareholders in the new "corporation," whose dividends consisted of a Christmas package of lentils every few years. In the days before Kickstarter, when the Internet was still in its infancy, crowd-funding depended on being able to locate an actual crowd—the very thing north-central Montana was known for *not* having.

Still functioning like a young start-up after twenty-five years in business, Timeless Seeds' biggest handicap was that they didn't have a line of credit. Operating exclusively on cash flow, the shoestring company's only option was "pay as you can," and certain times of the season were leaner than others. Dave hated to see tardy checks and unpredictable delivery schedules stretch farmers' tight budgets, and he was open to establishing penalties for late payment and delivery. The risk of a CSA-style contract, however, was more than he could absorb. The scale of his growers' operations—determined to some extent by the scale of the farm economy around them, from which they were never wholly independent—was simply too large in relation to the size of his business. "It would be neat to do what the pasta company does," Dave said to the Crabtrees, "but you've got to have a lot of money to do that. You have to be able to spread it out over lots of growers. It could kill us if a grower got hailed out and we still had to pay them."

The prospect of a predetermined schedule for cleaning and storing each type of lentil, one variety at a time, posed a similar difficulty. Given Timeless Seeds' limited operating budget, the company didn't have enough money to buy ahead on its thirty products—or enough warehouse space to store extra inventory. So Dave attempted to schedule deliveries from growers according to orders from buyers, which were maddeningly hard to predict. Restaurants, in particular, tended to place small, mixed orders, which fluctuated wildly according to food trends and consumer taste. Specialty distributors were just one step up the food chain from restaurants, chasing the same trends—and neither were eager to store extra product in their own warehouses, which were often located in high-rent areas like New York or San Francisco.

Timeless Seeds' diverse customer base was part of what made the company resilient, but it was also a source of uncertainty in its own right. Dave couldn't predict when he might get a big order for Belugas, or when the hot crop might be French Greens. So he managed his inventory much the way he'd always run his farm— adaptively. Sometimes farmers made the drive to the Timeless plant on short notice to help Dave fill an order—and more often, they stored crops for a year or two in their own bins while waiting for space to open up at the plant. The whole thing, Dave admitted, was "a big juggling act."

To be sure, Dave's flexible, somewhat freewheeling approach was baked into his character—this element of his personality was, after all, what had allowed him to go against the grain, succeed as an organic lentil farmer, and develop an unorthodox business. But it was also a survival strategy, born of the constant need to make do with less. Until Timeless had the resources to beef up its operating budget and double or even triple its warehouse space, its CEO had to take things one day at a time.

"FARMING IS A PROHIBITED BUSINESS"

Meanwhile, Doug and Anna had their own challenges, not the least of which concerned their struggles with lenders. On the list of institutions they wanted to reinvent—equipment manufacturers, trade associations, universities—banks were at the top of their agenda.

"Farm Credit Services, you think they'd provide credit and service to farmers, right?" Anna rhetorically queried Dave, frustration dripping from each word as she recalled the ordeal of buying her farm. "We did this whole six-month process. We were totally clear. We had budgets, we had all the cash flow lined out. Then right before we were supposed to close, they said we can't do this deal. So we went with another local bank to do the guarantee. We went up there thinking we were going to have this great conversation about what we're doing. The loan officer took us into the office, and he says, 'Why do you guys want to do this? Why do you want to farm?' This is the *ag* lender."

Once they'd convinced the agricultural lender that farming was a good idea, Anna went on, she and Doug had faced another hurdle. Having purchased a place to farm, they needed at least a little bit of operating credit before they could start seeding. Anna couldn't wait to launch into that story.

"We go to our bank here in Helena, where we have banked since 1999, and we apply for a line of credit for our business," Anna began. "They say yeah, sure. We get a credit card with a five-thousand-dollar limit and we're thinking that's great, that's all we need, just a little overdraft protection. They never asked us what the business was. So I get home, and I'm doing all the reconciling of the expenses, and I realize, what the heck, they attached it to our personal checking. No."

Doug interjected. "That was the whole point of getting a business account—to have it separate."

"So I go down to the bank," Anna continued, "and I ask what's going on. They say, 'Oh man, we really messed up.' I'm thinking, yeah, you messed up. So they canceled it and we had to reapply. This time, they asked us what our business was and we said a farm. The application comes back, and the underwriter says, "You're denied." What? The same exact information, the same people, the same credit—the only thing that changed is it said that it's a farm. They said, 'Sorry, farming is a prohibited business.'"

"Seriously—I want a T-shirt that says 'Farming Is a Prohibited Business,'" howled Anna, amused but fuming. "So I looked at the loan officer, and I go, 'You ask your underwriter who grew the wheat for his toast this morning.'"

Dave readily empathized with Doug and Anna's exasperation, because financial institutions had been a headache for him too. That's what had gotten him in the racket of sourcing "creative capital": leaning on AERO friends for labor, equipment, in-kind donations, and whatever other help they could offer. The community resource pool had kept the plant's doors open, but Dave had grown increasingly frustrated with the limitations of running a business like a bake sale, his hat perpetually in his hand. "Without money, it takes much more time to get something done," Dave admitted. "We're in three or four hundred stores, when we could be in three or four thousand, but that requires having a larger inventory to go out and sell those stores on the product. If we run out and can't deliver it, they won't come asking twice."

Since Timeless didn't have a line of credit, Dave explained, he couldn't build the grower base that would allow him to pursue markets strategically. That would be sticking his neck out too far. So instead, he'd had to play it conservative and stick with the opportunistic strategy that made it impossible to establish a regular schedule like Anna wanted. "The good news is that we've grown step by step, organically," Dave told me. "The bad news is that it's taken ten years to get where we could've gotten in three years with adequate funding."

THE RUMPELSTILTSKIN PROBLEM

At the crux of Dave's problem was the fact that the biological time of his plants and the financial time of his markets were not in step. Dave was forever attempting to reconcile these two types of time, to make Timeless a successful business without undermining everything it stood for. With everyone around them barreling along faster than their slow-release nutrients and long-term cropping cycles, both Dave and his growers were always feeling behind.

"It takes a long time to get there," Doug Crabtree told me. "I had twenty years to drive around and certify and look at what everybody else was doing and conceptualize what we wanted to do, but even at that, it's still going to be ten years before ours is any kind of a mature system."

"The frustrating part of that to me," Anna added, explaining how long it had taken to build up enough of a nest egg to even get to the point of tussling with bankers, "is that we had to wait until we were forty to start, so we're going to be fifty before we've actually seen two cycles of our rotation."

Thinking aloud, Doug estimated that it would take twice that amount of time—twenty years—before the Crabtrees could actually observe the impact of that rotation. "Oh shit," said Anna's face. "By that point, I'll be in my sixties." Two weeks earlier, I'd seen Anna nearly blow her top when a friend mentioned how taken she was with the patient approach of crop breeder Wes Jackson. Jackson had spent more than thirty years working to develop a perennial wheat variety and had recently proposed that Congress scrap its every-five-year agriculture legislation and lay out a strategic plan for the next half century instead. "We have things we can do right now," Anna had butted in, impatiently. "We don't have time to wait for another fifteen years of research or a fifty-year farm bill." Anna admired Jackson, but her trouble was that she had a foot in both worlds—the perennial one underground and the annual one above it. As her mounting frustration approached full-on folkloric tragedy, I worried Anna might pull a Rumpelstiltskin and tear herself right in half.

Doug was stretched to the limit too, and he'd been counting the days until July 9, when he was set to scale back from full-time organic program manager to three-quarter-time inspector. One of the reasons Doug was changing job descriptions was that he'd used all his vacation farming and couldn't see a way to keep the operation going without taking more. This was something I'd heard over and over again from Timeless farmers. They needed more *time*.

In the interim, resolute land stewards like Doug and Anna jam-packed their days like airplane passengers determined to fit everything in their carry-ons—and this morning was no exception. Having come to enough of an understanding about their 2012 contract to get their hands back in the dirt, the Crabtrees piled into an old farm truck and escorted Dave out to their crop. Fifteen minutes before their colleagues in Helena started their workdays, we were already on to the field tour.

LENTIL DETECTIVE

The first strip we passed was seeded to chickling vetch, a leguminous green manure that was starting to bloom with white and pink flowers. Dave waved Doug on. He'd love to nerd out on nitrogen fixation, but these days, the Timeless CEO's focus was on the soil builders his customers could eat.

Those edible legumes were to be found in strip 11, which the Crabtrees had sown with Black Belugas. We got out of the pickup and walked into the early-season lentil crop, an ankle-high confusion of green. Dave asked Doug and Anna a series of questions, recording the strip number, acreage, seeding rate, drill spacing, and date the Belugas had gone in the ground. Once he'd logged these details on a clipboard, Dave threw his hat out to randomly select a transect, then counted the number of plants per square foot. Realizing that my wrist was cramping, I set my pen down for a moment and took a deep breath. Vilicus Farms was a lot to take in. Technically speaking, Dave was surveying just three of Doug and Anna's sixteen crops—lentils, emmer, and flax—since the rest were headed to other buyers in the Crabtrees' diversified network. But there were several strips of each. Plus, each strip had a history.

The lentils in strip 11 were choked with weeds, and Doug chalked it up to the flax he'd planted there the previous year. Like lentils, Doug explained to me, flax was noncompetitive. That meant it had gotten weedy, giving Vilicus Farms' robust Russian thistles a head start on this year's Black Belugas—which the thistles needed like Jack Nicklaus needed a handicap. Instead of flax, Doug mused, he could have planted an aggressive grain like buckwheat in the year before the lentils. But then there would likely have been some buckwheat in the Black Beluga crop, which would have been a pain to sort out during harvest and processing. Much like Dave's juggling act at the processing plant, the rotation at Vilicus Farms was an educated guess, based on a long list of trade-offs.

After a disappointing first stop, Doug and Anna were pleased to discover that their second field of lentils—strip 16—was less weedy. "This might be your best one," Dave complimented them, equally relieved. Again, Doug cycled back through the rotation in his head. This field had also hosted flax before lentils, but—Doug racked his brain—what had come before *that*? Maybe it was the rye he and Anna had planted in the fall before the flax, he surmised. Since rye tended to outcompete pretty much every other plant on the farm, maybe it had knocked down the weeds enough to give the flax, and now the lentils, a better head start. It was sort of like the old woman who swallowed the fly, I suggested, chuckling. You had to trace a lot of steps backward to get to the bottom of things out here.

"HOW DO YOU FIGURE IN THE COVER CROP?"

Still wrestling with her Rumpelstiltskin problem, Anna couldn't decide whether to celebrate her farm's complexity or try to simplify it. "Going back to our Timeless board meeting and Dawn's idea that Timeless Seeds needs to focus on three to four things," she started in, citing money manager Dawn McGee's suggestion before stopping herself and considering the opposite position. "I have mixed feelings about that from a diversity/stability standpoint, but what do you think are our three to four key crops?"

Dave opted for the Socratic strategy he'd used the night before, inviting Anna to share the burden of answering her unrelenting inquiries. "Have you done the enterprise analysis I sent out?" he asked, turning the question back on her. Montana State had released the analysis tool to help farmers determine which plants to seed, based on the net benefit of each crop. Dave had forwarded it to Anna, figuring it would be right up her alley.

Doug pitched in. "We did some," he told Dave. "But it doesn't capture the integration of our system." The enterprise analysis, Doug explained, assumed that the costs and benefits of each crop could be assessed individually. But at Vilicus Farms, costs and benefits were realized across the whole farm system, in ways that were difficult to tease apart. "We have crops we harvest and crops we don't harvest," Doug said, playing right into Dave's Socratic method, "but they all serve a function, ecologically or agronomically."

"Right. How do you figure in the cover crop?" Anna added, using the more mainstream term for green manure, which highlighted its erosion-combating properties. Souring on the idea of paring down to three or four "key crops," Anna reminded herself that Dawn McGee's recommendations came from a business perspective, not an ecological one, and were certainly not directed at farming. Not everything that made sense for a business made sense on the ground—or, as Doug pointed out, *under* the ground.

How would he and Anna decide which of their crops were the highest value? Doug wondered aloud. The ones they harvested for a profit? Or the ones they plowed under to feed the soil? With a BS in agricultural economics from Purdue and an MS in plant science from South Dakota State, Doug was admittedly a somewhat black-and-white thinker, sympathetic to Dawn McGee–style logic. But every time he tried to calculate his way through Vilicus Farms, he stumbled into a morass of slippery variables that ensured he'd never emerge with a definitive equation. "On one hand, the ag economist in me would really like to have that nailed down, hung on the wall: It costs us thirty cents a pound to grow emmer, so anything we sell above that there's some profit," Doug continued. "But then I get stuck, because how much of the fuel that puts out the peas do you charge to the emmer because the peas provide the fertilizer to the emmer? Each crop is interdependent."

"NATURE'S STILL A LOT MORE IN CHARGE"

Although the complexity of Doug and Anna's system challenged their respective inner ag economist and inner engineer, on a fundamental level their approach made sound economic sense— in a way even some of their neighbors could appreciate. For one thing, the Crabtrees had been able to save a lot of seed, which cut down on the expense of buying it each spring. And of course, they also skipped another major spring expense: fertilizer and herbicides. Keeping costs down was particularly important in a place like Hill County, Doug explained to me, because the "benefit" side of the balance sheet was largely out of the grower's control.

"Nature is still a lot more in charge in this ecosystem than it is in the Midwest," the Ohio native observed. "If you're in an input-dependent system, you're going to put on the fertilizer and you're going to apply the herbicides and the fungicides whether or not you end up getting a crop, whether or not it rains—so you've got that one-hundred- to two-hundred-dollars-an-acre investment whether you get fifty bushels or zero. In our case, we might still get zero some years, but at least we've only got thirty or forty dollars an acre invested in it. And yeah, we're probably not going to get the top-end yield ever, but we don't need to."

Anna agreed. Given that she spent her weekdays finding ways

to trim environmental footprints, she loved the net-gain approach of lentils. "They take less from the soil than a wheat crop does every year," she told me, "and they give something back too, because they are a leguminous nitrogen fixer."

As if on cue, strip 19 presented Anna with a convincing visual aid. Two years earlier, this field had been split between lentils and oats, and the former crop line was now visible in the color of this year's seedlings. On the lentil side, the young emmer was a deeper green, indicating higher nitrogen content.

"Yeah, we're really not into yield," Doug continued. "If we can make equal revenue from a ten-bushel crop of flax instead of a thirty-bushel crop of wheat, I'll take the ten-bushel crop every time. It takes less out of the soil, it takes less moisture, it takes less trucking, it takes less storage, it takes less everything. It was an epiphany for me to start to think about that, that I would much rather grow a low-yielding, high-value crop than a high-yielding, low-value crop. I suppose at some level everybody couldn't do that or there wouldn't be enough food in the world, but most of the high-yielding crops aren't food in the first place." I could see Doug's mind's eye traveling back to his hometown in Ohio, where row after row of genetically modified corn stood ready to become ethanol.

Doug's rationale sounded good, and in many ways, recalled the philosophy Dave Oien had doled out in the AERO *Sun Times* back in the early eighties. But there was the Rumpelstiltskin issue. "We're trying to live in two different systems right now," Anna said, putting her finger on it. "We're trying to live in this system we're creating, but do it within the existing system that doesn't support it."

It's true that Doug and Anna live in their own universe, complete with its own language. Like Tuna McAlpine, the Crabtrees eschew the term "conventional" farming, preferring "chemically dependent." Doug can tell you exactly why. "We've been practicing agriculture for approximately twelve thousand years and using poisons in great quantities for just sixty of them," he reasons, "so to label that 'convention' is a huge insult to eleven thousand nine hundred and forty years of agriculture." Doug and Anna call sprayers "Orsons" (after Orson Welles's *War of the Worlds*), and time is marked as "BF" and "AF" (before and after the complete reorientation of their lives they refer to simply as "the farm").

The vision the Crabtrees were trying to articulate, Doug told Dave, was one in which their whole life would function like their "high-value, low-input" flax. By pursuing synergies—with compatible fellow growers as well as compatible crops—he and Anna hoped to live and farm less expensively. They imagined belonging to a network of a dozen farmers, trading labor and equipment. But that wasn't happening yet, because the Crabtrees' community was spread all over Montana. If he and his wife didn't spend so much time and money driving all over the place, Doug lamented, their style of farming could be tremendously cheap. "But how do you get from here to there, and how do you survive while you're doing the getting?" Exactly, Dave Oien was thinking. So how about that Chinese pea buyer?

Not ready to give up, Doug and Anna were determined to put their values at the center of their agriculture and compel everything else into some semblance of alignment. Given the considerable size and power of the conventional farm industry, this effort sometimes felt about as futile as trying to convince the earth to orbit the moon. But the Crabtrees kept on pushing. Each time a conventional institution presented a barrier, they set about inventing a workaround.

"FARMING IS A PROFESSION"

I'd first met this indefatigable couple in their home in Helena on a snowy Memorial Day weekend in 2012, the only time off they'd had since January. The foul weather had prevented the Crabtrees from driving up to their farm, which had been a relief to Anna but a source of anxiety for Doug. "You know those webcams some people have to keep tabs on their kids?" Anna said. "We need to get Doug one of those for our crops." Doug was online doing the next best thing: farm research. While Anna and I ate breakfast, Doug tried to ascertain how to make John Deere planters seed sunflowers.

This was the next institution the Crabtrees wanted to tackle: the implement dealer. "We don't want this great big equipment," Anna explained. "We're working with this one-size-fits-all industry, but the key to sustainability is that it has to fit your place." Frustrated with the direction of modern equipment manufacturing, Anna and Doug were forever hunting down older, smaller machines and modifying them to suit their unique farm system.

Russ Salisbury had explained this equipment issue to me too, I told Anna, seizing the opportunity to share some juicy tidbits from my research. As I'd walked through Russ's impressive stockpile of used and unused machinery, the ex-mechanic had pointed out several of his improvised contraptions. "Barley's simple," Russ had told me. "Everything works for wheat and barley, because that's what it's made for." But since Russ wanted to undersow clover and alfalfa into his barley, he'd had to experimentally remodel seeding drills year after year until he hit on something that worked. Bud Barta had made his own seeder too, I discovered, as had Farm Improvement Club program manager Nancy Matheson. I got the sense that for these stalwart AERO members, such

DIY gadgetry was more than a necessity; it was a point of pride. While flipping through the fall 1997 issue of the *Sun Times,* I'd spotted a picture of Russ next to a science fair–esque contraption, which he was gleefully contributing to the organization's live auction. "From last year's generator to this year's garden seeder," the photo was captioned.

Anna listened politely as I recounted these stories, but her vision of making do was a little different. Instead of a jerry-rigged generator, she wanted an iPhone app and a spreadsheet.

I'd never had the gall to ask Anna directly, but I had a pretty good hunch she'd been a straight-A student all through high school, college, her master's, and her PhD. She moved in circles where it was simply expected that offices would come stocked with snazzy monitors, homes with high-speed Internet and low-flow toilets. Anna worked just as hard as her colleagues did and took her job just as seriously. So she got frustrated with the assumption that choosing to farm was a de facto vow of poverty. As much as not getting the loan, that's what had really irked the Crabtrees at the bank. Farm Credit Services had raised an eyebrow at their living expenses, which included insurance, retirement savings, and the house payment on their place in Helena. The second-career farmers didn't see why they should have to defend their middle-class standard of living, but they knew the problem was bigger than one stingy loan officer.

"I think farming is a profession and you should be compensated as a professional, but that's a hard argument to make not only to financers but to other farmers," Doug said, looking up from his laptop. "There's an assumption in the ag community that you're supposed to struggle for the first forty years until you get the land paid for, and then you get to coast—apparently into retirement if you live long enough—by extracting enough rent from the next generation so that they're sure to struggle the way you did. At some point, there's got to be a better way."

Anna and Doug didn't think citizens' groups were enough to change this vicious cycle of rural debt. Although the Crabtrees belonged to the Alternative Energy Resources Organization, Doug was encouraging his fellow AERO growers to join the Organic Trade Association too. Instead of Farm Improvement Clubs funded by 800 dollars in philanthropic capital, Doug envisioned an OTA-supported organic "checkoff" program, modeled after those for agricultural commodities. If just a few cents of each retail organic purchase were siphoned into a dedicated account, he calculated for me, such a checkoff could support 30 million dollars for research and promotion. These were the kind of numbers you needed to make a difference, the Crabtrees felt.

"NONE OF THOSE GUYS EVER TALKED ABOUT RATIOS"

While an underground existence held a certain romance for folks like Russ Salisbury, the Crabtrees wanted to see their approach go mainstream. As we discussed financing and equipment, it became clear that Doug and Anna's goal was to propel Timeless from movement to enterprise. They wanted to scale up to the point that their stewardship could make a consequential impact. They wanted a decent income. And they wanted what Dave and Sharon had never had: a normal life.

"Dave is a great guy," Anna told me, "but he's got a degree in religious studies and this is not about making money for him. Whereas, for Doug and I, this is a business that supports us making money and living a good life."

On second thought, Anna wondered if she'd been too harsh and asked if I found her analysis unfair. But Dave had already told me much the same thing when I'd visited with him three weeks earlier in his own kitchen.

"I'm a religious studies major," Dave had said. "When I tell the bank what we pay our growers, they say this or that ratio isn't high enough for a commercial loan. I don't even know what they mean. These loan officers were business majors; they went to school for that. I did Heidegger and Black Elk. None of those guys ever talked about ratios."

Although Anna's inner engineer and Doug's inner ag economist routinely clashed with Dave's inner Zen master, the boyish old-timer was just as grateful for the Crabtrees' advice as he was for his accountant wife. Jostling back and forth between big ideas and little details, the unlikely allies worked out ways to go against the grain without sacrificing their livelihoods. Still, the Crabtrees weren't sure Dave had ever really moved beyond a black medic lens on the universe, a perspective so radically bottom-up that no one could say with certainty which seeds were going to germinate, or when. "Dave's idea of change is that you're still this little thing and others pick up on your idea and move with it," Doug told me. "Our idea of change is that *you* are the one that does it and scales it up."

GRAD SCHOOL FOR FARMERS

While they wrestled with Dave over the operational logic of Timeless Seeds, Anna and Doug were also working on their own strategy for scaling up the lentil underground: an incubator program for new growers. The structured three- to five-year apprenticeship would function like a professional master's or doctoral degree for beginning farmers, who would complete a series of courses and a capstone project, just like budding executives and engineers. Such an incubator could double as a "Rodale of the Northern Plains" for diversified farming systems science, inspired by the famous organic research facility in Pennsylvania. The Crabtrees even imagined converting the abandoned village surrounding the surveillance radar station into student dorms. A serious incubator program, they explained to Dave, could potentially solve a lot of the problems they'd been talking about.

To begin with, the Crabtrees' "Rodale of the Northern Plains" could address at least a piece of the research problem. Doug and Anna had supported the efforts of several other Timeless farmers to raise money through a nonprofit Organic Advisory and Education Council, but that group, much like the early AERO Ag Task Force, had been focused mostly on lobbying Montana State University researchers to study low-input systems, rather than commissioning or conducting its own studies. For once, the Crabtrees wanted to see *their* values steer the discourse. They were sick of tugging at a big ship that was anchored in an entirely different mooring.

Germinating a like-minded circle of farmers could also solve some of their equipment woes, Doug and Anna reasoned. Once their numbers reached a critical mass, these farmers could invest in a fleet of custom machines and share with one another. Such resources might even be managed by a formal cooperative, which could go a long way toward solving the financing problem. "It would be so much easier to be a beginning farmer if you could go down the road even fifty miles and trade work with another one or share equipment," Doug said, wistfully. "But we're the only ones within two hundred miles doing what we're doing. Sometimes I feel like I'm on an island."

Doug and Anna were philosophically committed to organics, and they'd built both a farm and a business that manifested their vision. But there was a fourth step to conversion: building a supportive community. As Doug and Anna's litany of frustrations made clear, even a solid group of collaborative farmers wouldn't be enough. The Crabtrees needed allies across the food system— from their seed suppliers to their grocery store to their creditors. They had made some headway with a few institutions directly connected to their business, but their ambitious model remained frustratingly separate from the fabric of everyday life in Havre. The Crabtrees' crops were putting down roots, but Doug and Anna still felt like outsiders.

Having endured several years as the laughingstock of Conrad, Dave Oien empathized with Doug and Anna's loneliness. He knew how hard it was to get to the point where you could refer to yourself and your farm without having to resort to the adjective "alternative." This final phase of conversion was so slow, in fact, that Dave was still working on it himself. As he gradually built up his business, he recruited prospective growers according to three criteria. They had to be good farmers. They had to be good businesspeople. But they also had to be good ambassadors.

I followed Dave thirty-five miles south from Doug and Anna's place, so I could tag along for another field visit. When we stopped off to grab lunch in Havre, Dave pointed out a few odd features of the local grocery store. They had started carrying organic produce. And local grass-fed beef. In fact, I noticed, the IGA supermarket was having trouble keeping up with demand for these new products, many of which were out of stock. When I asked why this meat-and-potatoes town had seemingly rediscovered kale as the forgotten element of some culinary holy trinity, Dave chuckled, telling me that Havre's residents were, in fact, picking this stuff up at church. But not from their pastor. The gospel of good food was the dedicated lay ministry of Jody and Crystal Manuel, a pair of independently minded conservatives who homeschooled their six kids, volunteered regularly with their fellow parishioners, and grew organic lentils on a 4,000-acre spread seven miles south of town. "I love this family," Dave divulged, as though he was letting me in on a secret. "They're not what anyone expects."

12

THE GOSPEL OF LENTILS

Sporting a pale-blue T-shirt, soiled jeans, and a dirt-stained Timeless cap, Jody Manuel spoke at about one-fourth the pace of Anna Jones-Crabtree. When he talked, that was. Given the option, Jody preferred to listen and observe instead. The taciturn rancher's hat shaded his entire face from the solstice sunlight, since his gaze nearly always pointed slightly down. Hoping to trick Jody into looking up for a moment, I remarked on the incredible views stretching out in all directions from his grandfather's homestead, which was every bit as spectacular as the county park it abutted. "Yeah, this is a pretty awesome place to go to work every day," Jody said reverently, as I gawked at the Bear Paw Mountains.

Before Dave Oien showed up in his life, Jody had found more time to look around, because he'd had only one job: handling cows. Jody's main interest in his family's place had always been the cattle, so he'd let his brother-in-law raise conventional wheat on the family's crop acreage. But when Jody's health-conscious wife, Crystal, started researching organics, the prospect of cultivating a more diverse array of plants had piqued the rancher's interest in farming for the first time.

The Manuels had started their foray into organic farming slowly, attending a 2007 trade association gathering in Great Falls to meet others who had taken the plunge. The Montana Organic Association conference had included a tour of the Timeless facility in Ulm, but Jody had been too shy to introduce himself to Dave at the time. Instead, he'd gone back to Havre and started doing his homework, gradually putting together a plan for transitioning his family's conventional wheat operation. On a sleepy January day in 2010, Jody had been paging through the MOA newsletter, when an advertisement got his attention. "Wanted: Ten Good Farmers," the spot read, followed by a list of desired attributes: "Commitment to Soil Health. Focus on Quality. Dedication to Crop Rotations." At the bottom of the ad, next to the Timeless Seeds logo, was Dave Oien's phone number. Jody decided he was ready, and he jumped in with both feet. By the time I tagged along with Dave for his June 2012 field visits, the Manuels were well into their second season of lentil farming, and they'd started growing emmer for Timeless as well.

The first thing Jody showed Dave was the field where he was experimenting with a "cover crop cocktail": a mix of vetch, red clover, ryegrass, flax, turnips, and radishes that he'd seeded in two waves in late April and mid-May. "Cover crop cocktail" was a flashy rebrand for soil-building intercrops, Dave explained to me, somewhat amused to hear from Jody that Montana State had recently sponsored a field day to promote the practice to conventional growers. Jody's version of this "cocktail" included both legumes (the vetch and clover, for nitrogen) and deep-penetrating root crops (the turnips and radishes, which performed a gentle version of tillage). The mix had cost 20 dollars an acre to seed, Jody estimated, but he thought it was worth it. "I think this cover cropping is—I can't think of anything that's going to be more beneficial," he told Dave. "I don't really think that I'm doing it primarily to benefit the land, because I am in business to earn a living, but at the same time I know that it's improving the soil."

Much as he had done at the Crabtrees', Dave moved swiftly from Jody's soil-building crops to Timeless Seeds' crowning edible: Black Belugas. Jody had ended up planting his lentils a little later than he wanted to this year, he explained to his buyer apologetically. Facing a serious bindweed problem in a field he was tilling for the first time, Jody had borrowed a sturdy tractor attachment from the Crabtrees to plow it down. He'd eventually succeeded in eradicating the weeds, but in the process, he'd sidelined his tractor—the same one he needed to plant lentils. Seeding day had had to wait on the mechanic.

BLACK BELUGAS AND BIBLE STORIES

I was happy to see that Jody had managed to get his Black Belugas in the ground before the season got away from him. When I'd first met the Manuels, four weeks earlier, the tractor had still been sitting idle in the field, and Jody was obviously concerned. And yet, I noted, he was also remarkably calm. I'd climbed into Jody's bright-red, three-quarter-ton Dodge Ram, expecting a swashbuckling roller-coaster ride of a ranch tour. There were miles of private mountain roads ahead of us, stunning snow-covered mountains behind us, and the man at the wheel was a God-fearing conservative. The scene had all the makings of a mud-slinging truck commercial, except that the driver refused to exceed fifteen miles an hour. The road was still mucky from the Memorial Day snow, Jody explained, expertly balancing a Holy Bible on his console, so he had to be careful not to get stuck. When we'd finished the first leg of our tour, Jody invited me to share lunch with his family. He sat down, took off his hat, and offered a simple blessing, giving thanks for the gifts of food, rain, and good health.

Crystal Manuel had prepared a four-course, farm-to-table lunch, complete with Black Beluga lentil soup. Describing her South Asian–inspired Desi dressing as she herded her four youngest children to the dining room, Crystal channeled the pride of an elite restaurateur without the slightest trace of preciousness. This had to be the nicest meal anybody ever ate at a table with crayons on it, I remarked. Crystal laughed. It was the middle of the school day, she explained. The Manuels were homeschooling all six of their children through the eighth grade, and the four pupils who joined us for lunch—Sawyer, Taliya, Teague, and six-month-old Shayna—were all current enrollees at Crystal Manuel elementary. Teenagers Sarah and Tristan had recently graduated from their mom's classroom and were finishing up their freshman and sophomore years at Havre High.

As I savored the tangy aftertaste of Crystal's soup, her four charges efficiently cleaned their plates, focused intently on the prize of recess. Eleven-year-old Sawyer was the first to finish, and the garage door banged shut as he dashed off to ride his four-wheeler. Four-year-old Teague was next: He wanted to show me his Bible story computer game. Once Teague and I had finished helping a slightly pixelated Queen Esther choose a dessert for her important dinner with King Artaxerxes, Crystal joined us in the Manuels' loft/classroom, offering it to me as guest quarters for the night. His computer time up, Teague ran off to draw pictures with his older sister Taliya, and I stayed for a few minutes to visit with Crystal about the elaborate meal she had prepared. It turned out that her training was in nutrition, and a major reason the Manuels had jumped into organics was Crystal's interest in health and wellness. In fact, she'd had her sixth child at home in a bathtub, grounds for serious street cred among the most rarefied natural health circles of San Francisco or Los Angeles. My jaw dropped as

Crystal nonchalantly told the story. She had booked a midwife from Great Falls in advance, but once Crystal's water broke, things had moved along rather quickly. When the Manuels realized the midwife couldn't possibly make the 120-mile journey in time for the birth, Jody had delivered their youngest daughter, Shayna, himself.

Jody, I gathered, was not an easy character to typify. Given that he had recently run for county commissioner as a libertarian Republican, I was surprised at how highly he spoke of Doug and Anna Jones-Crabtree, who worked for the government and socialized with Helena's staunchest Democrats. If Jody knew about his neighbors' liberal leanings, though, he wasn't concerned. Grateful to the Crabtrees for lending him a plow to deal with his bindweed, he was already talking to them about pooling seed orders, to cut down on hauling expenses. Even the ancient words the two families had chosen to express the idea at the heart of their farms bore a curious resemblance. While the Crabtrees had named their farm Vilicus, Latin for "steward of the land," the Manuels introduced me to the term *sozo,* an Ancient Greek word used in the New Testament. While *sozo* was typically translated as "salvation," Jody explained, he and Crystal were particularly fond of its extended definition: "to heal, preserve, and make whole."

Conventional political boundaries seemed to dissolve and realign in the presence of lentils and their farmers, which actually made sense once I thought about it. It wasn't that hard to understand why lentil farming might lead to a sort of third politics—a nuanced perspective on what needed to be shared at what scale in order to survive. I'd been focused on all the ways lentils behaved like good cooperative lefties. But you could also see the tiny legume as the ultimate libertarian—conservative and resourceful.

TROUBLE IN THE RHIZOSPHERE

Except that, at the time of Dave Oien's 2012 field visit, Jody's second field of lentils didn't appear to be very resourceful at all. Dave had dug up several plants, and he couldn't find any of the telltale white growths he was looking for on the tips of their roots. There were plenty of lentil sprouts poking up, but since the plants didn't have these nitrogen-fixing nodules on their roots, that meant none of them were making fertilizer. "I don't see a single nodule there," Dave told Jody, his hands clutching a rooty bouquet of bum lentils. "It seems like it would be an inoculant issue."

Jody sucked in a heavy breath. "Inoculant" was a key part of the support system that allowed his Black Belugas to thrive. As the greenhorn pulse farmer already knew, it wasn't actually his lentil plants that fixed nitrogen, but the symbiotic rhizobia bacteria that typically set up shop in the Black Belugas' root nodules. Some soils had rhizobia hanging around from previous legume liaisons. But that was an outside chance on ground like Jody's that had either come out of long-term fallow or recently exited an exclusive relationship with wheat and chemicals. So, like all the Timeless growers, Jody applied peat moss filled with specialized bacteria to his lentil seeds before planting them. These carefully chosen strains, selected for their affinity with peas and lentils, ensured that nitrogen-boosting microorganisms would be available to the tiny Black Belugas when they germinated. The bacteria-spiked peat moss was called inoculant. And it was what Dave was worried about.

"Did you get that inoculant from us?" the Timeless CEO asked Jody, who nodded. "Do you still have a bagful of it? I'd like to see." Having personally taught several of his growers about inoculant and how to use it, Dave hated the idea that he might have inadvertently doomed somebody's crop with a dud bag. Two of the sacks of inoculant used on these lentils were actually leftovers from Doug, Jody reported, remaining calm. Since the Belugas at Vilicus Farms were clearly nodulating their hearts out, that would seem to eliminate inoculant as the source of Jody's problem. The level-headed rancher asked resignedly if no nodules meant no lentils, ready to hear the worst. Not exactly, Dave said, but this wasn't good news. Starved of nitrogen, the crop would be short and probably not that productive. Jody nodded. Like cover crops and cash crops, inoculant and lentils went hand in hand. You couldn't get something for nothing. He walked back to his truck, in search of a better tool for digging up roots.

This was the Manuels' second season growing Black Belugas, Dave told me, and it was a crucible of sorts. Jody's Beluga crop had been a near-total loss last year, but he'd realized what went wrong and had agreed to try again. Once. Dave finished his sentence wordlessly, with a sober glance at the ground. He knew Jody had set aside his cleanest, most fertile field for the little black legumes, since they could be sold at a hefty premium and he liked working with Timeless. But Dave also knew that Jody's spelt crop was doing quite well, and if the lentils failed again this year, the Manuels would probably have to replace their Belugas with the robust heritage grain. Dave hated to lose such a promising new grower, and he felt no small sense of responsibility for encouraging Jody to take a risk on a tricky crop.

Plus, Timeless was fresh out of Black Belugas. Difficult to grow but increasingly popular, they were among the products Dave was most likely to run short on. If he had to say no to buyers too many times, they might stop calling. Given the delicate dilemma of supply, the business counted on symbiosis as much as their lentils did. While the plants relied on inoculant, cover crops, and rotations, Timeless counted on relationships, financing, and marketing—which was why Dave had to spend so much time on the phone, when he'd just as soon be building upcycled seeders and funky solar gadgets.

"I WANT OUR NEIGHBORS TO BE ABLE TO AFFORD IT"

Jody and Crystal, meanwhile, were working hard to create another series of relationships—with local consumers. The busy parents were bending over backward to sell meat directly to their hometown IGA supermarket, even though it would have been much easier to just send the whole herd to the natural beef company in Minnesota that was more than happy to buy from them.

"When I first went into the IGA to talk to the guy that's in charge of their meat department," Jody recounted, "it was almost like he already had his mind made up. He said, 'I just don't think people are going to be willing to pay those kind of prices'—and we hadn't even talked price yet. He was just assuming that since it was 'natural' . . ."*

Jody had almost given up on marketing locally, but instead he had asked the meat department manager what the IGA was paying for the conventional beef they were retailing. The manager had taken Jody back to his office and shown him his wholesale price list, which was broken down into various cuts: chuck roast,

---

* For now, Jody was stuck in the same position Dave had been decades ago—describing how his beef fit the organic paradigm with words like "natural," since it wasn't officially certified. But that was about to change. Meat had been included when the USDA passed its new *National Organic Program* rules in 2002, so once Jody's pastureland completed the program's requisite three-year transition period, his beef would became officially, certifiably organic.

T-bone, sirloin. Jody had done some quick math, attempting to mentally reassemble the spreadsheet of cellophane-wrapped packages into a living, breathing bovine. He had told the manager he thought he could sell his natural beef for a pretty comparable price. "In that case," the manager had said, "yeah, we could sure try it."

Now that he'd managed to talk them into it, Jody was committed to selling what he could to the local grocery store, even though it was more of a hassle. Jody explained that when he sent his cattle to Minnesota, not only did he receive a higher price, but also he could deliver a whole semi load at once. Retailing at the local IGA, on the other hand, meant processing one animal at a time. So even though the Manuels' ranch was just seven miles from the final point of sale in downtown Havre, Jody had to put in some serious driving time before his beef made it to his neighbors' shopping carts.

"IGA has a requirement that it has to be slaughtered at a USDA-inspected plant, and there's one in Shelby and one in Malta," Jody reported, estimating that it was about 100 miles to either of these "local" processors. "I can't even get the one in Shelby to return a phone call, they're so swamped. On their answering machine it essentially says that 'We might call you back or we might not.'" Since neither of his local packing plants would return his calls, Jody had researched a third option: the Little Rockies Meat Packing Company, owned by the Assiniboine and Gros Ventre tribes. Every two weeks, Jody made the ninety-minute trip to the tribes' facility on the far side of the Fort Belknap Indian Reservation, hauling exactly one cow.

"I tried to talk IGA into taking two animals at a time instead of just one," Jody continued. "You take these heifers, they're in a group, you know, just out in the pasture. By the time you bring two or three of them up to the corral, you sort off the one you want to take, load it in the horse trailer by itself, haul it a hundred miles . . . By the time you get down there, she's just going ballistic a lot of times, even if it's a nice, docile, gentle heifer. For no other reason than that, it'd be nice if they took two." Notwithstanding such difficulties, Jody had recently added another wrinkle to the Manuels' diversified crop and animal operation: direct-market pork. That had been a learning experience too, he confessed. At first, Jody had advertised his local pork in the classified section of the *Havre Daily News*, but after several weeks with no phone calls, he asked Casey Bailey for marketing advice. Casey told Jody to put the hogs on Facebook, and he quickly sold them all.

While Jody worked the phone and the Web, Crystal went straight for her neighbors' stomachs. I got a taste for the persuasiveness of Crystal's approach from the four-course lunch she'd made during my visit, which had included not just a hearty Black Beluga soup and green salad, but also rolls made from the Manuels' Kamut, and raspberry rhubarb crisp with millet topping. The rhubarb had come from the family garden, while the store-bought raspberries tantalizingly anticipated harvests to come—Crystal had just planted some bramble bushes. Offering up such mouth-watering fare, Crystal had started leading an annual nutrition workshop for the women at her church, beginning with relatively innocuous themes like raw food and healthy hydration.

The year before my visit, Crystal's workshop had tackled a much thornier issue—GMOs—and she'd been recommending the movie *Food, Inc.* to curious members of her church group. "They're starting to care about where their meat comes from," Crystal said, smiling broadly. "So this year, we're going to do a farm-to-fork tasting out in the cover crop cocktail once the pigs are in there grazing it down. I've invited all the women and their kids, and we have a church van lined up." I tried to imagine Havre's decent Christian women eating hors d'oeuvres in the cover crop. Leave it to Crystal to pull off white-tablecloth dining among pigs.

Although she'd been steeped in the constitutive irony of modern rural America—the bizarre industrial arrangement that leaves professional food producers among the least likely people to have access to fresh produce—Crystal was determined to bridge the gap between production and consumption, starting with her own family. In a place where it might snow on Memorial Day, however, this was no mean feat. The summertime window of reliably frost-free nights was brief in northern Montana, which meant vegetables started from seed might never mature. In order to have a successful garden, Crystal realized, she'd need to give her veggies a head start in a greenhouse. Since she didn't have one of her own yet, she decided to purchase some young plants in town for her first season.

So in the spring of 2010, Crystal Manuel had gotten in her minivan and headed off to downtown Havre to buy some heirloom, organic starts. The trouble was, nobody was selling them. Undaunted, Crystal not only got online and found a place to order them—she had five phone conversations with the Arizona-based supplier and brought him to town the following fall to chat with all her neighbors. "We had the organic gardening workshop in November and it was like twelve below zero that day," Crystal told me, "but we just invited people, and so many of them came." Crystal's greatest triumph had been convincing an elderly local greenhouse manager to show up. Now he, too, was a proponent of organic fertilizer. "He sells fish emulsion and seaweed now!" Crystal told me, delighted.

In a small town like Havre, you didn't have to be a person of faith to recognize that farm-to-table aspirations were pretty hollow unless you could a find a way to share the bounty with your whole community. Unless you organized your neighbors, you literally couldn't even get a start. And although Jody and Crystal had gotten their start—and their organic starts—they still felt as if they had a long way to go. Per capita income in Havre averaged just under 23,000 dollars a year, and 17 percent of residents lived in poverty. How many of those folks were going to buy fish emulsion and seaweed?

"One thing that bothers me about this whole industry is the cost," Jody said, when I bumped into the Manuel family a few months later at an organic conference. "It's tough for the average person, living paycheck to paycheck." Jody related the story of a missionary friend in the Philippines, who had lamented that local people there didn't have access to the fishery anymore, because all the crab and lobster was being shipped out on big commercial boats. "I can see how it's sort of like that here too," Jody reflected. "I mean, we're sending our meat to Whole Foods."

When I'd visited the Manuel place in May, Jody hadn't yet sold any beef to the natural-food chain because he was still transitioning his herd to organics. But since this season's newborn calves would be his first certified animals, he'd started exploring the option. A broker had already been out to the ranch to see if the Manuels' cattle looked like Whole Foods material, and the verdict was promising: The man thought Jody's animals would fetch a healthy premium. The business opportunity was a relief to the budget-conscious father of six. But the good news was bittersweet, since the Manuels' newly certified beef might never again grace the kitchen tables of Havre. "I think I am going to raise prices at IGA now that we have our first organic calves—to get a comparable price—but I don't want to," Jody told me. "I want our neighbors to be able to afford it." Three decades after Dave Oien had been forced to give up on his own organic beef business, he and the lentil underground had built enough of a support structure to allow Jody Manuel to make a go of it. But it still wasn't quite the closed-loop food system they were all shooting for.

As the movement went mainstream, ruggedly individual farmers found themselves sharing in ways they never had before. People like Jerry Habets were sharing knowledge, changing one another's minds. Having revamped their philosophy, people like Casey Bailey had started changing their farms, designing systems in which different elements complemented one another, rather than trying to maximize the yield of a single crop. Once they'd changed their farms, the lentil underground had realized that they couldn't make a living unless they drastically altered their business model. So people like Doug and Anna Jones-Crabtree had begun developing collective infrastructure and devising new financing models to spread risk. Jody and Crystal Manuel had taken this cooperative spirit beyond the farm community, determined to get the rest of their neighbors on board, even if it meant driving their cattle 100 miles, one at a time, and selling their products a little more cheaply at the local IGA.

At this point, the lentil underground hit the limit of what they could do by themselves. They had taken their movement mainstream, but they still hadn't diverted the prevailing current of the food system nearly as much as they wanted to. Most farmers still had to sell into markets warped by monopoly power, and most consumers still had to buy from those markets. So many bizarre incentives were lodged between food and reality that people couldn't afford to do what was truly economical—and sometimes they didn't even have the choice. Industrial food and farming remained artificially cheap. And in most little towns, the burger chain and the big grain elevator were still the only game in town. Dave and his accomplices had converted a little pocket of farm country, but what they really wanted to overhaul was the American way of eating, and that was a big job. They'd need a larger crew, since the obstacles they were running up against now—like the massive federal Farm Bill and its entrenched system of subsidies—were codified in law. Dave had found people to grow lentils, distribute lentils, and, in this meat-loving part of Montana, even eat lentils. But would they *vote* for lentils?

13

THE BIRDS, THE BEES, AND THE BUREAUCRACY

POLITICS AT THE POLLINATOR WORKSHOP

On Thursday, June 14, 2012, a steady stream of state and federal employees paraded into the Lewis and Clark Interpretive Center in Great Falls to learn about bees and butterflies. But when the projector hummed awake at nine fifteen A.M., the first ten eyes on the screen looked suspiciously alert for this hour of the morning. Lurking amid the nine-to-five crowd were five people clearly accustomed to beginning their day before dawn. From the looks of their focused gaze, they were here on a mission.

Doug Crabtree and Anna Jones-Crabtree had spent weeks enthusiastically spreading the word about this pollinator workshop, which was facilitated by a nonprofit conservation group called the Xerces Society. The training was geared toward Natural Resources Conservation Service staff but open to the public, and since Doug and Anna thought the discussion was important, they had worked hard to convince fellow farmers that it was worth leaving their farms behind for half a day in the middle of the growing season. Casey Bailey, Bob Bailey, and another Timeless Seeds grower—Jacob Cowgill—had signed up right away.

"Why aren't there more farmers here?" Jacob wondered aloud.

"They're probably out spraying," Doug answered wryly.

The sole producers in a room full of civil servants, the five

Timeless growers nonetheless made their presence felt. Greatly outnumbered by staff from NRCS, the Montana Department of Agriculture, the Bureau of Land Management, and the Forest Service, the sharp-witted quintet still managed to ask about half the questions. "Does tillage in the fall hurt ground-nesting bees?" Casey wanted to know. He and his buddies were here in good faith to learn about the sophisticated critters that pollinated their buckwheat and safflower. But they also had a thing or two to share with the NRCS.

When I first heard that an agency called the Natural Resources Conservation Service wasn't already tight with the Timeless crew, I was astonished. The legume strategy was all about natural resource conservation, right? Well, yes, the Timeless farmers explained to me, but the NRCS didn't always see it that way. Founded in 1935 as the *Soil* Conservation Service, the agency sometimes had a one-track mind about exactly which resource it was obliged to conserve. Intensely focused on combating soil erosion, the NRCS had become enamored of an agricultural method known as "no-till."

Zero-tillage farming, the lentil growers explained, was a farming approach that had become popular in the eighties. Rather than mechanically ripping out their weeds before seeding, no-till farmers left their plows in the shed and used chemicals to clear their fields instead. This way of farming had become even easier when plants like corn and soybeans were genetically engineered to resist herbicides, allowing farmers to spray all year round, right into their cropland. Not everybody thought the environmental downsides of this chemically based, GMO approach were worth the payoff, but since the NRCS had originally been established to prevent another Dust Bowl, the agency had a hard time resisting any approach that kept land in place—even chemically treated land. As no-till farming spread, the NRCS had taken to it like a sweat bee to a sunflower.

Unfortunately, this focus on no-till had driven a wedge between the NRCS and the sector of the agricultural community that should have been its staunchest ally: organics. By drawing a hard line on tillage but taking a relatively laissez-faire attitude toward herbicides and genetically engineered crops, the agency punished organic producers for the one industrial practice they relied on, without rewarding them for phasing out so many others. There were exceptions, the Timeless growers told me, but by and large the agency's incentive structure effectively discouraged organic farming.

Casey Bailey understood the NRCS's attraction to no-till systems because, at first, he'd felt the same way. After learning about the method in a college class, the fourth-generation farmer had been so excited about it that he'd gone right out and leased some land so he could experiment with tillage-free agriculture himself. The budding ecologist liked the idea of softening his touch on the underground world, so that earthworms and microorganisms could build his soil undisturbed. But since he wasn't plowing, Casey had to use a lot more herbicide to kill the weeds, and he couldn't help but wonder what that glyphosate bath was doing to all the other life in his soil. "I think the chemical companies capitalized on academic soil science when they said that we should be saving our organic matter and not tilling our soils," Casey concluded. Sure, there were environmental arguments for plowing less. But there were downsides to chemical no-till too: Applying more herbicides increased the risk of groundwater pollution and encouraged the evolution of herbicide-resistant superweeds. Farming wasn't an equation you could solve for one variable.

By the time I met him in 2012, Casey was still trying to minimize tillage, and he was excited about emergent research on organic no-till (some of it based on Timeless Seeds' original model, the Australian ley system). But he'd come to weigh that objective against several other indicators that he considered equally important to the health of his farm. That was why he had brought his dad to this Xerces Society workshop—so they could learn together about supporting the native bees that pollinated several of their crops. "It's amazing what these little critters can do," Bob Bailey said in awe. "It almost makes you think there's a God."

While his dad scouted for bees in the conference center's native plant garden, Casey queried one of the workshop leaders. Which was the best flowering legume to have in the rotation, from a pollinator standpoint? Was early tillage or late tillage better? And how about all that herbicide associated with the no-till strategy? Balancing these numerous considerations was a tricky matter, and it wasn't easy to reform agency programs so that they truly accounted for the complexity of diversified farming systems. But Casey and his fellow growers were determined to try.

"WHAT ABOUT THE TRADE-OFFS?"

"As an organic producer, we've found it challenging to fit the square peg of what we do into the round hole of NRCS practices," Doug Crabtree diplomatically explained. "We need to get to understand each other better."

Anna put the matter more bluntly. "I don't know what is up with the no-till water you guys are drinking," she said, taking issue with a study cited by one of the agency representatives. "What about the trade-offs? What about the chemicals and their impact on soil microbiology?"

Anna was frustrated because she and Doug had been invei-gled into alternating no-till with their rye crop in order to qualify for support from the NRCS Conservation Stewardship Program, a program that pays farmers for conservation performance by contracting with them to implement environmentally friendly "enhancements." One of these enhancements, "Use of Non-Chemical Methods to Kill Cover Crops," seemed like a great fit for certified organic farmers like the Crabtrees, who were al-ready committed to plowing down their cover crop (so as to con-trol their use of resources like soil water), rather than spraying it out. But the way the NRCS rules were written, producers could qualify for this enhancement only if they followed the tillage of their cover crop with a no-till cash crop. And therein, for the Crabtrees, lay the rub.

"The reason we grow rye in the first place," Doug explained to his district conservationist, Talana Klungland, "is because it's competitive and cleans things up for the next four years. But with this no-till thing, we got a poor stand, and the field's not as clean." Since the Crabtrees didn't use herbicides *at all,* Doug emphasized, they needed to do at least some mechanical weeding, or their crops would get choked out. Given all the ways their diverse, chemical-free system enhanced the soil, Doug tried to convince Talana, some modest tillage was a small price to pay.

The Crabtrees had invited Talana and two other NRCS staffers to visit their farm the day after the pollinator workshop, to demon-strate what they were talking about. Hill County's most deter-mined organic advocates seemed to be making some headway. Talana was impressed with the lack of erosion at Vilicus Farms, noting that such tenaciously adherent soil was tough to achieve in this windy area, even with no-till. NRCS state biologist Pete Husby, who was making his first-ever visit to an organic farm, gave the

Crabtrees an even more surprising vote of confidence. Thumbing through the *Pollinator Habitat Assessment Form and Guide* he'd been working on with Xerces, Pete suggested adding harvestable species as well as conservation plantings, since Doug and Anna had several crops that were clearly "great for pollinators." By the end of the half-day tour, it sure sounded like the Crabtrees had convinced at least two NRCS folks that an organic system with appropriate tillage could actually benefit the land.

As satisfying as it had been, however, the conservation show-and-tell session had also exhausted most of the daylight and nearly all of the Crabtrees' abundant energy. Reforming NRCS was even tougher than scouting for nodules or pulling up thistles, I remarked, wondering aloud if Doug and Anna ever tired of engaging with public programs that had been designed to support a completely different style of land management. They couldn't afford not to, Doug told me. Although he and his wife managed their business as carefully as they managed their soils, they couldn't control the weather—or the fluctuations of global markets, which were even more volatile these days, tied as they were to the machinations of Wall Street. Initiatives like the NRCS Conservation Stewardship Program helped buffer the Crabtrees' income and provided some semblance of the much larger government safety net (commodity crop subsidies and insurance) that their conventional neighbors relied on. Without better aligning those initiatives with their practices, Doug and Anna would have a difficult time weathering the start-up phase of establishing a new kind of farm and farm business—let alone convincing other farmers to follow suit. Doug didn't put it this bluntly, but I understood what he was getting at. The Crabtrees weren't just farming for themselves. They'd invested a lot of time and money in resources that benefited everybody: clean water, carbon sequestration, nutrient management, and yes, pollinators. If Vilicus Farms was providing public services for the common good, shouldn't it get some public support?

Truthfully, even passionate sustainability evangelists like Doug and Anna couldn't sponsor the soil health of an entire region. As the first generation of Timeless farmers had learned the hard way, their effort to revolutionize agriculture in the grain belt could only go so far without some policy changes. Reaching out to local civil servants and state agencies was a good start, but Timeless growers were already thinking ahead to the big prize: the federal Farm Bill. A month after the pollinator workshop, Doug, Anna, and Casey met up again for Timeless Seeds' summer field tour and barbecue. As it had since that first year at Bud Barta's place, the growers gathering offered farmers a rare opportunity to get together and troubleshoot problems. But these days, the strategy session moved swiftly from weeds to white papers. Casey Bailey was hosting this year's tour at his place in Fort Benton, and although he knew his fellow growers could give him several helpful pointers on his field operation, what he really wanted to fix was a lot bigger than his farm.

14
FROM THE WEEDS TO
THE WHITE HOUSE

On Friday, July 13, 2012, Casey Bailey hosted Timeless Seeds' annual field day and barbecue, his first major farm tour. Sweating his way through the scorching, humid affair, the thirty-two-year-old farmer was feeling the heat in more ways than one. It made Casey nervous to put his farm on display, just four years into his organic transition. The hot weather had thrown the Baileys' weeds into overdrive, and Casey couldn't shake the feeling that his fields were a bit too messy to debut, even among friends. He'd noticed that his crops were maturing quickly too, maybe a little too quickly, and he feared this historically droughty season might turn out to be a total loss. Several of Casey's neighbors had already concluded as much and weren't even planning to attempt a harvest.

The difference between Casey and his neighbors, however, was that conventional commodity farmers could typically count on federal crop insurance to keep them running in the black, even if they didn't have a single grain of wheat to show for the thousands of acres they'd seeded. That insurance—along with other federal programs tailored to incentivize a small handful of industrial commodities—played a much larger role in farmers' risk analysis than their guesses at the weather. Drought sounded like a natural disaster, but it wasn't wholly natural, or necessarily a disaster. Truth be told, the word lent an air of inevitability to a complex problem that was partly the result of its own "solution."

The problem known as drought was not just a matter of annual rainfall totals. It was created partially by industrial farming practices, which reduced soil water holding capacity over time, so that crops were more vulnerable to water stress in dry years. Unfortunately, these were the same industrial practices that helped farmers qualify for federal support programs that partially sheltered their *income* from the ups and downs of climate. Perversely, the ecological and economic strategies for weathering drought were working at cross-purposes.

Looking ahead to a lifetime of managing his family's farm, Casey knew he shouldn't waste too much time worrying about exactly when the rain was going to stop. That was obviously going to happen several times over the life of any central Montana farm, so what did it matter whether it was this year or next? The real question was how to create the right economic and policy incentives, such that farmers could plan for this inevitable climatic uncertainty. Why not reward people for planting drought-resilient crops and building up their organic matter to increase soil water retention? At the very least, they shouldn't be encouraged—often against their better judgment—to seed varieties that were almost guaranteed to regularly fail.

Much as Casey appreciated his fellow growers' suggestions about farming practices that might help him control his weeds and conserve moisture, it was these larger policy issues he really wanted to dig into. Escorting his guests out of his sweltering lentil field and back to the relative cool of the garage, Casey invited them to tuck into some barbecue. Once they'd loaded their plates with grass-fed burgers and farm-to-table potluck dishes, the Timeless growers and their guests started talking shop.

"WE NEED TO HAVE A VOICE"

"We farmers tend to focus on our operation first, but it really is important to share that experience with our national and state politicians," Casey encouraged his fellow growers. "They're there for us. At least they should be. And they can be if we speak up."

Casey was particularly concerned that no one was representing people like himself, whose lives and farms were "not black and white." He had vocal friends on both sides of the so-called national food fight—zealous urban community gardeners and proud conventional grain growers—but the space in between was a veritable echo chamber. It was uncomfortable to be the organic farmer who was still using diesel-based tillage, or the conventional producer who'd cut his herbicide use to nearly—but not quite—nothing. Since these folks didn't see their systems in progress as ideal, they tended to be very humble. And very silent. "The loudest voices in the organic movement are definitely not coming from the gray areas," Casey observed, "because when you get in the gray areas, you get quieter. But we need to have a voice."

If anybody in this crowd was determined to amplify the lentil underground's political voice, it was Doug Crabtree and Anna Jones-Crabtree. At least every couple of years, the pair marched straight into the offices of their elected officials in Washington, DC, as part of the "Farmer Fly-Ins" organized by groups like the Center for Rural Affairs, the Organic Trade Association, and the Farmers Union. Doug and Anna were also applying for every federal program they could possibly qualify for, convinced that each application presented an educational opportunity as well as a financial one. Rather than modify their farm system to fit the programs, as so many farmers had done to qualify for commodity payments, the Crabtrees were determined to use their farm as the starting point of the discussion—and challenge the agencies to improve on their models. Sustainable agriculture was a better form of stewardship than bare fallow, they told the NRCS, as part of their application for the Conservation Stewardship Program. Organic farming was a promising means of economic development, they encouraged the Environmental Protection Agency, volunteering to serve as a pilot site for the EPA's new Economy, Energy, and Environment program, in partnership with local extension agents.

Anna's fellow farmers weren't surprised to hear that a relatively progressive environmental agency was supportive of organic agriculture. But the fact that the Crabtrees were partnering with the extension service was newsworthy. A handful of agents had enthusiastically participated in AERO trainings and Farm Improvement Club field days, but the service as a whole still had a reputation for being skeptical of organic methods. Of course, they weren't nearly as bad as the no-till boosters at the Natural Resources Conservation Service. How was Anna faring with them? her fellow Timeless growers wanted to know.

Overall, NRCS had actually been pretty good to work with, Anna answered, acknowledging that it had taken some effort for both parties. She and Doug had sunk a lot of time into patient conversations with the agency, but it had paid off. The Crabtrees had received substantial funding for their ecological practices from both the Conservation Stewardship Program and another NRCS initiative called the Environmental Quality Incentives Program, or EQIP. Established in the 1996 Farm Bill, EQIP took a more proactive approach than previous conservation programs. Instead of paying people to leave their land alone, EQIP provided cost share to farmers who wanted to actively care for it—by planting windbreaks, for example, or buffer strips for wildlife. In 2008, the program had even begun offering cost share specifically to support organic conversion.

Plus, the local NRCS scientists who'd been receptive to the Crabtrees' ideas had made some real progress at the pollinator workshop, Anna reported. The partnership the Crabtrees were participating in—between NRCS and the nonprofit Xerces Society—was helping move the agency toward more organic-friendly policies. If a proposed grant came through, the pollinator conservation nonprofit would be helping NRCS rewrite some of their practices to better include organic systems, with Vilicus Farms as one of the pilot sites. "Really, a lot of those USDA programs that were in the Farm Bill have helped us, so those are important," Anna commented, hoping to plant seeds of advocacy among her more reticent fellows.

Anna's comment got her husband, Doug, going on another federal program that was ripe for reform: the commodity checkoff. Like all farmers, Doug explained, organic growers were contributing to checkoff programs for whatever commodity they raised—wheat, barley, beef. But all this money went to marketing conventional grain, conventional meat. Doug's deep voice made for a hilariously faithful imitation of the Beef Council's ubiquitous television ad, "Beef, It's What's for Dinner." Having gotten his fellow farmers' attention, he asked if they knew who had paid for all those beef ads. Do you raise cattle? Doug asked, eliciting several nods. "Then you paid for it," Doug finished. "That was the checkoff."

If organic growers could opt out of those commodity checkoffs and pool that money into a multicommodity fund of their own,

Doug explained, that would add up to 30 million dollars for organic research and marketing. Imagine a clever organic lentil spot running on Super Bowl Sunday! But that policy change would require at least two amendments to the Farm Bill, so they'd better start calling their representatives.

THE GREAT WHITE COMBINE

Of course, a checkoff-supported marketing fund—organic or otherwise—would only help people who had a crop to sell. Sooner or later, every one of these farmers knew they would hit a bad year or a drought. Most of them had already lost a harvest to "the great white combine": hail. The scariest thing about converting to diversified organic production was that there was no solid fallback plan. "The reason we farm like we do out here," Casey explained, pointing to the herbicide-resistant Clearfield wheat that his dad had planted on the Baileys' remaining conventional acreage, "is the safety net. If this crop fails, we've got crop insurance. But if my organic crops fail, that's a big risk."

Grain farmers have long joked that they are "farming the government" rather than the land, and as Casey's remark indicated, they haven't had much choice. The key to their livelihoods lies in aligning their management with farm programs, even if they know it's not the most prudent way to coax food from soil. Like Orville Oien, Casey's dad understood this economy, and he knew his best bet was to stick with the protocol that brought the money in, crop or no crop. That protocol, of course, was dictated by federal and state law, which was why Casey had invited several non-organic neighbors to this tour. He needed to get them on board.

"I want to be an organic farmer who's respected by conventional farmers," Casey said emphatically. "I want to make this work for all of us. It's going to take changing subsidies and crop insurance. It's these policies—and there are so many power players involved—that really steer what we do out here, that make our landscape look like it does."

Support for farming organic legumes had improved markedly since Dave had started doing it thirty years earlier. In the 2012 Farm Bill, the USDA had finally rolled out a whole farm revenue insurance program. Now that it was possible to insure lentils—as well as a number of other diverse crops—the Crabtrees were planning to sign up. "We spend more on crop insurance than fuel," Doug told me. "It's our biggest expense." Still, Doug and Anna couldn't cover their rye, and the insurance available for several of their other crops wasn't that great. As Jerry Habets had explained to me when I'd oohed and aahed over his intercrop, buckwheat could be insured only under the oxymoronically titled Non-insured Crop Disaster Assistance Program. "It's basically little to nothing," Jerry told me.

Plus, like the existing checkoff program and Montana State's enterprise analysis, all these federal insurance options assumed that each field contained only one crop. I got an earful about that from the guy who'd brought his grass-fed burger to the barbecue, Timeless grower Jess Alger. Jess ran an integrated farm and livestock operation fifty miles south of the Baileys in Stanford, Montana, and like Jerry Habets, he used intercrops—sometimes even spontaneous ones.

"We had a whole bunch of winter wheat coming up in the peas," Jess told me, "so we left it for the winter wheat. By the time the winter wheat got ripe, well, then the peas had climbed on the wheat, so we had about half wheat and half peas. Well, that was a hassle with the federal crop insurance. They were not impressed.

'Well, you called it peas.' 'Well, yeah, it is.' 'Well, you've got wheat.' 'Well, yes we do.' . . . On and on, it was, round and round and round we went." Since it wasn't immediately clear which of his plants was *the crop,* Jess had the insurance adjusters thoroughly flummoxed.

"WE'RE NOT A CIVILIZED NATION"

Timeless growers like Jess Alger continued to press their representatives in DC to provide better insurance for their crops, but what they needed even more urgently was better insurance for themselves. It wasn't a conversation these proud farmers tended to initiate, but health care posed the single biggest economic risk for most of the people who were at the barbecue.

Jess was lucky: As a retired Air National Guard member, he was eligible for federal Tricare. But when he'd lost a kneecap several years earlier, he hadn't had any coverage. The surgery he'd needed had cost 5,000 dollars, which had been a major hardship for the penny-pinching rancher. Even more worrisome for Jess had been the fact that his other knee had also been weakened by his injury, so he was pretty sure he'd need the same procedure again in a few years. But by that time, Jess had been covered by Tricare, which cost him just 233 dollars a year. The federal insurance policy had paid for every cent of Jess's second operation.

Most of the families at the Timeless gathering had solved the insurance problem with another form of subsidy—one partner, typically a woman, worked a job in town. They were in good company: In 2012, small farms (defined by the USDA as those grossing less than 350,000 dollars) relied on off-farm sources for a whopping 67 percent of their income. These weren't hobby farmers, but people who reported a positive farm income and considered agriculture their "major occupation." The USDA didn't ask farmers *why* they took off-farm jobs, but if they had, they would've gotten a talking to from people like Doug Crabtree.

"I'm a type 1 diabetic," Doug told me matter-of-factly, carefully avoiding the dessert table, "so not having health insurance is really not an option. At least one of us has to keep a job that has insurance because we're not a civilized nation where we provide that basic service to our population." Since she was a federal employee, Anna explained, her husband was covered on her plan. If she died tomorrow, Doug would still have health insurance for the rest of his life. And it was good insurance. On one of their Farmer Fly-In trips to DC, the Crabtrees had proposed allowing all participants in the Farm Bill's beginning farmer programs to buy into this same federal employee health plan. It would be a win-win, Doug and Anna figured: The farmers would have access to affordable care and the influx of young policyholders would lower the median age in the pool.

"I think that's an idea that actually could have some legs," Doug said, "but two years ago, we went to DC as they were debating the health thing, and—"

"Our good senator Baucus told us, we'll take care of it, it'll be fixed in two years," Anna finished. "Yeah, right."

"YOU JUST KIND OF SNEAK BY"

Health coverage had also been an unrelenting headache for Sharon Eisenberg, ever since the New York native moved to rural Montana to wed a renegade lentil grower. As a self-employed accountant married to a self-employed farmer, Sharon's only option was the private insurance market—which was more or less highway robbery. "It was astronomical; it was just crushing really," Sharon told me, "but we always had it, because I figured if we didn't, you're banking the farm against the medical system. Guess who's gonna win that one?" Health insurance premiums had eaten up 10 to 15 percent of her family's budget, Sharon estimated, and this was for a policy with a 5,000-dollar deductible. If they could barely afford private health insurance, they definitely couldn't afford to actually use it. So they'd done so just once—when Dave had to have an appendectomy. Apart from that operation and childbirth, they'd had virtually no interaction with their local hospital. "So that's your health insurance, being healthy?" I asked, half joking. "Yep," Dave said. "Exactly, that's exactly right."

Since she did people's taxes for a living, Sharon knew her family wasn't the only one in Conrad with inadequate health care access. At least half her clients had no insurance at all, Sharon estimated, and a lot of those were farmers. Although it was expensive, Sharon tried to talk her neighbors into getting some kind of coverage, because she knew they were continually exposed to occupational hazards, on top of the usual risk of medical problems. "They're just hoping nothing is going to go wrong," Sharon said. "Well, you dig around in most modern American families and you're gonna find some health issue of some kind."

"I don't know if we're lucky or if it's just because we've eaten extremely well for thirty years," Dave mused, grateful that his biggest health issue had been that appendectomy. Both Jon Tester and Jess Alger were missing digits, and Dave had noticed Doug Crabtree periodically checking his insulin levels during his farm tours at Vilicus. "It's probably some of both," Sharon concluded. "You just kind of sneak by."

But more likely, Sharon had learned, you don't sneak by. You get caught. "Everybody comes up short when you actually have some issue, like if you have a child with some illness or something," she told me. "If that had happened to us, I probably would've closed my office and gotten a job at a big employer in Great Falls. That's what you have to do—you need to be in a group where they can't turn you down. So I'd have been commuting to Great Falls with everybody else in Conrad. When I first moved here, nobody was doing that, and now it's extremely common—and it's a pretty good hike." But after spending two hours a day on I-15 for several years, many of Dave and Sharon's neighbors had run out of time, patience, or gas money. Eventually, they'd made that commute to Great Falls one last time—in a U-Haul.

Especially if you had a family member with a chronic illness, Sharon explained matter-of-factly, it became harder and harder to stay on the homestead. If your spouse or your kid got really sick, it would be virtually impossible to stick with a livelihood like organic agriculture—in which your *crops* weren't even insured. People around here might tell you it was bindweed that forced them to quit organics—or stop farming all together. But once you got to know them as well as their accountant did, you started uncovering other reasons.

One such reason I'd heard a lot about in these rural communities was breast cancer. When someone in Conrad or Havre or Fort Benton was diagnosed, it was common for neighbors to respond with their long-standing tradition of mutual aid. But cancer treatment was expensive, and no matter how generously rural families pooled their resources to help one another out, it was seldom enough to cover hospital bills. Sharon had just seen this happen with one of her uninsured friends, Dorothy (not her real name), who had recently been diagnosed with a malignant tumor and needed surgery. Dorothy and her husband had held an auction sale, but Sharon knew the proceeds would pale in comparison to Dorothy's medical expenses. From Sharon's point of view, the only real solution to this problem was a single-payer health care system: Medicare for all. She didn't think recently passed federal legislation—the Affordable Care Act—went far enough, but it might be a good start. If it ever got implemented. "We'll see what the Supreme Court does with this Obamacare," Sharon remarked. "But if they toss it, what are we supposed to do—have a bake sale for Dorothy? Okay, we can bake some brownies and raise a few bucks for Dorothy's medical bills."

"They better be marijuana brownies if she's got cancer," Dave cracked.

In truth, I learned, Dave and Sharon had discovered a reasonably praticable legal stopgap solution, at least for themselves and their staff: a state-administered small business health care program called Insure Montana. Since 2006, Timeless Seeds had been able to cover their employees—though not their growers—under this program. The company paid half the premium, the state kicked in a portion based on the policyholder's income and family size, and most of the Timeless staff got health insurance for less than 100 dollars a month.

Interestingly, it was the firsthand experience of another Timeless grower that had led to the development of Insure Montana. Back when he was in the Montana legislature, Jon Tester had sponsored a bill to establish the state-administered insurance program, aware that rural families were desperate for better access to medical care. Subsequently elected to the US Senate in 2006, Tester had gone on to help pass the Obamacare law that Sharon was now tracking with such curiosity. The issue was still a personal one, Jon told his constituents. If he lost his next election, he wasn't sure he'd be able to afford health care himself. He could probably find a less intense off-farm occupation, but in many ways the senator was doing the same thing his neighbors were: working a second job for the insurance.

Of course, Jon Tester wasn't in DC just to pick up his federal benefits. He and the lentil underground had an ambitious legislative agenda to tackle. They'd made some progress on issues like health care, crop insurance, and conservation programs, but they were about to face their toughest battle yet. If they lost this one, it could put them out of business for good.

SEEDS OF TROUBLE

When he heard, in 2002, that Montana was already hosting three to four dozen test plots of genetically engineered wheat, Jim Barngrover was troubled. He figured the crop would hit the market within the next two years, and then the genie would definitely be out of the bottle. Personally, Jim's biggest reservations about GMOs, or genetically modified organisms, concerned their potential impacts on human health and the environment. But as a seasoned activist, he knew the most convincing argument for a precautionary approach to the new technology was economic.

Montana farmers sold about 60 percent of their hard red spring wheat to countries that did not accept genetically modified grain, Jim explained in a 2003 AERO *Sun Times* article. If the state's wheat supply became contaminated, growers could lose up to 900 million dollars a year. Lambasting the legislature's failure to curb or at least regulate GMOs, the Timeless partner found himself in the ironic position of defending the integrity of conventional wheat—against the genetic drift of an even less desirable plant.

Despite the state government's track record of inaction, Jim promised, AERO, the Northern Plains Resource Council, and the Montana Farmers Union would force the GMO issue with a more aggressive suite of bills in 2003. The legislation they sought to pass would not only mandate stringent state regulation of genetically engineered crops but would also require labeling of GMO products, establish manufacturer liability, and require seed companies to ask farmers' permission before sampling their crops and filing a patent infringement lawsuit.

The GMO fight was clearly an uphill battle against deep-pocketed interests, so the Timeless farmers had to dramatically extend their political network. Intent on building a strong enough coalition to fight back against genetically engineered wheat, Jim found himself collaborating with a number of unlikely allies. The lefty activist met with libertarian populists, consumer groups, lobbyists from the famously conservative Farm Bureau and Montana Grain Growers—anyone who thought a foray into genetically engineered crops merited at least a bit of caution. It wasn't enough to push a bill through in 2003, but momentum was building.

In 2005, AERO launched the Grow Montana coalition, convening a diverse group of aligned organizations to consolidate their influence in Helena. As the 2009 legislature approached, it appeared the alliance had a decent shot of passing the most popular piece of its legislative package: the Farmer Protection Bill. As sponsor Betsy Hands explained, the Farmer Protection Bill would establish a standard crop-sampling protocol for patent holders to follow when investigating farmers, something GMO seed companies had been doing with increasing frequency. If a grower acquired patented plant material unknowingly—by planting contaminated seed or via pollen drift—they couldn't be held liable for patent infringement. After several years of failed attempts, it looked like the farmer protection measure finally had the necessary votes to pass. The bill sailed through the Montana House of Representatives on a 57–43 vote, and Jim Barngrover started thinking ahead, imagining how he might leverage this majority to pass some of his more far-reaching GMO-related proposals.

And then, before it could reach the floor of the state senate, the Farmer Protection Bill was tabled in committee. Two days later, an investigative reporter from the Associated Press offered an explanation. Monsanto had hosted a dinner for members of the Senate Agriculture, Livestock, and Irrigation Committee at a private club in Helena. Somewhere between the steak and the dessert, the legislators had changed their minds about patent infringement.

"Eventually we did get a GMO bill that was very significant," Jim Barngrover told me. The political veteran finished his story on an upbeat if not fully resolved note. Following the embarrassing steak dinner scandal, the state department of agriculture had aggressively championed farmer protection and had helped pass a revised version of the bill in 2011. "It still isn't where I want to be, by any means, but it protects farmers," Jim told me.

"And I should also mention," he added, "when Tester was president of the state senate, he got a resolution through the senate and the house and signed by the governor. That resolution stated that there would be essentially no commercialization of GE wheat in Montana until or unless our major markets, principally in Asia, accept GE wheat. I was in the office with him when he and [Kamut farmer/entrepreneur] Bob Quinn authored that resolution together."

WE ARE A PART OF OUR ENVIRONMENT

Offering his own take on the genetic engineering issue between bites of farmer Linda Lassila's famous lentil cake, Casey Bailey appeared ready to take up where the previous Timeless generation had left off. He'd been following a California proposition to label GMOs, which he strongly supported. "When companies have to make society more ignorant to succeed, that really irritates me," Casey said, explaining his position. "And, really, we don't know if these genetically altered plants are changing—I mean, we are a part of our environment. It's foolish to think that we can play around like this without feeling the consequences."

Casey's holistic ecological perspective had him fired up about another policy issue as well, which steered the barbecue conversation back to the shortcomings of federal conservation programs. Casey was annoyed by the preservationist view that all human impacts were bad, and he shared Doug and Anna's opinion that federal cost share should reward good stewardship instead of essentially telling farmers to give up. The no-till trend was one thing, but the real agrarian cop-out, from Casey's perspective, was the way some people took advantage of the Conservation Reserve Program. One of the most popular government programs in this area since its inception in 1985, the CRP was paying farmers—handsomely—to do nothing.

Like the NRCS, the Conservation Reserve Program had been formed in response to concerns about erosion. Originally launched as a minor part of the USDA Soil Bank Program in the 1950s, CRP got going in earnest when the heartland started hemorrhaging topsoil thirty years later, following a decade of "fencerow to fencerow" farming. While Dave Oien offered his desperate neighbors legumes, the 1985 Farm Bill had tempted them with something far more attractive: cash money. Concerned that too much land was being farmed, the federal government had revamped CRP, offering to lease "highly erodible" parcels to keep them out of production. All farmers had to do was establish permanent vegetative cover, and they would get a check every year. The program had been rightly celebrated as a triumphant case of voluntary resource conservation—it had significantly reduced erosion. But it had also become a victim of its own success, at the expense of rural communities.

Whether or not they were conservation minded, drought-weary growers had flocked to the CRP's guaranteed income, and the acreage enrolled in the program had ballooned. Within a few years, a far greater share of rural America (and nearly all of the state of Montana) had been classified as "highly erodible," and Congress had added several new means of qualifying for conservation reserve status as well. Wetlands, saline seep, and wildlife habitat were all grounds for a conservation lease, and the 1996 Farm Bill even allowed farmers to enroll sensitive ground that had been cropped for two of the previous five years—a pretty low bar in a region where many growers fallowed every other season.

Congress had bumped the "heavy cropping" requirement up to four years out of six in 2002—since people had been buying land and farming it for two years just to qualify for CRP. But by then, the basic character of the program had been established. With the federal government paying higher rent than the going rate for cropping, conservation had become the highest and best use of agricultural property. It didn't matter if the land was highly erodible or not. The economical thing to do was to put it in CRP.

You couldn't blame CRP for the fact that it had to operate

within the increasingly absurd context of the American food system, but clearly, the program was suffering from some unintended consequences. In the absence of a thoughtfully legislated social safety net, inventive American farmers had repurposed the federal conservation initiative into rural America's de facto retirement program. Anna Jones-Crabtree didn't begrudge her neighbors for hanging up their farm hats in their golden years, but it bugged her that so many CRP checks were being spent outside the rural economies that had sustained those farmers for most of their lives. "It's ridiculous," Anna Jones-Crabtree exclaimed. "You should not have a program that pays people to take their entire farms out and take the money to Arizona."

Although the CRP might have good intentions of combating soil erosion, Anna felt, the program was partially responsible for another form of erosion, painfully evident across the grain belt: the attrition of farmers and farming knowledge. A lot of young people didn't know how to farm anymore, Anna explained, because their parents had left the family tractor idle in the shed while they sat on fifteen-year CRP leases. The standards for "vegetative cover" in the early years of the CRP program had been fairly minimal, so it was entirely possible that some of this farmland would actually have been better off under the management of diversified organic farmers like the Crabtrees. "You can't tell me that CRP that has almost no diversity in its grass mixture is really providing any more wildlife habitat or care than our farm," she argued. "I don't know for certain, but I'd like to see some studies on that."

"WE CAN'T COMPETE WITH THE
FEDERAL GOVERNMENT"

Five-year-old Kale O'Halloran cut this discussion short, bouncing into Anna a step ahead of older brothers Lucas and Quin, who were tracking the green beacon of Kale's John Deere cap in hot pursuit. Parents Brandon and Mariah followed, walking. The thirty-three-year-old music teacher and thirty-two-year-old home-steader mom were too hot to chase after their sons, but they were glad to see the boys burning off some steam. The family had spent much of the summer meticulously weeding the emmer they were growing for Timeless, whose founding farmers were longtime ac-quaintances of Mariah's dad, Scott Lohmuller.

Although Kale didn't know it, the boisterous five-year-old had landed his parents in an all-too-familiar conversation. The Conservation Reserve Program was a sore subject for the O'Hallorans—the main reason the family had been living in what amounted to farm limbo. Brandon's family owned 3,000 acres in the Shields Valley, south of Bozeman, where both Bran-don and Mariah had grown up. Brandon's folks had separated, and none of his siblings or cousins wanted to take over the farm, so the family had taken the land out of production and put it in CRP. Brandon and Mariah were itching to farm and had offered to step in. But Brandon's relatives balked. They were making more money off the CRP lease than Brandon and Mariah could afford to pay as organic producers, and they were not particu-larly eager to take a pay cut.

So instead, Brandon and Mariah were doing their best to im-provise a farm system on the 160 acres they *did* have access to: the spurge-challenged parcel attached to the place where Mariah's parents had retired, on the outskirts of Lewistown. The weedy suburban farm was both too much and too little for the young family: too much work and too little income. To make ends meet, Brandon directed choir for the Lewistown Public Schools, which meant it was often dark by the time he made it out to check his crop. The O'Hallorans' agricultural methods might have been sustainable, but their lives were not.

Frustrated with the challenges of part-time farming, Brandon and Mariah had started talking to other growers in the Timeless network about the need to overhaul the Conservation Reserve Program. Without a policy change, the O'Hallorans worried, they'd never have a farm of their own. "We can't compete with the federal government," Mariah told me. "What—thirty bucks an acre? There's no way; we just can't do it."

"Do you have a commercial driver's license?" Casey Bailey asked Brandon, changing the subject. Having discovered that the friendly band director had grown up on an operation much like his own, Casey had started scheming up a plan. He chuckled to himself, recalling the day he and his college buddy had perplexed a nearby rancher with their harvesttime bebop. A trio would really keep his neighbors guessing.

"Oh, sure," Brandon answered nonchalantly. "We did a bunch of custom haying when I was a kid, and I would haul the swather." In fact, the O'Hallorans' swather—the machine that leveled their neighbors' fields of alfalfa into neat rows of hay—was just the first of many things Brandon had hauled around. He'd driven talc for mining companies in college, and for a couple of years he'd made some extra cash building roads.

Casey was sold. "Can you come back up here for harvest in

about ten days?" he asked. Brandon brightened. Helping with the Baileys' crop would keep him from dwelling on that CRP lease on his family's land. Plus, Casey's fields really were looking good this year. Whether it was the scrupulous youngster's diligent weeding or a streak of meteorological luck, it appeared that all those diverse plants were going to generate an impressive bounty.

Still, as the mercury climbed, it became clear that central Montana was in the throes of a particularly punishing drought. In the company of his fellow Timeless growers, Casey felt good about the bet he'd placed, on the long-term ecological wisdom of organic rotations, rather than the short-term protection offered by the conventional farm industry and its system of subsidies. But as he said good-bye to his guests, Casey began to wonder about this wager. Would his lentils make it?

V

HARVEST

15
THE MOMENT OF TRUTH

On a scorching afternoon in late July, I returned to the Bailey place, hoping to lend a hand. Casey and the crew were in full swing, scrambling to cut all their crops before Mother Nature beat them to it.

As soon as I turned off on Clearlake Road, I saw Casey in his combine. "Everything's coming on at once," his girlfriend, Kelsey, told me, pressing a glass of water into my hand. "Peas, lentils, hay." Casey and his college friend Bob were cutting peas at the moment, Kelsey explained, and then they'd need to clean out the combine before they could get to the lentils. "We go until two A.M. sometimes at Casey's," Bob admitted, as I rode along for a few passes of the pea harvest. I noticed he'd stashed a sandwich and some chocolate in the cab.

The crew worked until eleven that night, and they were back at it right away the next morning, even though it was a Sunday. While his buddy gathered the last of the peas, Casey tried to decide what to harvest next. He was tempted to try the spelt (the ancient grain he rotated with lentils), but the stand hadn't matured evenly. Some of the seed heads looked perfect, probably just a day or two shy of falling off the stalk. And yet, other plants looked as if they could use another week to soak up the plentiful sunshine.

Not sure what to do, the fledgling organic farmer asked his dad. Bob Bailey had never even heard of spelt until his son started growing it, but he'd had to make this kind of call every summer of his life—and Casey trusted his judgment.

"Looking out here, it looks ripe," Bob said to his son.

"Will the combine cut it?" Casey asked. He was worried because there was still a lot of "green" in the crop—it didn't seem to be quite dried down.

"Well, you're here now," Bob said, "and it might hail tomorrow night. How tough is the straw? How dry was it last year?"

"Well, last year we swathed it, so it's hard to judge," Casey answered. Swathing—the method typically used to cut hay—was a good option for growers who were nervous about too much moisture in their grain. Swathers cut plants off at the stems, leaving a neat windrow to dry in the sun until the combine gathered it up. But this two-step process required an extra pass through the field, which was both expensive and time-consuming. And if it rained, you were screwed.

"Shoot, I think I'd cut it if it was mine," Bob said, careful to phrase his advice in a way that emphasized Casey's role as the decision maker.

"Why don't you jump on the combine with me," Casey suggested. "Let's cut a little bit and see how we feel."

Kelsey watched the father-son team take off slowly down the row, Casey's brow furrowed in concentration. "He definitely gets stressed-out during harvest," she sighed. As the duo made their way back toward us a few minutes later, however, the younger Bailey's expression had completely transformed. The spelt was ready all right, and it was a bumper crop. "This stuff is crazy," Casey gushed. "That's a full load just down and back."

Kelsey and I hustled to clean out a bin for the prolific ancient grain, which was evidently going to get harvested right now. The hesitation of a moment ago had been replaced with an exuberant sense of urgency. "We should be able to finish all the spelt today if we run both combines," Casey calculated, already revving up for another pass.

As Casey's dad had reminded him, the forecast was calling for showers sometime in the next twenty-four hours—maybe even hail. A perfectly ripe crop was an attractive target for north-central Montana's great white combine, so the Baileys were anxious to get that abundant spelt safely stashed. The crew took a quick meal break just before five, anticipating a long evening. When I went to bed at ten thirty, they were still cutting, their headlights illuminating the field.

I barely glimpsed Casey on his way out the door the next morning, a piece of Kamut bread in his hand as he raced back out to the combine. Last evening's rainstorm had passed him by, but he knew today could be an entirely different story. "We finished the field of spelt and it filled the bin exactly," he told me, not pausing to rest on his laurels. "Today we'll go look at another field to see if that's ready." I had a ranch tour to attend, so I bid farewell to the Bailey harvest crew for the next couple of days, wishing them clear skies.

By the time I got back to Fort Benton, forty-eight hours later, Casey had a whole new set of issues on his mind. "We were half-way done with the lentils and the combine broke down," he said dejectedly. "Those French Greens look so good." Once again, Casey found himself at the mercy of Mother Nature. Until he could get his precious seeds squirreled away, they were subject to the vicissitudes of Chouteau County's unpredictable climate.

"My emotions just go like this during harvest," Casey sighed, making dramatic up-and-down motions with his calloused hands. "I'm happy, but I'd be happier if I was cutting lentils." And yet, he had a million things to do in the meantime, Casey reminded himself. Rather than lose precious moments to worry, he jogged off to start haying, making a mental note to check in with Brandon O'Halloran. Following up on the conversation he'd had with Casey at his farm tour, the fellow Timeless grower had made good on his promise to lend a hand with the Baileys' harvest, and he was now busy helping Casey's dad bring in the family's conventional grain.

But before he could make it out of the driveway, Casey spied a familiar compact hybrid coming toward him, with its telltale TIMELSS plates. It was Dave Oien, of course (who else would arrive at the precise moment when things were in their most chaotic state of disarray), but he wasn't alone. A broad-shouldered man in a collared white shirt stepped out of the vehicle that had been tailing Dave, and vigorously shook Casey's hand. By now, Casey knew how to recognize a prospective Timeless buyer on a field trip, and he pivoted deftly into tour-guide mode. The broad-shouldered man wanted to know how many bushels of peas the Bailey Farm was going to bring in this year, and he liked to get his information firsthand. His Connecticut-based company was interested in brokering the deal Dave had told Doug and Anna about in June—shipping Montana-grown peas to China for nutritional supplements.

"Did you get your combine fixed?" Dave asked his protégé, while the pea dealer checked out Casey's samples. The veteran farmer was as nervous as his greenhorn grower about the delay of the lentil harvest. Timeless Seeds had one other French Green producer this year, but the drought was so bad at his place that the crop was likely to fail. If the Baileys got hailed out, Dave would have to spend the next twelve months explaining to broad-shouldered, white-collared businessmen why he couldn't supply the popular variety. "They're flying in the part tomorrow morning," Casey reported reassuringly. "We'll be back at it before lunch."

Casey Bailey would break down three times in his lentils, but he escaped the threat of hail and ended up with a bin-busting crop. I first heard the news from Dave, when I went by the Timeless plant in late October to get a rundown on the 2012 season. By the time I arrived, central Montana was cloaked in a billowy layer of snow. but since this year's harvest was complete, that was okay. With the fruits of their labor stashed safely in their elevators, Timeless Seeds' farmers could finally take a deep breath. The CEO's peak season, however, was just getting started.

When I rolled into Ulm at eleven o'clock on that crisp fall morning, the Timeless parking lot was full. Operations manager Leni Yeager greeted me at the door, pausing midstride to give me a hug in the lobby before racing back to the hard-hat zone. Peering after her, I caught a glimpse of Loren Nicholls, who was busy cleaning what appeared to be emmer. A few paces beyond him, Jason Roberts was packaging product to ship out on the FedEx truck. Even the gentle former Peace Corps volunteer who used the Timeless facilities on a work-trade basis had gotten caught up in the hectic pace. The fair trade rice importer, Mary Hensley, was whirring away on her computer.

Amid all the commotion, Dave had somehow found the time to talk to a University of Montana environmental studies major, who was conducting an interview for a class project. "We started in 1986, just four farmers," I could hear him cheerfully narrating for the millionth time. When the student researcher began asking about net and gross and pounds of product, I piggybacked on the conversation, anxious to hear about this year's yields. I'd spent the past couple of months back on my own campus—in Berkeley, California—and I'd been hearing dire news about crop loss in the grain belt. Eighty percent of US agricultural land had experienced drought in 2012, the most extensive dry spell since the 1950s. According to some projections, the future of American farming was in doubt. "How was the crop?" I asked Dave, preparing for the worst.

"Jon Tester brought us some beautiful purple barley," the Timeless CEO raved, surprising me, "and Jody's lentils were really nice."

"So the Manuels' plants had successfully developed nitrogen-fixing nodules after all?" I asked, relieved to be starting the conversation on a happy note.

"Yep, Jody's lentils kicked in," Dave answered. "Nine hundred pounds per acre, which is more than four times what he got the year before. Unfortunately, the driver he hired for harvest turned his farm truck over. Jody called me—it wasn't the middle of the night, exactly, but it was pretty late. I picked up the phone and Jody said, 'What should I do? My hired man tipped the truck over.'" Not only had the hired man spilled four hundred bushels of lentils, Jody divulged, but he'd been hauling them across pasture, so the Manuels' cattle were presently chowing down on this unexpected midnight snack.

Dave had counseled Jody through the process of shooing away the cows and salvaging about half of the Black Belugas. Now Crystal was joking with all her Timeless buddies about how much the cows had enjoyed their "lentil cereal." Once they'd developed a taste for those gourmet Black Belugas, Crystal quipped, they'd become "lentil junkies." In fact, the Manuels' herd had been so desperate for another lentil fix that they'd broken into the pigpen. Jody and Crystal had been feeding their pigs lentil "screenings"— rejects from the cleaning process at the Timeless plant—so that the hogs would be accustomed to a legume diet by the time the Manuels turned them out in the cover crop cocktail. The cows had sniffed out their new favorite food, tromped right through the pigs' fence, and feasted.

"Maybe you had the right idea from the beginning, huh?" I teased Dave, as we cracked up over Crystal's legume-crazed cattle. Central Montana's original Black Beluga farmer had of course fed the same lentil chow to his own cows—on purpose—back when he was the only one in the area experimenting with Canadian plant breeder Al Slinkard's "Indianhead" variety. "Yep," Dave said. "But that's an expensive cattle ration these days." As Dave's voice got more solemn, I braced myself again. Perhaps now I'd get the story of the drought, I thought, trying to formulate a polite question about how much money Timeless had lost this year. But Dave was already on to another upbeat story.

"Jody had a great success with the foundation emmer seed," Dave reported, hopeful that diversifying into the seed market would help Timeless and other similar businesses reduce their dependence on large companies. "Brandon and Mariah had six really nice acres also. Loren just got that cleaned. So now we need to build markets, because we've got this pedigreed seed that would be a shame to feed to somebody, even if it was the French Laundry or whatever. It's like, this is too good for you guys even; this needs to go back in the ground."

Since Dave seemed so determined to focus on good news, I decided to take a more direct approach. If I was going to get a straight answer about Timeless Seeds' losses, I realized, I'd have to ask the question point-blank. After thirty years of hard work, this historic drought year had presented the lentil underground with a moment of truth. They'd started their journey in the eighties, when similarly devastating droughts had killed off their crops. They'd tried to change their farming system—and to some extent, the whole food system—to make it more resilient. But were they really any better off now? I readied myself for an uncomfortable pause, bad news, even the possibility that my study might be done for. But nothing could have prepared me for Dave's response.

"The drought wasn't so bad for us really," Dave informed me nonchalantly, delivering the stunning news as though it was an afterthought. "Our yields were actually surprisingly good, given the weather we had through the summer." Although growing season precipitation had dipped 40 percent compared to last year, Dave estimated, Timeless Seeds' farmers had still realized 80 percent of their normal yields, thanks to their carefully chosen crops and all that stored soil moisture.

"So overall, you're down about twenty percent of your typical yield?" I calculated, trying to get the figures straight. Nope, Dave said. The high quality of the Timeless farmers' harvest had made up for the slightly lower volume, so the net effect was a normal inventory. I wanted to be sure I had that right. Historic drought year. Zero losses. How was that possible?

Dave seemed a little puzzled by my question, as though I wasn't asking quite the right one. As I tried to follow his train of thought, it slowly dawned on me that he'd become such a perennial thinker that he couldn't even conceive of farms in annual terms any more. As he kept talking, I began to question my own understanding of this exceptional season. These weren't really this year's lentils, I reflected, watching several tons of legumes pass by en route to the color sorter. Although the seeds had gone into the ground this spring, the water and nitrogen and bacteria and organic matter that had helped them grow had a much deeper history. In a sense, Timeless Seeds had had three decades to prepare for this summer. No wonder it didn't seem like such a big deal.

"Yeah, we got plenty of lentils," Dave sighed. "That's why I'm stuck here cleaning them." Dave was jealous because I was on my way to the annual AERO meeting, once a treasured ritual for the Timeless CEO. Back when Dave was strictly a farmer, he could count on getting a break by the last weekend in October, when AERO always scheduled its conference. But now that he was responsible for processing and distributing his friends' crops, Dave couldn't take a day off until December. He'd see me then, Dave promised, at the Montana Organic Association conference in Helena. I felt a little sad as I drove off in the snow. The season was over. But as Dave reminded me, another season was just beginning.

16
THE NEXT GENERATION

Dave Oien didn't cut his own crop in 2012. For the sixty-three-year-old CEO, running Timeless Seeds was more than a full-time job. So he was leasing his land to Jerry Habets, the formerly skeptical neighbor who had become one of his most enthusiastic growers. And for the past four seasons, Dave and Sharon had also been incubating an innovative small farm operation on the fifteen acres next to their house. From Dave's perspective, this fledgling family farm was probably the most successful "harvest" he'd ever grown.

When a graduate student at the University of Montana offered to do a sustainability analysis for the new processing plant Timeless had opened in 2006, David Oien probably saw a little bit of himself in earnest Jacob Cowgill. A central Montana native whose journey through environmental studies had led him back to his rural roots, Jacob was excited to graduate and start farming—and since his girlfriend, Courtney, had grown up on a farm just south of Conrad (long since sold, unfortunately), that seemed like the place to look for land. Having watched so many neighbors move away,

Dave was thrilled to meet a young couple who were actually thinking about moving in. He encouraged Jacob to accept a nearby apprenticeship, and when the young man successfully completed two seasons with his desire to farm still intact Dave and Sharon offered the recently married Cowgills an inexpensive lease on the field in front of their house.

For Jacob and Courtney, the offer to start farming at Dave's place had seemed almost too good to be true. Dave's well-amended soil was the ideal foundation for launching the diversified vegetable farm they had in mind, and the heritage turkeys they wanted to raise could go in his greenhouse. Timeless Seeds would buy the Cowgills' lentils and heirloom grain, and most of the implements Jacob and Courtney needed were available in Dave's equipment yard. Since Dave's place was already under organic certification, they could get started right away, without the usual three-year transition period. Loading all their worldly possessions into two flatbed trailers, three pickups, and two cars, the Cowgills moved out to Conrad in March of 2009.

While visiting Dave and Sharon over the course of the summer, I'd had the chance to watch Jacob and Courtney's young farm and family blossom, as they chased toddler Willa through rows of chard and squash and carrots. Four seasons in, Prairie Heritage Farm was supplying fresh produce to eighty-seven local families through their community supported agriculture program—a pay-in-advance arrangement that was essentially a weekly farm subscription. In the winter, the Cowgills offered a grain CSA as well, one of the first such businesses in the region. And they were famous for their heritage turkeys, which had become Thanksgiving favorites across western Montana.

Dave monitored the Cowgills' development with the pride of a father, bringing surprise treats out to the field on long harvest days and teaching Jacob how to fix his tractor. So it was bitter-sweet when Jacob and Courtney came to him and told him he'd succeeded in helping them achieve their dream. After four years at Dave and Sharon's farm, they'd sufficiently developed their field operation, their customer base, and a small nest egg. They were ready to buy a farm of their own.

In September 2012, Jacob and Courtney moved from Dave and Sharon's land onto their new place in Power, Montana. The thirty-acre homestead was forty miles closer to their main customer base in Great Falls and Helena, and the new property came outfitted with a butcher shop. Dave helped the Cowgills clean out the turkey coop they'd erected in his former greenhouse, and lent them his horse trailer to move the birds down to Power. If they needed extra acreage, Dave told the Cowgills, they could always keep farming some grain at his place. It was going to be awfully quiet around here.

"IT'S ALMOST LIKE A WILDERNESS"

Before the first snows of 2012 blanketed north-central Montana, Jerry Habets prepared the Oien farm for winter. He was experimenting with a new cover crop called sorghum Sudan grass, known for its deep-penetrating roots. While they were alive, these roots exuded a compound called sorgoleone, known to suppress several species of annual weeds. And when the Sudan grass died, the gargantuan mass of decaying roots made a substantial meal for underground microorganisms. Postharvest feasts weren't just for people, Jerry explained. You needed to feed the soil too.

Down the road in Valier, Tuna McAlpine was also tending a cover crop of sorts. Tuna hadn't grown any lentils to sell to Timeless this year, but he was planning to plant some as ground cover and just see what happened. "If the lentils don't make it," he told me, "they're still a good plowdown. Wheat, you can't do that." Tuna's youngest son, Lane, had expressed interest in taking over the farm someday, and the fifty-four-year-old rancher wanted to leave the land in good shape for the next generation of McAlpines. So he'd been seeding more legumes, and each autumn, he'd been leaving more of his plants in the earth.

Back when he was a kid, Tuna told me, people farmed in circles. Starting with the perimeter of their field, they spiraled inward until they got to the middle. Tuna drew a picture on my notepad to illustrate the method. "You see," he said, pointing to the corners of the paper, "it leaves them skips, because you can't turn in a square." When farmers reached the center of their inward spirals, Tuna explained, they went back to pick up these triangular "skips" left at the corners of the field.

In the eighties, Tuna continued, people decided that it was more efficient to make a few outer rounds and then just go back and forth all the way across the field, so they didn't have any corner skips to deal with at the end of the process. At first, Tuna had followed in line. He was happy enough going back and forth, and in fact, he might never have considered the circular method again, had it not been for a seemingly unrelated development: the advent of "net wrapping" for hay bales. This new technology allowed farmers to speed up the time it took to tie a bale of hay—but net wrap was also three times as expensive as the twine it replaced. Tuna hated the thought of spending money for something he didn't really need, so he considered whether there might be another way he could make up a little time while haying. And then it hit him: circles. When he used the back-and-forth system, Tuna's baler was idle for a moment every time he made a turn. But when he went in circles, there was no need to pause—he just kept right on making hay until he got to the center of the field.

"So I went back to round and around," Tuna said, "but that leaves them skips. It's not really that much you're leaving out there, but in a bug's eye or a bird's eye it can make the difference between total removal of all the habitat and leaving some. Where do insects go, ladybugs, little birds? A pheasant could weather a storm in there. It's a way of farming things but still leaving something."

But Tuna wasn't just leaving something. He was also putting something back. In May, he'd invited me out to visit the ranch, to see the restoration projects he'd been working on for the past two decades. I was disappointed to arrive just as the weather turned to blowing rain, but Tuna was unfazed. "I've already saddled up the Japanese quarter horses," he said enthusiastically, pointing to a pair of four-wheelers parked just outside his door. "You ready?" Tearing up and down hills he'd known all his life, Tuna proceeded to lead me through a harrowing three-hour obstacle course. Plunging straight into the creek that snaked through the middle of his property, he yelled back through the whipping wind for me to follow. Just in time, he pointed out the electric fence strung above the water, which was fast approaching at eye level. "Duck," Tuna yelled back at me. "It's hot."

The creek, Tuna explained as I caught my breath, was one of his projects. He'd noticed it getting narrower and deeper as he managed his grazing to allow for regrowth of riparian vegetation. Although Tuna had made some immediate, obvious changes on his ranch—12,000 new trees, five new wetlands—it was gradual recovery processes like the shifts in this creek bed that he found most fascinating. In several places where he once grew crops, Tuna told me, he had decided that wasn't the most appropriate use of the land, so he'd turned it back to pasture—which was now looking so healthy it could have passed for native range. Another spot he'd formerly farmed had been flooded out year after year, and Tuna had eventually realized the water was coming from the ground. He'd remade the natural spring, which had pleased both his cattle and the deer. Restoration farming raised food too, Tuna pointed out. "Both of my sons shot their first deer in this coulee," Tuna told me proudly, "so we have some deer to eat that way. You get to feeling like you're part of the place. It's a symbiotic relationship."

Tuna was just a stone's throw away from Glacier, the spectacular national park that had always existed in some degree of tension with the agricultural communities to its east. Other ranchers in this neighborhood complained about the wildlife that came across the park boundary and ate their crops. They were particularly upset about federal protection of gray wolves, which occasionally made off with one of their cows. But Tuna saw things differently. "If you drop down in the bottoms," he reflected, showing me his favorite part of the ranch, "it's almost like a wilderness. I think everything could be more wild, like these wetlands. I think farms could add more wilderness. This production system isn't just about taking everything for your own benefit."

When we came out of the bottoms, Tuna and I spotted something running on the hill across the coulee. I knew it wasn't one of his cows—it was running too fast. It occurred to me that it might be a deer or a pronghorn antelope, but it looked too big.

"I think that's a griz," Tuna declared, squinting. "Yep, two of them." I did a double take. Grizzly bears were a relatively uncommon sight even in the park, and downright rare as far east as Valier. Of all the incredible things I'd seen at Tuna's ranch, this seemed like the best piece of evidence that his restoration projects were working. Tuna's agricultural practices were clearly providing what my professors called "ecosystem services"—known simply to these bears as food and a place to hang out. Instead of policing a strict partition between civilization and wilderness—what academics called "land sparing"—Tuna was implementing the cutting-edge ecological strategy of "land sharing." The hard-nosed rancher seemed to have known all his life what conservation scientists were just beginning to appreciate: The fundamental ecological processes that supported farms were the same ones that supported national parks. So if farmers managed for these basic environmental goods—nutrient cycling, natural pest control, carbon sequestration—they could grow food and steward the land at the same time. Nature and agriculture weren't competitors. They were, as Tuna had said, symbiotic.

I reached for my camera to document the remarkable grizzly sighting. And then I hesitated. What would Tuna think? Grizzly bear reintroduction was a hot-button issue in rural Montana, and a lot of ranchers felt that federal wildlife protections had over-reached. After a summer of tagging along with Timeless Seeds' growers, I had a feel for the razor-thin margins of this way of life, and I couldn't blame Tuna if he was concerned about whether the bears might harm his cattle. He had his kids' college education to worry about. Having come to respect the rancher's dedication to responsibly stewarding his land, I didn't want to come off as a know-it-all environmentalist from Missoula. Who was I to say that a bear sighting was something to celebrate?

It seemed like an eternity to me, but I managed to hold my tongue until Tuna spoke. "That's awesome," he said, as the bears bounded over the hill. "We haven't seen them on the place in three years. Did you get a photo? I can't wait to show Anne and the kids."

17

LOOKING BACK, LOOKING FORWARD

When I walked into the Montana Organic Association meeting on the final day of November 2012, the first person I saw was Casey Bailey. Laughing over drinks with a couple of his buddies, he looked nothing like the self-described gerbil I'd seen rushing around at harvest. "It's been good to get some rest," Casey admitted. Everybody I ran into at the Helena conference was more relaxed than usual: Jerry Habets, Jody Manuel, even Anna Jones-Crabtree.

Jerry was particularly chipper, keen to update me on his intercrop. Miraculously, the buckwheat, Black Kabuli chickpeas, and Petite Crimson lentils he'd planted together had ripened at the same time, so he'd harvested the whole lot at once. Big Sky Seeds—less than half an hour north in Shelby—had been able to separate them out, and they'd bought all Jerry's buckwheat. Before leaving for the conference, Jerry had delivered the last of his lentils and chickpeas to the Timeless plant in Ulm, where he'd been heartily congratulated on his successful experiment. Determined to repeat it, Jerry was already talking about next season.

I also got good news from Jim Barngrover, who'd enjoyed a successful harvest too. I had to follow up with Jim by e-mail to get the full tally of what all he'd raised, between his two community garden plots and his small backyard: "Onions, peppers, peas, potatoes, carrots, cabbage, garlic, shallots, spinach, kale, squash, beans, broccoli, corn, tomatoes, strawberries, raspberries, and various herbs. Then there are the couple of gallons of sauerkraut in the crock in the basement. I also have numerous freezer bags of pesto." Jim was proud to report that he'd helped Helena Community Gardens donate one and a half tons of produce to the local food bank. And he had bagged a deer on his annual hunt at Bud Barta's place.

Bud hadn't made it to Helena for the organic association gathering. A decade earlier, he'd decided his day job building green homes was enough work for one person and had started looking for a like-minded tenant. For the past five seasons, he'd leased his land to Ole Norgaard, the farmer who was milling heirloom corn at the Timeless plant. In addition to this corn, Ole was also growing a panopoly of other organic crops on the 650 acres he rented from the Bartas: wheat, barley, peas, sainfoin seed, triticale, alfalfa, grass hay. "It's good to have Ole out there," Bud said. "We think kinda the same about farming, and also about business." Although Bud wasn't at MOA, Ole was, and he was beaming. He had just managed to get his Montana Morado Maize corn bread and pancake mixes stocked at the natural foods market in Great Falls, and he had a promising lead at another store in Missoula.

BORN ORGANIC

Amid the jovial scene at the Montana Organic Association meeting, Dave Oien was the one person who seemed nervous. Both his mauve-colored Timeless ball cap and flannel shirt were spotlessly clean, and the typically chatty CEO was uncharacteristically silent. Dave sat quietly through dinner, keeping one eye glued to MOA president Daryl Lassila. When Daryl announced that it was time to present the organization's Lifetime of Service Award for the year, the Timeless CEO rose from his seat. "And to introduce our winner," Daryl told the 140-person crowd, "I'll turn the microphone over to David Oien."

"This award recognizes an individual who has made outstanding contributions to Montana's organic community over the course of their life," Dave read. "But," he interjected, "this year we are giving it to two people, because it's hard to separate their contributions from their partnership."

These two had been the first to pitch in for everything, Dave told the crowd. Founding members of two co-ops, and among the first applicants for Montana's organic certification program, one or the other of them had truly "been there when." When the AERO Ag Task Force began meeting. When Dave needed farmers to plant medic. When the lentil pool was formed *and* when the Trader Joe's deal went bust. The pair had helped Jerry buy the Habets homestead, and they'd made sure Tuna didn't lose the McAlpines'. They'd helped Danish immigrant Ole Norgaard get a green card and provided financing for another business Timeless had incubated, Big Sky Organic Feed. "This year's Lifetime of Service awardees have been critical to the existence of Timeless Seeds," Dave acknowledged, "and to sustainable agriculture in Montana. Please give a big round of applause to Russell Salisbury and Elsie Tuss."

The roomful of organics advocates—many of whom hadn't even been alive when Russ Salisbury planted his first certified crop—leapt to their feet. When Dave finally managed to quiet the crowd, he passed the microphone to Russ.

"Dave didn't reach back to what I'm most proud of," Russ said, as his friend handed him a framed certificate. "He probably wasn't born then."

"When I was conceived—" The audience laughed, interrupting Russ's story after just four words. They didn't know he was going to reach back *that* far. The zany farmer's conception seemed a rather intimate topic for such a public setting. "You know, we have these little competitions about who's been organic the longest," Russ continued. "But I started out producing organic fertilizer that first day."

"Now, was that *green* manure, Russ?" someone behind me asked, as the room erupted in giggles. Leave it to Russ to skip over seventy years of noteworthy accomplishments and bring it back to basics.

As usual, however, Russ's outlandish humor had more than a nugget of truth in it. He wasn't kidding about the influence of his down-home childhood. Proudly outfitted in his Farmers Union vest, he was now telling some of his young fans what it had been like in those days, back when the trip to Great Falls had been a major expedition. Meanwhile, the life partner Russ had met shortly after helping finance Timeless Seeds—Elsie Tuss—had attracted an entourage of her own. With the commanding voice of a woman who, at age eighty, thought nothing of climbing atop a John Deere to survey her livestock, the former nun recounted memories from her own girlhood on a Montana homestead.

A lot of people would assume that such simple, rural upbringings would have made Russell Salisbury and Elsie Tuss provincial. That had certainly been the attitude at my high school in Missoula, where the cowboy section of the hallway was a ridiculed no-man's-land two floors below the lunchtime haunts of the jocks and the environmentalists. But when I'd worked alongside Elsie in her kitchen, I'd gotten a globe-trotting lesson in geopolitics.

Each time I'd asked Elsie about an issue she and Russ faced on their farm, the savvy Internet user had deftly knit together a worldwide web of interconnected events. From hybrid seed deals in India to oil spills in the Gulf of Mexico to shifting cultivation in Belize, Elsie truly saw the big picture. Her worldview was a direct descendent of the scrappy home economics she'd gleaned from homesteading dryland prairie through the Depression—but with the "family budget" reimagined at the scale of the global village.

Russ and Elsie spent money only on necessities, which is to say, the things *they* deemed necessary: donating to Doctors Without Borders, for example, or covering the remaining balance of a responsible rancher's mortgage payment. They didn't think of these extra-household expenditures as philanthropy. To Russ and Elsie, these were contributions toward essential public services, as though worldwide public health and sustainable resource management were things their extended neighborhood might budget for like road repair or the rural fire department. But as generous as they were with the money they hadn't spent on themselves, Russ and Elsie were best known for contributions in kind. Over the years, the Salisbury place had become an unofficial, statewide lending library, where pretty much any item of machinery that was still ambulatory was fair game. As Dave Oien put it, "Russ is the kind of guy who will give you anything if you need it, but won't sell it to you."

Now I knew the main reason Timeless Seeds and their crops had weathered the drought. It seemed trite, but it wasn't. They were humble. And they shared.

ALL THE WEALTH OF THE EARTH

While I was in Helena, I spent an afternoon rummaging through the bookshelves in the AERO office on Last Chance Gulch Street. I wasn't looking for anything in particular, but the nonprofit's bulging cache of newsletters and annual reports seemed like the best stack of papers to comb through to make sure I hadn't missed something important.

Most of what I found at the AERO office was pleasantly familiar. A *Sun Times* ad for the previous year's Timeless Festival promised workshops with Captain Compost and cooking demos with Leni Loves Lentils. The proceedings from the 1988 Soil-Building Cropping Systems Conference faithfully documented Jim Sims's rousing address, and the text of a 1999 radio commentary featured characteristically opinionated Elsie Tuss.

But wedged among Farm Improvement Club evaluations and grower surveys was a piece of AERO history I'd never expected to dig up. Back in 1993, the citizens' organization had launched a curriculum development project, geared toward fourth, fifth, and sixth graders. AERO had interviewed several farmers for the teaching package, Nancy Matheson had told me, but they'd run out of funding and the project had never been completed. The footage was pretty good, as Nancy recalled, but because AERO had since moved offices and changed directors, it was probably lost to history.

And yet, here it was. I recognized Dave Oien's name on the handwritten label of a VHS, following the words "curriculum project." Curious, I located a video production shop at the edge of town that was able to convert the tape to DVD. As soon as I got it home, I popped it into my laptop and hit play. The recording didn't start with Dave. But uncannily, the opening scene unfolded just a stone's throw from the current Timeless plant.

Ulm farmer Greg Gould looked directly into the camera, his face shaded by a plain brown ball cap on what was evidently a very sunny day. Perched serenely atop loosely folded legs in the midst of his crop, the bearded farmer responded thoughtfully to his interviewer's questions, with an astonishing economy of both speech and motion. Gould's lower body remained still as he methodically traced his fingers over a buckwheat plant, demonstrating the magic of phosphorous conversion.

The grainy, shadow-drenched picture and Gould's meditative voice lulled me into the reverie of a midsummer Montana afternoon. Since this footage had never been edited into curriculum—and I wasn't a sixth grader anyway—I let my focus drift. But fourteen minutes in, Greg beckoned me to listen up.

"There is something that we should remember today," Gould said emphatically, "even if we forget everything else." The Zen-like farmer had ditched the buckwheat plant, I noticed, and he was now caressing a handful of soil, passing it lovingly between his palms. "There are more organisms living beneath the soil than there are above it," Greg instructed. "From this life comes all the wealth of the earth. We are merely promoting a system that doesn't kill this life but can supply us with enough food."

AN ECOLOGICAL BIOGRAPHY

As I drove back over MacDonald Pass, Greg's words lingered with me. I had come to central Montana to trace the case study of a remarkable green business, to investigate the "triple bottom line" that generated good livelihoods from organic specialty lentils. Such values-based supply chains have become an increasingly popular model for simultaneously serving "people, profit, and planet." Grocery stores are now filled with grass-fed lamb, wildlife-friendly rice, *organic* fair trade tea, *domestic* fair trade wheat. Ventures like this are notoriously difficult to sustain, so I thought it would be a good idea to take a closer look at one that had survived for two and a half decades.

But when you begin to excavate the bottom line of Timeless Seeds, I discovered, it's not really the bottom line at all. What makes this lentil business go is a complex belowground ecology that reaches back to century-old grain pools, through the living rooms of stubborn ranch women, and across the political spectrum from counterculture political theater to populist revolt. Like Greg, Timeless and its growers are always trying to be a little gentler, to participate in the market in a way that doesn't kill their delicate underground, which is where it's really at.

The company—ostensibly the story I'd been following all summer—was merely the humble crop harvested out of a complex social ecology. What I'd realized as I spent time with the Timeless farmers is that most of what they were doing was tangential to the business, at least in mainstream economic terms. But if so many of these farmers' activities fell outside the purview of a typical enterprise, I could see how their broad-based efforts were nonetheless integral to their success. As they carefully stewarded an ecosystem, a social movement, and an information network, the lentil underground had introduced me to a very different form of economy. In the process, my neatly bounded case study had morphed into a sort of ecological biography. Timeless, much like the components of an ecosystem, could be understood only through its connections.

In making these connections, the plants and people of the lentil underground bore a curious resemblance to one another. Both initiated change in their communities that could only be described as radical. In the literal sense of that word, the underground allies sought fundamental transformation at the very root of their respective systems. Surrounded by producers, they insisted on lives as regenerators. "I can't sell things, but I can fix them," Russ Salisbury had told me. "That's what we do," his friend Scott Lohmuller had philosophized. "Clean up, rebuild." But as Scott's daughter Mariah had discovered when she and her husband attempted to launch an organic farm, being a regenerator was an underappreciated, largely invisible role. Socially and ecologically indispensable, it remained economically near impossible.

"YOU CAN'T DO IT ALONE"

Much like a newly initiated legume farmer, I want to think that lentils are a straightforward substitute for synthetic fertilizer, a cheaper, more environmentally benign alternative. To some extent, this is true. But if that was really all there was to it, there would be no lentil underground—just a smattering of savvy growers rationally applying plant-based nitrogen instead of expensive ammonium nitrate. But the fact is that biological fertility is more than just a different nutrient management approach. It's an entirely different way of life—one in which time and space broaden considerably, and the illusion of control falls apart.

Building your soil biologically is not a precise prescription for a particular crop, but a contribution to a larger ecology, subject to independent variables, geologic time, and global biogeochemical cycles. You will not capture all the value on this farm, in this year. You cannot individualize your return. To build biological fertility is to build community—to accept interdependence with other creatures and foster a common benefit. This way of life cultivates a new kind of awareness, a new empathy. You have to pay attention beyond this homestead. You have to pay attention beyond this season. You cannot spray and then forget about it and go to the lake.

Planting organic lentils—and all the other crops that go with them—becomes part of who you are, what you are conscious of, how you see the world. It forces you to listen more deeply, more expansively. And it softens, to some extent, the borders of the self. This is the great irony of the lentil underground, or perhaps its secret. What rugged individualism brought together, only community can sustain. When I'd asked Casey Bailey to reflect on the biggest lesson he'd learned by bucking the corporate farm industry, he'd paused for a full ten seconds, then answered firmly. "That you can't do it alone."

Since they know they can thrive only as part of a team, the members of the lentil underground are unceremoniously selfless. "I don't care if it's not benefiting me," Bud Barta told me flatly. I'd asked the hardworking builder if it bothered him that the money currently being made in organics didn't seem to be flowing back to the movement's originators. "As long as more people are moving in that direction," Bud said, "I'm happy. I mean, that's why we did it." Another Timeless grower was angry about proposed cuts to Farm Bill programs, but not the ones he benefited from. "I don't care if they cut my corn payments," Jerry Sikorski had told me in frustration. "I don't deserve payments, but for Christ's sake, don't cut the food to the poor people."

Bud and Jerry have long since refused the enduring myth of the lone ranger. They know it's false, because they've actually tried to live it. They've managed to carve out some of the independence they were looking for—but, perhaps paradoxically, not by themselves. Far more capable of truly going it alone than 99 percent of contemporary Americans, these people who can build or fix most anything are nonetheless intimately aware of their reliance on communities larger than themselves.

Part of this radical humility is letting go of the mentality that "bigger is better," that more grain is unquestionably merrier. Jerry Sikorski and his wife, Kathy, live in a part of eastern Montana hot enough to grow corn, which has proven to be a profitable crop for many of their neighbors. The Sikorskis have included the prolific grain in their rotation, but they pay attention to annual rainfall totals and reduce their seeding density accordingly. "We don't shoot for a hundred bushels to the acre," Jerry told me, "but we keep a plant population down around thirteen thousand plants per acre. It means less grain, but it also means fewer plants to use the available moisture."

Another hallmark of the lentil underground is their openness to new people and ideas. They aren't bound by an unquestioning loyalty to the way Granddaddy did it, or by a suspicious wariness of outsiders. The heritage and heirloom crops they grow manifest deep relational ties and long experience, but these carefully chosen plants are certainly not xenophobes. Black medic made its way to Montana from the American Southeast. Ley cropping came from Australia. Lentils were domesticated 10,000 years ago in the

Middle East, and breeders like Al Slinkard borrowed liberally from international collections when developing varieties for North America.

Like their seeds and systems, the people of the lentil underground trace their own development along paths that meander well beyond Montana. Dave Oien has made half a dozen trips to East Asia. Casey Bailey traveled and studied in Guatemala. And seventy-three-year-old homesteader Russ Salisbury ultimately hopes to leave his place to a nephew-in-law who was raised on a smallholding in Belize. "Carlos is my best teacher," Russ says of his younger relative and farm manager.

The Timeless farmers pursue neither uncompromising allegiance to tradition nor a wholesale break from previous generations in the name of progress. They worship neither past nor future. Instead, change and continuity find themselves intertwined into a way of life more cyclical than linear. As they revisit their grandparents' mutual-aid agrarianism, these farmers imbue this tradition with a newfound appreciation for the global reach of their neighborhood.

For each member of the lentil underground, this journey eventually arrives at the same question with which it began: how to save the family farm. Their problems haven't gone away. But they've learned to see them differently. Instead of noticing the immediate obstacles in their path—weeds and drought—they've begun to observe more systemic ones. The infinitely interconnected farm they now see before them presents a suite of daunting management challenges, but unlike rain and plant evolution, farmers can do something about at least some of them.

This Montana lentil harvest is no fairy-tale success, but a complicated saga of adaptation, learning, and even some hard times. The story of Timeless Seeds is not a heroic one, but then again these fragile plains are not a place that needs heroes. "What I'd tell beginning farmers who want to do this," Anna Jones-Crabtree told me, "is, yes, believe in yourself; but also, every season you learn something new, and every season you adjust and rework your plan."

People like Anna don't tend to make headlines as organic industry leaders, because their aim is not runaway success, but resilience. Anna and her fellow Timeless growers attempt to create a workable niche for themselves in the food system, while simultaneously questioning the very foundations of that system. By finding creative ways to stay in the game without fully accepting its rules, the lentil underground alters the landscape slowly, subtly, subversively. This is why they can withstand challenges that bring the rest of American agriculture to its knees, like the 2012 drought. Instead of building farming systems that are maximally productive under ideal conditions, they're designing dynamic agroecosystems for the long haul, which can both survive adverse conditions and adapt to them. The many dimensions of the lentil underground—from the diverse community of microorganisms beneath the surface of the soil to the diverse community of people organizing for change beneath the surface of red state America— are at the root of this supple strength. This is not the strength of the mythological Westerner, who can outcompete all rivals. This is the strength of generations of real Westerners, who know how to work together to weather life's storms. In a world made increasingly volatile by climate change, this is the kind of strength we need.

BEYOND THE FOODSHED

The thing is, Timeless Seeds only does enough business to contract with about twenty farmers. Sure, they've helped spawn a movement that includes other such companies, which also support a diversified organic approach. Loyal friends and family members are in on the action, as are dedicated scientists and nonprofit staffers, enthusiastic chefs, and passionate consumers. A couple dozen Timeless investors help spread some of the risk, and larger networks provide various forms of support. Anna Jones-Crabtree has her circle of sustainability professionals, while Jacob and Courtney Cowgill are bolstered by their CSA members and a tight-knit crew of University of Montana environmental studies alumni. Dave helped piece together the Oien family's livelihood with his parents' Social Security check, and Jess Alger got his knee surgery covered by Tricare. But as charming as this homespun patchwork is, it's full of gaping holes, which are anything but romantic. The social and environmental challenges these farmers endeavor to address are more than they can handle on their own.

Like it or not, standardized "factories in the fields" have become firmly ensconced in US policy, institutions, culture, and, indeed, our very psyche. Diversifying the American food system—not just the organic vegetable suppliers on the urban outskirts, but mainstream farms too—requires changing all those things. It is not going to happen overnight. We've spent decades building rural life around industrial logic: annual returns, simplification, and efficiency. It will take a lot of work and creativity to reshape it according to biological logic: multiyear cycles, diversity, and flexibility.

Perhaps the most insidious thing about monoculture is that

getting out of the habit of working with other species has also gotten us out of the habit of working with one another. We've bought out the neighbors with whom we used to share tips, tractors, harvest help, and good old-fashioned moral support. Getting back in touch with ourselves as biological farmers rather than industrial ones isn't just a technical matter. It's a wholesale shift. Entire farm communities need to adopt the ways of the dynamic world underground, where the long haul is what really matters and a shared prosperity is the only kind there is.

In other words, to have a healthy belowground ecology in our soils, we need a parallel one in our rural society. And, for that matter, in our urban foodsheds. From the looks of all the kale-enamored soccer moms and overall-clad hipsters, it would appear that such a transformation is well under way. But unfortunately, the good-food craze sweeping American cities hasn't been as helpful for the lentil underground as you might think.

While this highly gastrocultural moment has boosted the fortunes of artisanal cheese makers and suburban vegetable growers, it's actually a tough time to be an organic lentil marketer, given the food movement's recent turn toward locavore diets. Timeless Seeds, much like fair trade businesses in the developing world, has always relied on a strategic partnership with affluent consumers in population hubs like San Francisco. Such consumers understand that their purchases support ecologically appropriate land management and sustainable livelihoods in economically disadvantaged rural Montana. There's even a growing movement promoting such partnerships—domestic fair trade. The ten-year-old Domestic Fair Trade Association counts several retailers, manufacturers, processors, and nongovernmental organizations among its thirty-eight members. But the DFTA is swimming upstream, as a far greater share of North American foodies pledge to reduce their "food miles" and eat within a 100-mile radius of their homes.

Sustainability analysts have long since discounted the "food miles" approach as overly simplistic. When you break down the source of greenhouse gas emissions in the global food system, transportation to the final point of sale accounts for only about 4 percent. What we ought to be worried about are things like synthetic nitrogen, which generates 300 million metric tons of CO_2 emissions a year—and several marine dead zones. Even if lowering your carbon footprint is all you care about, you'd be much better off supporting legume-based nitrogen fertility in Montana than buying conventionally fertilized local food. As a team of international researchers calculated in a recent review paper, legume crops and legume-based pastures use 35 to 60 percent less fossil energy than chemically fertilized grains, and the inclusion of legumes in cropping sequences reduces the average annual energy usage over a rotation by 12 to 34 percent. Of course, there are many other social and environmental reasons to support businesses like Timeless Seeds, but with grocery stores and restaurants increasingly posting the food miles of their products, it's been hard to sell consumers on a more nuanced approach to a righteous diet. Plus, local fruit and vegetables—those charismatic megafauna of the supermarket—benefit from decades of cultural and commercial associations with health. Everybody knows an apple a day keeps the doctor away and that leafy greens are a superfood. But lentils? Most Americans don't even know what they are, let alone how or why to eat them.

The real problem, though, isn't knowledge. It's money. Even in decidedly nonepicurean central Montana, Timeless growers have found a surprising number of people who are excited about eating organic lentils. They just can't afford them. "What can we tell people when they say our food costs too much?" Courtney Cowgill asks earnestly. "That we're going to leave our land better than when we found it, or water quality is going to be better because of us, or maybe fewer people are going to get sick because we don't use chemicals or pesticides? It's just really hard to quantify that for people when they're on a limited budget."

So long as they have to operate within a cheap-food economy that externalizes its social and environmental costs, both farmers and eaters will be forced into the false choice between a healthy environment and their own bottom line. Timeless Seeds has prepared fertile ground—and an incredible demonstration of what's possible. But they can't fix the food system alone. That's a job for all of us.

EPILOGUE

If you walk into the Timeless plant today, you'll get a glimpse of two other projects the company is currently incubating. Their equipment and distribution network support a fair trade business that imports heirloom rice from 2,000-year-old terraces in the Philippines. They're also hosting a small mill that aims to replace industrial hybrid corn with more nutritious, sustainable varieties. The organic feed venture that got its start at Timeless has graduated to a larger facility in nearby Fort Benton, where the screenings and surplus of the lentil underground become a nutrient-packed meal of heritage grains and legumes for livestock and backyard chickens across the West. And Prairie Heritage Farm, the community supported agriculture operation that began on Dave Oien's land, is just down the road in Power.

Here, in sleepy central Montana, is a snapshot of what the future of food could look like. Unlike the food system we've got now, it wouldn't be focused on one crop or one strategy. Instead of a few massive farms, we'd have lots of them, in several shapes and sizes. Urban gardeners would grow local produce and raise chickens. Rural growers and researchers would go back to breeding nutritious, ecologically adapted grains, instead of eking out marginal-yield gains at the expense of human and environmental health.

Fair trade distribution would allow city dwellers to support responsible farmers who take care of our planet's support systems—whether those farmers happen to live just across the mountains or halfway around the world. We're still a long way from the widespread belowground network that will be required to realize that kind of food system. But this little victory in Montana proves that it's possible, one seed at a time.

As for Timeless Seeds itself, and the characters in this book, here's where things stood when I went back to visit in February 2014, just a few months before *Lentil Underground* went to press:

A quarter century after four central Montana farmers dreamed of an agricultural revolution, Timeless Seeds had nearly closed the loop between farm and fork. Back in 1986, when they started a small seed business, Dave Oien and his three farmer friends had made their first foray into the rest of the food system beyond their own fields. Over the years, they'd linked their renegade farms to other parts of the food chain, diversifying into processing, wholesale distribution, and branded marketing. And this spring, they were taking the final step: a retail packaging facility. Bud Barta had just sent Dave a set of plans for the new packaging room at Ulm, which would be constructed by Barta Built in April and ready to roll by September.

Twenty-five years after he'd drawn his last paycheck from Timeless Seeds, Jim Barngrover was also back in action: as a grower relations and procurement representative. With the company poised to triple its contracted acreage, Dave was short staffed, so he'd handed over the best part of his job to his longtime friend. In a few weeks, Jim would be headed out for preseason visits with the seventeen folks who'd agreed to grow for Timeless this year.

Tom Hastings was the only one of the original Timeless partners who wasn't involved in the business anymore. Tom had left the company a decade ago, but he'd held on to one piece of it: an abandoned grain elevator that Timeless had purchased in the early 1990s for a dollar. Dave still went by the old elevator a couple of Saturdays a month to visit his former business partner's quirky pop-up, Timeless Tom's Second Hand.

Jim Sims, the cowboy scientist who'd helped Timeless launch its first product, had called it quits as well. After a thirty-year career at Montana State University, Sims had retired in 1996 to a quiet neighborhood on the outskirts of Bozeman. His Canadian counterpart, Al Slinkard (aka Dr. Lentil) had retired from the University of Saskatchewan in 1998. Meanwhile, the lentil underground had found a new academic champion: MSU nutritionist Alison Harmon. Harmon, a driving force behind the university's Sustainable Food and Bioenergy Systems program, had teamed up with Dave and the Crabtrees, and she was putting together a resource guide for chefs and food service professionals. Playing on Montana's mining history and official nickname, Harmon had devised a catchy title for the project: "Lentils: Gems in the Treasure State."

Sharon Eisenberg, just two years away from drawing Social Security, was ready to pass the buck to the next generation too. Already overburdened with tax-season work for her private clients, Timeless Seeds' CFO had spent many hours this winter studying the new health care options available under the Affordable Care Act. Obamacare had survived its Supreme Court challenge, but Sharon wasn't particularly impressed with the new menu of expensive insurance plans. "The dental coverage is a little better," she sighed, "but we should have just done single payer." Hopefully, it wouldn't be her problem for much longer, Sharon told me. Dave and the Timeless Seeds Board had started interviewing candidates for a new general manager position, which would relieve Sharon of some of her duties and help Dave with some of his. Timeless hadn't advertised, but people had been calling Dave out of the blue, asking if the growing company had any job openings. The inquiries came from surprising places—the Montana Department of Agriculture, a much larger processor in Great Falls, even an enormous grain plant in eastern Montana. "I was astonished when that guy called me about working here," Dave said. "He was earning more than the entire staff of Timeless combined."

While deeper-pocketed admirers knocked on Dave's door, Timeless Seeds original financier, seventy-four-year-old Russ Salisbury, was still farming, as was his eighty-one-year-old partner, Elsie Tuss. The couple had gone to Arizona for the winter in one of their most roadworthy vehicles, but they'd be back soon, Sharon Eisenberg told me. She had to file their tax returns.

Tuna McAlpine had already called Sharon about his taxes. He had two fewer dependents this year: His oldest son had earned his bachelor's degree and landed a job as a farm appraiser, and his oldest daughter had graduated from the University of Montana with an MS in speech pathology. Tuna wasn't contracting with Timeless for any crops this season, but he and his wife, Anne, occasionally saw Dave and Sharon when the two families picked up groceries from their buying club.

The Alternative Energy Resources Organization—the nonprofit that had introduced Timeless Seeds' four partners and recruited Tuna McAlpine to join its Farm Improvement Club program, was entering its fortieth year as the northern plains' voice for renewable energy and sustainable agriculture. AERO no longer sponsored Farm Improvement Clubs, but the model had been taken up by others: the Center for Rural Affairs, Iowa State University, even the Ecological Farmers of Ontario.

Blu Funk was still serving Montana-grown Black Beluga lentils at ShowThyme, the restaurant in Bigfork that had first picked up Timeless Seeds' signature crop in 1998.

Jerry Habets had renewed his lease on the Oien place, and he'd also started custom hauling for Timeless and several of his fellow growers. Jerry was planning to plant his triple intercrop again this year, and Dave had promised to buy the understory: Petite Crimson lentils. Jerry's "Montana Milpa" wasn't the greatest thing from a processing standpoint, Dave admitted, since it was a bit of a hassle to separate everything out. But it sure was great for the land.

Casey Bailey had a Timeless contract too—for 100 acres of French Green lentils. He was still transitioning his parents' place to organics, 200 acres at a time, and he'd grown his cattle herd to 150, so he could rotate into alfalfa more often and let the cows graze down his cover crop.

Doug Crabtree and Anna Jones-Crabtree had welcomed their first apprentice the previous season, and they were planning to hire two for 2014. Doug had left his position at the Department of Agriculture to farm full-time, and Anna was doing most of her day job remotely. Still, the busy couple didn't seem to have enough hours in the day. Despite swearing to pare down their sixteen-crop repertoire, the Crabtrees had seeded twenty-one in 2013. Now they were considering a whopping two dozen for the coming season, including 238 acres of Black Belugas for Timeless Seeds. Timeless still wasn't quite as organized as the Crabtrees would have liked, but they were delighted that the company had finally obtained a line of credit in December, so it could pay farmers more promptly. Meanwhile, the Crabtrees had made some modest progress initiating cooperative projects with fellow growers: They were planning to grow some heritage grains for Jacob and Courtney Cowgill's

CSA and they were already sharing a semi truck and trailer with their Havre neighbors Jody and Crystal Manuel.

The Manuels had three Timeless crops ready to go in the ground for 2014: chickpeas, emmer, and Purple Prairie barley. They had decided to take the Whole Foods distribution deal for their grass-fed beef, but they were still selling directly to local individuals too, including a few members of Crystal's church group. Two years ago, some of those ladies had been taken aback when Crystal invited them over for hors d'oeuvres in the pig pasture. But apparently, those brave enough to take her up on it had spread the word, and the Manuels' farm-to-fork ranch tour was well on its way to becoming an annual Havre tradition.

Having narrowly won reelection in 2012, second-term US senator Jon Tester was contracting with Timeless too. He still had some seed from the bumper lentil crop that had funded the down payment on his house, and he was planning to grow it out for the first time in years. Dave had a buyer who was interested in that variety—Sunrise Reds—so he'd asked Big Jon if he thought the old seed was viable enough to generate a commercial yield. Somehow, the senator had found time to do a germination test, and it had turned out well. "I'm dancing," he wrote Jim Barngrover, who had asked the senator whether he wanted to "tango" with Timeless.

Brandon and Mariah O'Halloran had nearly quit farming at the end of 2012, after Brandon's relatives sold the family's land in the Shields Valley. Although they'd seen it coming, Brandon and Mariah hadn't quite let go of their dream of somehow, someday turning the place into an organic farm. When the door had shut firmly on that possibility, it had taken a bit of the wind out of their sails. But when a café had come up for sale in downtown Lewistown, the opportunity gave the O'Hallorans a second wind—and a new dream. The couple had turned the Rising Trout into a local food showcase, featuring organically raised meat, eggs, and produce from the area, as well as fresh-baked bread made from their own grain. To complement all that nitrogen-feeding grain, which they were still raising at Mariah's parents' place, they needed some legumes. So they were contracting with Timeless to grow several acres of chickpeas.

Thirty-three miles up the road in Power, life was busy for Dave's former tenants Jacob and Courtney Cowgill. The owner-operators of Prairie Heritage Farm hadn't slowed down on veggies, turkeys, and ancient grains. On top of that, they'd added a thirty-nine-tree fruit orchard to their operation, in partnership with extension researchers at MSU. And the previous season, the couple had also formed a seed co-op, with the idea of collaborating with other farmers to develop locally adapted vegetable varieties. Life beyond the farm was eventful for the Cowgills too. They'd had a second child in May, and Courtney was working part-time as an editor while teaching a distance education class for the University of Montana. Jacob was also teaching online for UM, and he had two other side jobs too: substitute rural mail carrier and lobbyist for the Farmers Union. Given the historic volume of snow, it looked as if 2014 would be an unusually intense year for Jacob's postal service job, but that was nothing compared to the firestorm about to hit his other one. The lentil underground had made some progress on federal policy—the recently passed Farm Bill had authorized money for pulse crop nutrient analysis and incentives to add more pulse crops to school lunch. But closer to home, a familiar battle was brewing: genetically modified organisms. Monsanto had been purchasing land near Great Falls for wheat-variety trials, and few locals trusted the corporation's assertion that none of the seeds planted there would be GMOs.

At the Timeless plant in Ulm, OSHA-savvy operations man-ager Leni Yeager was still holding court in her pink hard hat, watching over Loren Nicholls and Jason Roberts like a mother hen. But things were hardly the same. "You remember then," Loren welcomed me dramatically, as I walked into the bustling fa-cility. "Well, this is now." When he swung open the doors to the hard-hat zone, the tidy warehouse that greeted me bore little re-semblance to the falling-down elevator Timeless had left behind just eight years ago. Neatly stacked pallets of legumes and grains were inventoried, in crisp printing, on a shiny new whiteboard. On the processing floor, a new decorticator was removing skins from a batch of Petite Crimson lentils. A supportive buyer had helped Timeless finance this machine, Loren reminded me, which meant they no longer needed to contract this job out to a larger processing plant. Once Bud finished the retail packaging line, Loren continued, Timeless would have its whole supply chain in-house, right up to the final point of sale. That meant more work, of course, so the Timeless plant had added a second shift, bumping its workweek hours to six A.M. to eleven P.M. "I don't think Dave will ever add a graveyard, though," Loren said, with a knowing wink. What Dave had added, though, were two new employees: of-fice manager Heather Hadley and plant foreman Mike Ferrara.

What should I put down for *your* title? I teased Dave. On the Timeless website, he was listed as CEO and founding farmer, but he didn't spend his days like any other CEO I knew. Today, for ex-ample, Dave had made an impromptu trip to Fort Benton to pick up eleven bags of Kamut. It was a time-sensitive errand, and Dave wasn't sure if a delivery truck would be available in time. So he'd decided to fetch the ancient grain himself—in his Honda Civic hy-brid. The previous day, Dave had made a personal trip to pick up French Green lentils from the nonprofit vocational center he'd been working with since 1994, now known as Quality Life Concepts. This was apparently something Dave had done before: He knew the names of nearly every developmentally disabled client there, even the ones who didn't work on his packaging jobs.

I rode along as Dave shuttled product around central Montana, eavesdropping on the calls he made from his Bluetooth headset. Picking up what I could from Dave's half of one of these conversations, I gathered that a conventional buyer looking to diversify was asking about organic lentils. Things sure had changed, I said to Dave, noting an incredible statistic I'd just learned from Alison Harmon: Montana now produced about half of the lentils in the United States—enough to supply six servings a day to each of the state's 1 million residents. Dave was surprised by the big numbers, but not the trend. "Some of the farmers that saw the first lentil in their life up on our plots here, they're probably doing three or four or five hundred acres of lentils now," he told me. "There's hardly anybody anymore that's doing just one crop, even conventional guys." No sooner had Dave finished his thought than his phone rang again. One of his buyers wanted him to certify the Timeless plant as kosher, so he started calling around to get a recommendation for a rabbi. Dave had learned to delegate some things, I'd noticed, but there was a limit to how much he was willing to simplify his diverse life. He liked things this way.

On the final day of my visit, Dave took his household newspapers and cardboard to the Conrad recycling center. We weren't planning to stay long. It was four degrees outside, and I had a plane to catch. But when Dave pushed a button to pop his trunk and get his recyclables, nothing happened. He turned his key in the ignition, but the car wouldn't start. He couldn't even get a chug-chug-chug out of the hybrid engine. It was completely dead. After calling Sharon to ask for a jump, Dave started rooting around for his jumper cables. And then he remembered—those were in the trunk too. After a split second of panic, a light bulb went on somewhere inside Dave's head. The next few moments went by so quickly, I hardly knew what was happening. Suddenly the trunk was open, the hood was propped, cables were hooked up, and a faint ding signaled the Civic's resurrection. "I guess the battery lost connection," Dave explained, showing me the bolt he'd just tightened before loading his jumper cables back into the car. "That's never happened to me before."

"Well, that was an adventure," I said to Dave, once we'd called off Sharon and were safely back on the road. Dave's ungloved hands were bright red, and he was blowing on them to warm them up. "A brief adventure, luckily," he answered. "And a learning experience." I tried to figure out what it was I supposed to learn from Dave on this journey. I imagined myself, like Joseph Brown consulting Black Elk, distilling some nugget of wisdom from all the conversations we'd had over the past three years. What profound teaching had I received? What lesson would I convey from this homegrown sage? Before I could figure it out, Dave interrupted my meditation. "Never buy a car that won't let you get into both the trunk and the hood mechanically," he instructed me. "Now let's get you to the airport."

ACKNOWLEDGMENTS

A number of busy people spent long hours sharing their stories and their knowledge with me. I am deeply grateful to David Oien and Sharon Eisenberg, Jim Barngrover, Bud Barta, Russell Salisbury and Elsie Tuss, Jim and Toni Sims, Doug Crabtree and Anna Jones-Crabtree, Jody and Crystal Manuel, Jerry Habets, Casey Bailey, Jacob and Courtney Cowgill, Daryl and Linda Lassila, Clay and Anne McAlpine, Mariah and Brandon O'Halloran, Susan and Scott Lohmuller, Jerry and Kathy Sikorski, Jess Alger, Laura Leibner, Cathy and Mick Odden, Mark and Monica Goldhahn, Ole Norgaard, Bruce and Melinda Pester, Leni Yeager, Loren Nicholls, Jason Roberts, Heather Hadley, Mike Ferrara, Mary Hensley, Neva Hassanein, Grant Jackson, Bruce Maxwell, Perry Miller, Fabian Menalled, Chengci Chen, David Wichman, Alison Harmon, Al Slinkard, Kenny Keever, Nancy Matheson, Jonda Crosby, Barbara Rusmore, Maxwell Milton and Joan Bird, Dawn McGee, Birdie Emerson, Kye Cochran, John Cawley and Christine Marshall, Blu and Rose Funk, Ann Sinclair, Robert Boettcher, Tom Bump, Jack Reams, Margaret Misner, Bob Herdegen, Dave Christensen, Scott Sproull, Andre Giles, Sam Schmidt, Bob Quinn, Wes Gibbs, Jan and Rich Boyle, and the staff and volunteers of the Alternative Energy Resources Organization and Montana Organic

Association. I am humbled by your generosity and your wisdom, and I am truly honored that you would trust me with telling some of your stories. Any shortcomings, of course, are my own.

I would never have met this extraordinary cast of characters had I not had the pleasure of working for one them, US senator Jon Tester. My stint as a legislative correspondent in Senator Tester's Washington, DC, office was quite the learning experience, and I am grateful to all the members of Team Tester for educating me, introducing me to several of the people in this book, and sending me off to grad school in California without too many snickers. I owe especial thanks to Matt Jennings, Andrea Helling, James Wise, Lili Snyder, Daniel Stein, Amanda Arnold, Susan Cierlitsky, and of course, Jon and Sharla Tester.

As a graduate student in geography at UC Berkeley, I enjoyed two great luxuries during the research and writing of this book: a lot of time and a lot of support. I am particularly grateful to my dissertation committee—Nathan Sayre, Jake Kosek, Ryan Galt, and Claire Kremen—for their wise counsel and uncommon patience. Several other colleagues and mentors at UC Berkeley were invaluable allies, among them Annie Shattuck, Maywa Montenegro, Albie Miles, Nathan McClintock, Alastair Iles, Shannon Cram, Erin Collins, Adam Romero, Mike Jones, Natalia Vonnegut, Marjorie Ensor, Christopher Bacon, Kathryn DeMaster, Ann Thrupp, Jennifer Sowerwine, Christy Getz, Miguel Altieri, Alex Tarr, and the members of the Sayre and Fortmann Labs, Center for Diversified Farming Systems, Berkeley Food Institute, and Center for Science, Technology, Medicine, and Society. Beyond Berkeley, I've also been inspired by my colleagues at the Sustainable Agriculture Education Association and by my indefatigable undergraduate adviser, Kay Kaufman Shelemay.

My research was financially supported by the National Science

Foundation, the PEO, Soroptimist International's Founder Region, and the Charles Redd Center; and Michael Sacramento at UC Berkeley's Graduate Division was my guru of grantsmanship. The librarians at the Montana Historical Society provided expert assistance with my archival work, and Yeu Olivia Han helped me transcribe interviews.

When it came time to put pen to paper, two consummate storytellers at Berkeley's Graduate School of Journalism mentored me through the complex process of authoring my first book. Michael Pollan and the members of his fall 2012 writing workshop helped me outline the project and thoughtfully commented on multiple drafts of the introduction. The following spring, under the auspices of a three-credit independent study, Edwin Dobb read two full drafts of the manuscript and provided thorough, incisive feedback. Both Michael and Edwin offered critical advice and encouragement as I worked through multiple revisions and pitched the book to agents and editors. I have them to thank for my formation as a writer. I am also grateful to four superb fellow storytellers—Annie Shattuck, Lynne Carlisle, Patrick Archie, and Nathan Hodo—who read the manuscript in its final stages and helped me improve it.

In New York, my first debt of gratitude is to my agent, Jessica Papin, who took a chance on a completely unproven first-time author with a pitch about lentils. Jessica totally got this book, and she championed it as if it were her own. Her suggestions on my proposal were so good that many of them are reflected in the final text of the prologue. Before I started working with Jessica, another insightful literary agent, Mollie Glick, also helped me hone my pitch. At Gotham Books, I've had the pleasure of working with editor Charles Conrad, who has an uncanny ability to get inside a story and identify what's missing. Two other people at Gotham helped shape the text: Leslie Hansen offered perceptive editorial suggestions and copy editor Eileen Chetti saved me from several embarrassing errors.

Writing is a weird job. A social science PhD is an equally weird job. Putting them together is a mental health risk and definitely calls for the buddy system. In addition to the folks mentioned above, several other kindred spirits helped me find meaning in my solitary work, even during those long months when I had very little to show for it. The world's most gracious landlady, Ruth Silverman, provided a beautiful live-work space, and her team of assistants—Su Evers, Araly Cruz, Evelyn Serrano, and Katya Kostyukova—made sure I had human contact even on my most intense writing days. Several stalwart friends had my back: Yan Xu, Lauren Merker, the Razon family, Sibyl Diver, Margot Higgins, Lauren Withey, Allison Rogers, Peiting Li, Simona Balan, Sepideh Sadaghiani, Rose Hardy, and Stephanie Bortz. My grandmother Helen Gordon inspired and encouraged me, both with her passion for growing things and with cautionary tales from her Dust Bowl childhood on a western Nebraska farm. My brother, Andrew Holder, has been a staunch supporter and stimulating interlocutor throughout. And my parents, Lynne and Ray Carlisle, contributed in innumerable ways to this project, not the least of which involved driving all the way from Missoula to Great Falls to bail me out when I got a flat tire.

Here in Berkeley, California, it's normal usage to refer to your significant other as your "partner." But Patrick Archie truly is one, in every sense of the word. Maybe I could have written this book without his unwavering intellectual, practical, and moral support. But it wouldn't have been nearly as much fun.

NOTES ON SOURCES

This is a work of nonfiction. I have used real names of people and places, with the written permission of identified sources. Contemporary scenes are reported from direct observation. To reconstruct the historical scenes narrated in Chapters 1–8, I have drawn on both the memories of those involved and archival materials: photographs, journalism, newsletters, nonprofit and business records, and a small amount of video. Direct quotes are taken either from statements made in my presence (as transcribed from digital audio recordings or handwritten notes) or from written records. In some cases, I represent individuals' recollections of their earlier statements as direct quotes, but in only a few instances have I corrected a grammatical error or deleted "umms" or "uhhs." Most of the research for this book was conducted while I was a graduate student at the University of California, Berkeley, according to a protocol approved by the university's Office for the Protection of Human Subjects. Although I conducted dozens of formal interviews and a small survey, my primary method of research was in-depth ethnography. Grounded in participant observation, ethnography allows social science researchers to develop partial cultural literacy in the communities where they conduct research, such that we can attempt to understand things about people and events beyond what is directly expressed in response to an interview question. Thus, some of the quotations and dialogue in this book were overheard as I shadowed farmers in their daily lives. Sparingly, I have attempted to report on these farmers' internal meditations—by reading between the lines of their words and observing actions and body language. While all these characterizations of people and events reflect my own limited perspective, I shared them with sources before publication, to confirm that they felt fairly and accurately represented. All remaining errors, however, are my own.

In the notes on sources, I retrace the steps I took to construct the narrative. In the bibliography, I cite selected sources that deepened my understanding of several issues I touch on in the book. I suggest these bibliographic sources as further reading for those who wish to dig deeper into these topics, or those looking to substantiate statements made by characters in the narrative.

I. FERTILE GROUND

Throughout the first eight chapters, I draw heavily on the *Sun Times,* a periodical published by the Alternative Energy Resources Organization from its founding in 1974 to the present. Nearly all the events chronicled in this opening section of the book were documented in the reported articles, columns, calendar listings, and classified advertisements of the *Sun Times,* complete with photographs, detailed descriptions, and direct quotations. I am indebted to the dedicated reporters and editors at AERO for recording this history as it happened. I am also grateful that nearly all the protagonists in these chapters were in good health and willing to spend several hours sharing their stories with me. Interviews with David Oien and Sharon Eisenberg, Jim Barngrover, Bud Barta, Jim Sims, Russell Salisbury and Elsie Tuss, and Nancy Matheson and Jonda Crosby helped me fill out and corroborate the story of Timeless Seeds' founding and early days. In addition, I drew on the following sources for specific chapters:

CHAPTER 1

E-mail correspondence with Scott Sproull—who shared photographs and materials from his alternative energy workshop—helped me tell the story of the night school class that first turned Dave Oien on to DIY renewable energy. An essay on the history of agriculture in Montana, submitted by the Montana State University Library as part of the National Preservation Program for Agriculture Literature, provided key details on the early-twentieth-century history of north-central Montana. I accessed this essay at the following website: http://harvest.mannlib.cornell.edu/node/24.

CHAPTER 2

The proceedings of AERO's 1984 Sustainable Agriculture Conference substantiated and supplemented the recollections of those present.

II. SEEDS OF CHANGE

CHAPTER 3

Several current and former researchers tutored me in the history, agronomy, and ecology of legume farming on the northern Great Plains: Jim Sims, Al Slinkard, Bruce Maxwell, Perry Miller, Chengci Chen, and Grant Jackson. I retraced Jim Sims's research on the Gallatin Valley Seed Company with the aid of the Internet,

which led me to the company's website: http://gallatinvalleyseed
.com/history.php.

David Oien's collection of articles about Jim Sims's research
and black medic was invaluable:

Cramer, Craig. "Water Saving 'Weed' Replaces Chem-
  Fallow." *New Farm,* September–October 1987, 28–30.
Hay and Forage Grower. "Black Medic Turns Fallow Green."
  March 1991, 16–17.
Henkes, Rollie. "Forages for All Reasons: Seeds of a New
  Revolution?" *Furrow,* Special Hay and Forage Issue,
  Spring 1992, 10–12.
Henkes, Rollie. "Taking a Closer Look at Annual Legumes."
  Furrow, Prairie ed., March–April 1994.
Kessler, Karl. "Homegrown Fertilizer for Wheat." *Furrow,*
  Northern Plains ed., September–October 1983, 6–7.
Kessler, Karl. "New Ways to Summerfallow." *Furrow,* North
  Plains ed., March–April 1993, 22–23.
Northcutt, Greg. "Forages Are a Natural." *Hay and Forage
  Grower,* February 1990, 28.
Oien, David. "Black Medic: A New Prescription for Worn
  Out Soils." *Synergy* 3, no. 1 (1991): 24–25.

CHAPTER 4

Although I did overhear several stories about Russ Salisbury at
farm tours and demonstration days, my favorite source on Russ's
life and philosophy was his correspondence with Alternative Energy Resources Organization staff, which I found in an archival
file at the nonprofit's Helena office. Russ's poignant essay "Land,"
which I found attached to one of these letters, belongs alongside

the writings of Wendell Berry and Fred Kirschenmann as a modern agrarian classic.

The history of AERO is well recorded in the organization's archives and the *Sun Times,* but interviews with Kye Cochran, Birdie Emerson, Nancy Matheson, Jonda Crosby, and numerous current and former AERO members added colorful details and a firsthand perspective. An oral history session I convened at AERO's 2012 annual meeting elicited additional juicy tidbits, and I am grateful to all who participated. Key events in the history of the Farmers Union are detailed on the organization's website, and Lawrence Goodwyn's *The Populist Moment* provided helpful context on agrarian cooperative movements in the early twentieth century. Kye Cochran's 1979 article in *Mother Earth News* recounts the history of the Northern Plains Research Council and can be accessed online: http://www.motherearthnews.com/nature-and-environment /strip-mining-consolidation-coal-company-zmaz79zsch.aspx.

CHAPTER 5

The Proceedings of AERO's 1988 Soil Building Cropping Systems Conference—complete with a lengthy transcript of Jim Sims's remarks—are a researcher's dream. AERO also provided me with extensive records from the ten years of the Farm Improvement Club program, including club applications and year-end reports, newspaper clippings from local and trade publications, and reports to funders. Clay (Tuna) McAlpine graciously toured me around his ranch and answered questions.

III. TIMELESS GROWS UP

CHAPTER 6

Quotes from Jon Tester are taken from a 2012 interview and visit
to his farm. Ann Sinclair's remarks were published in a 1995 interview with the AERO *Sun Times,* but I corroborated the story in a
2014 phone interview.

CHAPTER 7

I learned about Saskatchewan's conventional lentil industry from
Al Slinkard, who directed me to several references on the websites
of the Saskatchewan Pulse Growers and Pulse Canada.

CHAPTER 8

Al Slinkard was an equally helpful resource on the lentil variety
he released as Indianhead, for use as a green manure crop. To
trace the journey of this lentil before it made it into Slinkard's
hands, I consulted the USDA's Germplasm Resources Information
Network; and to follow it forward, to its emergence as the specialty food lentil Black Beluga, I referenced David Oien's article
"Indianhead Lentil," in the winter 1991 issue of *Synergy* magazine, as well as Dorothy Kalins's *Newsweek* article "The Taste-
makers," published September 18, 2005. In interviews, Oien
clarified that a key reason for developing a new trade name for the
lentil was the hurtful connotation of "Indianhead," the name of
the Agriculture and Agri-Food Canada research station that had
been researching lentil-based cropping systems. The station itself
had been named after a town in Saskatchewan that was report-
edly rife with unburied indigenous bodies after the smallpox epi-
demic that followed the arrival of fur traders. When Dave decided
to instead market the lentil under the name Black Beluga, he took

the additional step of registering this phrase as a trademark, to be held by Timeless Seeds. Mindful that the organic industry was on the verge of rapid growth, Dave wanted to protect his "deep green" product from co-optation. Within a few years, several of his peers across the country would find themselves outcompeted and undersold—by corporations who were interested in organic premiums but had no allegiance to organic principles.

Born and raised in western Montana, I ate at ShowThyme several times before I ever dreamed I would write this book. (When I was first served Black Beluga lentils, I thought they were some kind of exotic wild rice.)

IV. RIPE FOR REVOLUTION

In this section, I shift from archival and oral history sources to my own interviews, photographs, and field notes.

CHAPTER 9

Although other sources contributed to my understanding of the events in this chapter, it is based primarily on interviews and ethnography conducted with Jerry Habets and David Oien. Dawn McGee at Good Works Ventures, LLC, added key details.

CHAPTER 10

This chapter is based primarily on interviews and ethnography conducted with Casey Bailey and his family.

CHAPTER 11

Doug Crabtree and Anna Jones-Crabtree generously provided documentation to help me make sense of what I observed on their farm, including maps and a rotation plan. With the Crabtrees' permission, these documents have been published as an appendix to my *Ecology and Society* article, "Diversity, Flexibility, and the Resilience Effect: Lessons from a Social-Ecological Case Study on the Northern Great Plains, USA," and are available on the journal's website: http://www .ecologyandsociety.org/vol19/iss3/art45/appendix1.pdf.

CHAPTER 12

Three generations of Manuels helped me construct this chapter. The Timeless Seeds advertisement I describe is from the Winter 2010 Montana Organic Association newsletter, and the Havre demographics are 2008–12 averages reported by the US Census Bureau: http://quickfacts.census.gov/qfd/states/30/3035050.html.

CHAPTER 13

I reported this chapter at the Xerces Society's Pollinator Conservation Planning Short Course, held on June 14, 2012, at the Lewis and Clark Interpretive Center in Great Falls, Montana. For additional references on the history of the Natural Resources Conservation Service, see the bibliography.

CHAPTER 14

While most of the reporting for this chapter was conducted at Timeless Seeds' 2012 field tour and barbecue, I added quotes and information taken from interviews held before and after this event, where I felt they helped to clarify or explain. For the section on AERO's campaign to regulate GMO wheat, I drew on interviews with Jim Barngrover, as well as reporting by the AERO *Sun Times,* and two other journalists' coverage of the "steak dinner" scandal concerning the Montana Farmer Protection Bill:

Deines, Kahrin. "Biotechnology Seed Bill Tabled by Senators." *Associated Press/Helena Independent Record,* March

26, 2009. http://helenair.com/news/local/govt-and-politics
/biotechnology-seed-bill-tabled-by-senators/article
_05b7387e-08b4-56d6-9b3c-558eac25bc54.html.

Lowery, Courtney. "Did a Monsanto Hosted Dinner Kill the
Montana Farmer Protection Bill?" *New West,* March 25,
2009. http://newwest.net/topic/article/monsanto_hosts_din
ner_for_montana_legislators_on_seed_sampling_bill
/C559/L559/.

I also looked up the text of the bill on the Montana Legislature's
website (http://leg.mt.gov/bills/2009/billhtml/HB0445.htm) and con-
firmed membership of the Grow Montana coalition on that organization's website (http://growmontana.ncat.org). For sources on the
history of the Conservation Reserve Program, see the bibliography.

V. HARVEST

CHAPTER 15

This chapter is based on visits to Casey Bailey's farm and the
Timeless Seeds plant in Ulm, Montana. For more on the 2012
drought, see the bibliography.

CHAPTER 16

To construct the first section of this chapter, I drew on interviews and ethnography with David Oien, Sharon Eisenberg,
Jerry Habets, and Jacob and Courtney Cowgill, as well as the
Prairie Heritage Farm website: http://www.prairieheritagefarm
.com. The second section is based on interviews with Tuna
McAlpine and my visit to his ranch. Further reading on working
lands conservation and ecosystem services is suggested in the
bibliography.

CHAPTER 17

The first section of this chapter was reported at the 2012 Montana Organic Association Conference, held at the Holiday Inn in Helena, Montana, from November 29 to December 1—augmented by interviews conducted before and after the event. The middle section, "All the Wealth of the Earth," is based on unreleased video footage recorded for the Alternative Energy Resources Organization's Sustainable Agriculture Curriculum Development Project, 1993–94. Quotations and factual information presented in the final section are taken from interviews conducted in 2012 and 2013. Sources on the limits of the "food miles" approach to conscientious consumption are cited in the bibliography.

BIBLIOGRAPHY

AUTHOR'S NOTE

On the Industrialization of American Farming:

Berry, Wendell. *The Unsettling of America: Culture and Agriculture.* San Francisco: Sierra Club Books, 1977.

Hauter, Wenonah. *Foodopoly.* New York: New Press, 2012.

Pollan, Michael. *The Omnivore's Dilemma.* New York: Penguin, 2006.

Schlosser, Eric. *Fast Food Nation.* New York: Houghton Mifflin, 2001.

On Nitrogen Pollution and Marine Dead Zones:

Diaz, R. J., and R. Rosenberg, "Spreading Dead Zones and Consequences for Marine Ecosystems. *Science* 321 (2008): 926–29.

Eggler, Bruce. "Despite Promises to Fix It, the Gulf's Dead Zone is Growing." *Times Picayune,* June 9, 2007. http://blog.nola.com/times-picayune /2007/06/despite_promises_to_fix_it_the.html.

Millennium Ecosystem Assessment (MEA). Washington, DC: Island Press, 2005.

Tilman, D., K. G. Cassman, P. A. Matson, R. Naylor, and S. Polasky. "Agricultural Sustainability and Intensive Production Practices." *Nature* 418 (2002): 671–77.

On Jon Tester's US Senate Race:

Continetti, M. "How the West Was Won: Is Montana Senate Candidate Jon Tester the New Face of the Democratic Party?" *Weekly Standard* 12, no. 7 (2006). http://www.weeklystandard.com/Content/Public/Articles/000/000 /012/846btide.asp.

Egan, Timothy. "Fresh Off the Farm in Montana, a Senator-to-Be." *New York Times,* November 13, 2006. http://www.nytimes.com/2006/11/13/us /politics/13tester.html?pagewanted=1&_r=2.

Lowery, Courtney. "The 'Good Guy' Running for US Senate." *New West,* August 29, 2005. http://newwest.net/main/article/the_good_guy_running _for_us_senate/.

On the Life and Work of Joseph Epes Brown:

Brown, Joseph Epes. *The Sacred Pipe: Black Elk's Account of the Seven Rites of the Oglala Sioux.* Norman: University of Oklahoma Press, 1953.

Brown, Joseph Epes. *The Spiritual Legacy of the American Indian: Commemorative Edition with Letters while Living with Black Elk.* Edited by E. Brown, M. Brown Weatherly, and M. O. Fitzgerald. Bloomington, IN: World Wisdom, 2007.

PROLOGUE

On the 2012 Drought:

Eligon, John. "Widespread Drought Is Likely to Worsen." *New York Times,* July 20, 2012. http://www.nytimes.com/2012/07/20/science/earth/severe -drought-expected-to-worsen-across-the-nation.html?pagewanted=all.

Scheer, Roddy, and Doug Moss. "Dust Bowl Days Are Here Again." *Scientific American,* June 9, 2013. http://www.scientificamerican.com/article /dust-bowl-days-are-here-again/.

US Department of Agriculture Economic Research Service. "U.S. Drought 2012: Farm and Food Impacts." http://www.ers.usda.gov/topics/in-the -news/us-drought-2012-farm-and-food-impacts.aspx#.Ufk-rFOKQfo.

On Secretary of Agriculture Earl Butz and 1970s Farm Policy:

Critser, G. "Up, Up, Up!" In *Fat Land: How Americans Became the Fattest People in the World,* 7–19. New York: Houghton Mifflin Harcourt, 2004.

Friedmann, Harriet. "The New Political Economy of Food: A Global Crisis." *New Left Review* 197 (1993): 29–57.

Friedmann, Harriet. "The Political Economy of Food: The Rise and Fall of the Postwar International Food Order." *American Journal of Sociology* 88 (1982): 248–86.

On the Problems with Grain Monoculture:

Manning, Richard. *Against the Grain.* New York: North Point Press, 1994.

Pollan, Michael. *The Omnivore's Dilemma.* New York: Penguin, 2006.

Scott, James C. "Taming Nature." In *Seeing Like a State: How Certain Schemes to Improve the Human Condition Have Failed,* 262–306. New Haven, CT: Yale University Press, 1998.

On the Agronomy and Ecology of Lentil Farming:

Biederbeck, V. O., C. A. Campbell, V. Rasiah, R. P. Zentner, and G. Wen. "Soil Quality Attributes as Influenced by Annual Legumes Used as Green Manure." *Soil Biology and Biochemistry* 30, nos. 8–9 (1998): 1177–85.

Campbell, C. A., R. P. Zentner, F. Selles, V. O. Biederbeck, and A. J. Leyshon. "Comparative Effects of Grain Lentil–Wheat and Monoculture Wheat on

Crop Production, N Economy and N Fertility in a Brown Chernozem." *Canadian Journal of Plant Science* 72, no. 4 (1992): 1091–107.

Chen, Chengci, Karnes Neill, Macdonald Burgess, and Anton Bekkerman. "Agronomic Benefit and Economic Potential of Introducing Fall-Seeded Pea and Lentil into Conventional Wheat-Based Crop Rotations." *Agronomy Journal* 104, no. 2 (2012): 215–24.

Miller, P. R., Y. Gan, B. G. McConkey, and C. L. McDonald. "Pulse Crops for the Northern Great Plains. II. Cropping Sequence Effects on Cereal, Oilseeds, and Pulse Crops." *Agronomy Journal* 95, no. 4 (2003): 980–86.

Miller, P. R., B. G. McConkey, G. W. Clayton, S. A. Brandt, J. A. Staricka, A. M. Johnston, G. P. Lafond, B. G. Schatz, D. D. Baltensperger, and K. E. Neill. "Pulse Crop Adaptation in the Northern Great Plains." *Agronomy Journal* 94, no. 2 (2002): 261–72.

On the Limitations of Locavorism and the "Food Miles" Approach:

DeWeerdt, S. "Is Local Food Better?" *Worldwatch Institute,* 2009. http://www.worldwatch.org/node/6064.

McKie, R. "How the Myth of Food Miles Hurts the Planet." *Observer,* March 22, 2008. http://www.theguardian.com/environment/2008/mar/23/food.ethicalliving.

Schnell, S. M. "Food Miles, Local Eating, and Community Supported Agriculture: Putting Local Food in Its Place." *Agriculture and Human Values* 30 (2013): 615–28.

Weber, C. L., and H. S. Matthews. "Food-Miles and the Relative Climate Impacts of Food Choices in the United States." *Environmental Science and Technology* 42, no. 10 (2008): 3508–13.

CHAPTER 1

On the Land Sharing/Land Sparing Debate:

Fischer, J., Berry Brosi, Gretchen C. Daily, Paul R. Ehrlich, Rebecca Goldman, Joshua Goldstein, David B. Lindenmayer, et al. "Should Agricultural Policies Encourage Land Sparing or Wildlife-Friendly Farming?" *Frontiers in Ecology and the Environment* 6 (2008): 380–85.

Perfecto, Ivette, and John Vandermeer. *Nature's Matrix: Linking Agriculture, Conservation, and Food Sovereignty.* Sterling, VA: Earthscan, 2009.

Scherr, S. J., and J. A. McNeely. "Biodiversity Conservation and Agricultural Sustainability: Towards a New Paradigm of 'Ecoagriculture' Landscapes." *Philosophical Transactions of the Royal Society B—Biological Sciences* 363 (2008): 477–94.

Tscharntke, T., Yann Clough, Thomas C. Wanger, Louise Jackson, Iris Motzke, Ivette Perfecto, John Vandermeer, and Anthony Whitbread. "Global

Food Security, Biodiversity Conservation and the Future of Agricultural Intensification." *Biological Conservation* 151, no. 1 (2012): 53–59.

On the History of Grain Agriculture on the Great Plains and the Agricultural Treadmill:
Cochrane, Willard W. *The Development of American Agriculture: A Historical Analysis*. Minneapolis: University of Minnesota Press, 1979.

Cronon, William. *Nature's Metropolis: Chicago and the Great West*. New York: W. W. Norton, 1991.

Matheson, Nancy. "Overcoming Barriers to Sustainable Agriculture." *AERO Sun Times,* November/December 1983: 9–12.

Matheson, Nancy. "There's No Taste Like Home." *Montana Magazine,* January /February 2000: 39–44.

On the 1980s Farm Crisis and the Cost-Price Squeeze:
Davidson, O. G. *Broken Heartland: The Rise of America's Rural Ghetto*. Iowa City: University of Iowa Press, 1996.

Harl, N. E. *The Farm Debt Crisis of the 1980s*. Ames: Iowa State University Press, 1990.

On the Environmental and Health Impacts of Agrichemicals:
Carson, Rachel. *Silent Spring.* New York: Houghton Mifflin, 1962.

Harrison, Jill. *Pesticide Drift and the Pursuit of Environmental Justice*. Cambridge, MA: MIT Press, 2011.

Pimentel, David, H. Acquay, M. Biltonen, P. Rice, M. Silva, J. Nelson, V. Lipner, S. Giordano, A. Horowitz, and M. D'Amore. "Environmental and Economic Costs of Pesticide Use." *BioScience* 42, no. 10 (1992): 750–60.

On Climate Change and Agriculture:
Jensen, E. S., Mark B. Peoples, Robert M. Boddey, Peter M. Gresshoff, Henrik Hauggaard-Nielsen, Bruno J. R. Alves, and Malcolm J. Morrison. "Legumes for Mitigation of Climate Change and the Provision of Feedstock for Biofuels and Biorefineries: A Review." *Agronomy for Sustainable Development* 32 (2012): 329–64.

Lappé, Anna. *Diet for a Hot Planet.* New York: Bloomsbury, 2010.

Lemke, R. L., Z. Zhong, C. A. Campbell, and R. Zentner. "Can Pulse Crops Play a Role in Mitigating Greenhouse Gases from North American Agriculture?" *Agronomy Journal* 99, no. 6 (2007): 1719–25.

Vermeulen, S. J., B. M. Campbell, and J. S. Ingram. "Climate Change and Food Systems." *Annual Review of Environment and Resources* 37, no. 1 (2012): 195.

On the Chicago Counterculture and the Weather Underground:
Berger, D. *Outlaws of America: The Weather Underground and the Politics of Solidarity*. Oakland, CA: AK Press, 2006.

Gitlin, Todd. *The Sixties: Years of Hope, Days of Rage.* Rev. ed. New York: Random House, 1993.

Miller, James. *Democracy Is in the Streets: From Port Huron to the Siege of Chicago.* Rev. ed. Cambridge, MA: Harvard University Press, 1994.

The Weather Underground. Directed by Sam Green and Bill Siegel. New York: Docurama, 2004. DVD, 92 min.

CHAPTER 2

On the Commodity Payment System and Its Consequences:

Imhoff, Daniel. *Food Fight: The Citizen's Guide to the Next Food and Farm Bill.* 2nd ed. Healdsburg, CA: Watershed Media, 2012.

Winders, Bill. *The Politics of Food Supply: U.S. Agricultural Policy in the World Economy.* New Haven, CT: Yale University Press, 2012.

On the Early Organic Farming Movement in the US:

Belasco, Warren. *Appetite for Change: How the Counterculture Took on the Food Industry.* New York: Pantheon Books, 1989.

Conford, Philip. *The Origins of the Organic Movement.* Edinburgh, Scotland: Floris Books, 2001.

On Agroecology, Green Manures, and Biological Nitrogen Fixation:

Altieri, Miguel A. *Agroecology: The Science of Sustainable Agriculture.* 2nd ed. Boulder, CO: Westview Press, 1995.

Altieri, Miguel. "The Ecological Role of Biodiversity in Agroecosystems." *Agriculture, Ecosystems, and Environment* 74, no. 1 (1999): 19–31.

Crews, T. E., and M. B. Peoples. "Legume Versus Fertilizer Sources of Nitrogen: Ecological Tradeoffs and Human Needs." *Agriculture, Ecosystems, and Environment* 102, no. 3 (2004): 279–97.

Gliessman, Stephen R. *Agroecology: The Ecology of Sustainable Food Systems.* 2nd ed. Boca Raton, FL: CRC Press, 2006.

Magdoff, Fred, and Harold van Es. *Building Soils for Better Crops.* 3rd ed. Beltsville, MD: Sustainable Agriculture Network, 2010. http://www.sare.org/Learning-Center/Books/Building-Soils-for-Better-Crops-3rd-Edition.

Peoples, M. B., H. Hauggaard-Nielsen, and E. S. Jensen. "The Potential Environmental Benefits and Risks Derived from Legumes in Rotations." In *Nitrogen Fixation in Crop Production,* edited by David W. Emerich and Hari B. Krishnan. Agronomy Monograph Series 52. Madison, WI: American Society of Agronomy, Crop Science Society of America, Soil Science Society of America (ASA-CSSA-SSSA), 2009.

Vandermeer, John. *The Ecology of Agroecosystems.* Sudbury, MA: Bartlett and Jones, 2010.

CHAPTER 3

On Black Medic and Ley Farming:

Bell, Lindsay W., J. Lawrence, B. Johnson, B. O'Mara, and D. Kirby. "Ley Pastures—Their Fit in Cropping Systems." GRDC Advisor Updates. Canberra, Australia: Grains Research and Development Corporation. March 3–4, 2010. http://www.grdc.com.au/Research-and-Development/GRDC -Update-Papers/2010/09/LEY-PASTURES-THEIR-FIT-IN-CROPPING -SYSTEMS.

Chen, Chengci, with Jess Alger, Bob Bayles, David Buschena, Clain Jones, James Krall, Jon Kvaalen, Roy Latta, and John Paterson. *Survey and Economic Analysis of Montana Farmers Utilizing Integrated Livestock-Cereal Grain (Ley Farming) Systems.* Project Final Report. Sustainable Agriculture Research and Education. US Department of Agriculture, 2009. http://mysare.sare.org/mySARE/ProjectReport.aspx.

Clark, Andy, ed. "Medics." In *Managing Cover Crops Profitably.* 3rd ed., 152–59. Beltsville, MD: Sustainable Agriculture Network, 2007. http://www .sare.org/Learning-Center/Books/Managing-Cover-Crops-Profitably -3rd-Edition/Text-Version/Legume-Cover-Crops/Medics.

Lloyd, D. L., B. Johnson, K. C. Teasdale, and S. M. O'Brien. "Establishing Ley Legumes in the Northern Grain Belt—Undersow or Sow Alone." In *Proceedings of the 9th Australian Agronomy Conference,* edited by D. L. Michalk and J. E. Pratley. Wagga Wagga, Australia: Charles Stuart University, July 20–23, 1998. http://www.regional.org.au/au/asa/1998/3/019lloyd.htm.

Puckridge, D. W., and R. J. French. "The Annual Ley-Pasture System in Cereal-Ley Farming Systems of Southern Australia: A Review." *Agriculture, Ecosystems, and Environment* 9 (1983): 229–67.

On the New Western Energy Show:

Chaney, Albert O. "An Examination and Film Documentation of the New Western Energy Show 1976–77." Master's thesis, University of Montana, 1978.

On Parathion and Human Health:

Azaroff, L. S., and L. M. Neas. "Acute Health Effects Associated with Nonoccupational Pesticide Exposure in Rural El Salvador." *Environmental Research* 80, no. 2 (1999): 158–64.

Garcia, S., A. Abu-Qare, W. Meeker-O'Connell, A. Borton, and M. Abou-Donia. "Methyl Parathion: A Review of Health Effects." *Journal of Toxicology and Environmental Health Part B: Critical Reviews* 6, no. 2 (2003): 185–210.

Wright, Angus. *The Death of Ramón González: The Modern Agricultural Dilemma.* Austin: University of Texas Press, 2010.

CHAPTER 4

On the History of the Alternative Energy Resources Organization and the Northern Plains Resource Council:

AERO Sun Times, Summer 1994 (special twentieth-anniversary issue).

Charter, Anne Goddard. *Cowboys Don't Walk: A Tale of Two.* Billings, MT: Western Organization of Resource Councils, 1999.

Cochran, Kye. "Montana Rancher Resists Consolidation Coal Company's Attempts to Strip Mine His Property." *Mother Earth News,* January/February 1979. http://www.motherearthnews.com/nature-and-environment /strip-mining-consolidation-coal-company-zmaz79zsch.aspx.

On Progressive-Era Agrarian Populism and the Farmers Union:

Field, Bruce E. *Harvest of Dissent: The National Farmers Union and the Early Cold War.* Lawrence: University Press of Kansas, 1998.

Flamm, Michael W. "The National Farmers Union and the Evolution of Agrarian Liberalism, 1937–1946." *Agricultural History* 68 (1994): 54–80.

Goodwyn, Lawrence. *The Populist Moment: A Short History of the Agrarian Revolt in America.* Oxford: Oxford University Press, 1978.

National Farmers Union. "National Farmers Union History." http://www .nfu.org/about-nfu/history.

Pratt, William C. "The Farmers Union, McCarthyism, and the Demise of the Agrarian Left." *Historian* 58 (1996): 329–42.

CHAPTER 5

On the Decline of Public Agricultural Research Funding:

Buttel, Frederick H. "Ever Since Hightower: The Politics of Agricultural Research Activism in the Molecular Age." *Agriculture and Human Values* 22 (2005): 275–83.

Kloppenburg, Jack. *First the Seed: The Political Economy of Plant Biotechnology.* 2nd ed. Madison: University of Wisconsin Press, 2005.

On AERO's Farm Improvement Club Program:

Matheson, Nancy. "AERO Farm Improvement Clubs." *Journal of Pesticide Reform* 13, no. 1 (1993): 11.

Matheson, Nancy. "Montana's Farm Improvement Clubs Are a Collaborative Learning Community." *Sustainable Farming Quarterly* 5, no. 1 (1993): 1–5.

Rusmore, Barbara. "Reinventing Science Through Agricultural Participatory Research." PhD diss., Fielding Graduate University, 1996.

CHAPTER 6

On the Growth of the Organic Industry in the 1990s and 2000s:
Howard, Philip H. "Consolidation in the North American Organic Food Processing Sector, 1997 to 2007." *International Journal of Sociology of Agriculture and Food* 16, no. 1 (2009): 13–30.

Pollan, Michael. "Behind the Organic Industrial Complex." *New York Times Magazine,* May 13, 2001.

Raynolds, L. T. "The Globalization of Organic Agro-food Networks." *World Development* 32, no. 5 (2004): 725–43.

CHAPTER 7

On the Growth of the Conventional Lentil Industry in Saskatchewan:
Saskatchewan Pulse Growers Association. http://saskpulse.com.

Slinkard, A. E., and A. Vandenberg. "Lentil." In *Harvest of Gold: The History of Field Crop Breeding in Canada,* edited by A. E. Slinkard and D. R. Knott, 191–96. Saskatoon, SK: University Extension Press, 1995.

CHAPTER 8

On the History of Black Beluga/Indianhead Lentils:
Beiderbeck, V. O. "Replacing Fallow with Annual Legumes for Plowdown or Feed." In *Proceedings of the Symposium on Crop Diversification in Sustainable Agriculture Systems,* 46–51. Saskatoon: University of Saskatchewan, 1988.

Carlisle, Liz. "Making Heritage: The Story of Black Beluga Agriculture on the Northern Great Plains." *Annals of the Association of American Geographers* (forthcoming).

Carlisle, Liz. "Pulses and Populism." PhD diss., University of California, Berkeley, 2015.

On the Trade-off Between Crop Yield and Nutrient Density:
Benbrook, Charles M. 2007. "The Impacts of Yield on Nutritional Quality: Lessons from Organic Farming." Paper presented at the American Society for Horticultural Science Colloquium, "Crop Yield and Quality: Can We Maximize Both?" Scottsdale, AZ, July 18, 2007. http://www.organic-center.org/reportfiles/Hort_Soc_Colloquim_July_2007_FINAL.pdf.

Davis, Donald R., Melvin D. Epp, and Hugh D. Riordan. "Changes in USDA Food Composition Data for 43 Garden Crops, 1950 to 1999." *Journal of the American College of Nutrition* 23, no. 6 (2004): 669–82.

Fuhrman, Scott. "Nutrient Density." https://www.drfuhrman.com/library /article17.aspx.

Halweil, B. "Still No Free Lunch: Nutrient Levels in US Food Supply Eroded by Pursuit of High Yields." Organic Center, 2007. http://www.organic -center.org/reportfiles/YieldsReport.pdf.

On the Expansion of Organic and Conventional Lentil Farming in Montana:

Harmon A., T. Reusch, M. Fox, and M. Gaston. *Lentils: Gems in the Treasure State*. Bozeman: Montana State University, 2014.

CHAPTER 9

On Organic Conversion as a Philosophical, Existential Shift:

Bell, Michael. *Farming for Us All: Practical Agriculture and the Cultivation of Sustainability*. University Park: Pennsylvania State University Press, 2004.

Hassanein, Neva. *Changing the Way America Farms: Knowledge and Community in the Sustainable Agriculture Movement*. Lincoln: University of Nebraska Press, 1999.

Kirschenmann, Frederick L. *Cultivating an Ecological Conscience: Essays from a Farmer Philosopher*. Edited by Constance L. Falk. Lexington: University Press of Kentucky, 2010.

On Intercropping and the Mexican Milpa System:

Gliessman, Stephen R. "Chapter 15: Species Interactions in Crop Communities." In *Agroecology: The Ecology of Sustainable Food Systems*. 2nd ed., 205–16. Boca Raton, FL: CRC Press, 2006.

Liebman, M. "Polyculture Cropping Systems." In *Agroecology: The Science of Sustainable Agriculture*. 2nd ed., edited by Miguel A. Altieri, 205–18. Boulder, CO: Westview Press, 1995.

Malézieux, E., Y. Crozat, C. Dupraz, M. Laurans, D. Makowski, H. Ozier-Lafontaine, B. Rapidel, S. de Tourdonnet, and M. Valantin-Morison. "Mixing Plant Species in Cropping Systems: Concepts Tools and Models: A Review." *Agronomy for Sustainable Development* 29, no. 1 (2009): 43–62.

Vandermeer, John. *The Ecology of Intercropping*. New York: Cambridge University Press, 1989.

Wright, Angus. "Technology and Conflict." In *The Death of Ramón González: The Modern Agricultural Dilemma*, 140–87. Austin: University of Texas Press, 2010.

On the Use of Rotations and Cover Crops for Nutrient Management:

Davis, A. S., J. D. Hill, C. A. Chase, A. M. Johanns, and M. Liebman. "Increasing Cropping System Diversity Balances Productivity, Profitability

and Environmental Health." *PLoS ONE* 7, no. 10 (2012): doi:10.1371
/journal.pone.0047149.

Magdoff, Fred, and Harold van Es. *Building Soils for Better Crops.* 3rd ed.
Beltsville, MD: Sustainable Agriculture Network, 2010. Available for free
online at http://www.sare.org/Learning-Center/Books/Building-Soils-for
-Better-Crops-3rd-Edition.

Rick, T. L., C. A. Jones, R. E. Engel, and P. R. Miller. "Green Manure and
Phosphate Rock Effects on Phosphorus Availability in a Northern Great
Plains Dryland Organic Cropping System." *Organic Agriculture* 1, no. 2
(2011): 81–90.

CHAPTER 10

On Weed Ecology, Organic Weed Management, and the Agronomic Challenges Associated with Organic Transition:

Altieri, Miguel A. "Weed Ecology and Management." In *Agroecology: The
Science of Sustainable Agriculture.* 2nd ed., 283–306. Boulder, CO: Westview Press, 1995.

Menalled, F., C. A. Jones, D. Buschena, and P. R. Miller. "From Conventional
to Organic Cropping: What to Expect During the Transition Years."
Montana State University Extension Guide. http://msuextension.org
/publications/AgandNaturalResources/MT200901AG.pdf.

Mortensen, D. A., J. F. Egan, B. D. Maxwell, M. R. Ryan, and R. G. Smith.
"Navigating a Critical Juncture for Sustainable Weed Management."
BioScience 62, no. 1 (2012): 75–84.

CHAPTER 11

On the Conflict between Biological Time and Capitalist Time:

Boyd, William, and Michael Watts. "Agro-Industrial Just-in-Time: The
Chicken Industry and Postwar American Capitalism." In *Globalising
Food: Agrarian Questions and Global Restructuring,* edited by Michael
Watts and David Goodman, 139–65. London: Routledge, 1997.

Cronon, William. "Railroad Time." In *Nature's Metropolis: Chicago and the
Great West,* 74–80. New York: W. W. Norton, 1991.

Mann, S., and J. Dickinson. "Obstacles to the Development of a Capitalist
Agriculture. *Journal of Peasant Studies* 5 (1978): 466–81.

CHAPTER 12

On Rural "Food Deserts" and Improving Access to Organic Food:

Davio, Stephanie, Chris Ryan, and Jay Feldman. "The Real Story on the Affordability of Organic Food." *Pesticides and You* 31, no. 3 (2011): 9–18. http://www.beyondpesticides.org/organicfood/documents/true-cost .pdf.

Larsen, Steph. "Welcome to the Food Deserts of Rural America." *Grist,* January 21, 2011. http://grist.org/article/2011-01-21-welcome-to-the-food-deserts -of-rural-america/.

Morton, Lois Wright, and Troy C. Blanchard. "Starved for Access: Life in Rural America's Food Deserts." *Rural Realities* 1, no. 4 (2007): 1–10.

Pollan, Michael. "The Food Movement, Rising." *New York Review of Books,* June 10, 2010. http://www.nybooks.com/articles/archives/2010/jun/10/food -movement-rising/.

CHAPTER 13

On Agriculture and Pollinator Health:

Buchmann, Stephen L., and Gary Paul Nabhan. *The Forgotten Pollinators.* Washington, DC: Island Press, 1997.

Kremen Lab. University of California, Berkeley. http://nature.berkeley.edu /kremenlab/.

Rosner, Hillary. "Return of the Natives: How Wild Bees Will Save Our Agricultural System." *Scientific American,* August 20, 2013. http://www .scientificamerican.com/article/return-of-the-natives-how-wild-bees -will-save-our-agricultural-system/.

Xerces Society. http://www.xerces.org.

On US Agricultural Conservation Policy:

Cain, Zachary, and Stephen Lovejoy. "History and Outlook for Farm Bill Conservation Programs." *Choices* 19, no. 4 (2004): 37–42. http://www .choicesmagazine.org/2004-4/policy/2004-4-09.htm.

Franklin, Tim. "Land Program Looks Different to Investors, Farmers." *Chicago Tribune,* March 30, 1988. http://articles.chicagotribune.com/1988 -03-30/news/8803040790_1_farmland-ownership-conservation -reserve-program-farm-crisis.

Helms, Douglas, ed. *Readings in the History of the Soil Conservation Service.* US Department of Agriculture, 1992. http://www.nrcs.usda.gov/Internet /FSE_DOCUMENTS/stelprdb1043484.pdf.

Imhoff, Daniel. "The Conservation Era Begins—Again." In *Food Fight: The Citizen's Guide to the Next Food and Farm Bill.* 2nd ed., 48–52. Healdsburg, CA: Watershed Media, 2012.

McGranahan, D. A, P. W. Brown, L. A. Schulte, and J. C. Tyndall. "A Historical Primer on the U.S. Farm Bill: Supply Management and Conservation Policy." *Journal of Soil and Water Conservation* 68, no. 3 (2013): 68A–73A.

Orr, Richard. "Generations-old Soil Bank Idea Resurrected." *Chicago Tribune,* April 22, 1985. http://articles.chicagotribune.com/1985-04-22/news /8501230926_1_conservation-reserve-government-farm-programs -commodity-prices.

Wuerthner, George. "The Problems with the Conservation Reserve Program." *Counterpunch,* April 11–13, 2008. http://www.counterpunch.org /2008/04/11/the-problems-with-the-conservation-reserve-program/.

On the Problems with Chemical No-Till:

Mortensen, D. A., J. F. Egan, B. D. Maxwell, M. R. Ryan, and R. G. Smith. "Navigating a Critical Juncture for Sustainable Weed Management." *BioScience* 62, no. 1 (2012): 75–84.

Teasdale, J. R., C. B. Coffman, and R. W. Mangum. "Potential Long-Term Benefits of No-Tillage and Organic Cropping Systems for Grain Production and Soil Improvement." *Agronomy Journal* 99 (2007): 1297–1305.

Venterea, R. T., J. M. Baker, M. S. Dolan, and K. A. Spokas. "Carbon and Nitrogen Storage are Greater Under Biennial Tillage in a Minnesota Corn-Soybean Rotation." *Soil Science Society of America Journal* 70 (2006): 1752–62.

On the Financialization of Food:

Clapp, Jennifer. *Food.* Cambridge, UK: Polity Press, 2011.

Isakson, S. R. "Food and Finance: The Financial Transformation of Agrofood Supply Chains." *Journal of Peasant Studies* (2014): doi: 10.1080/ 03066150.2013.874340.

Russi, Luigi. *Hungry Capital: The Financialization of Food.* Hampshire, UK: John Hunt, 2013.

CHAPTER 14

On Farming for Better Soil Water Holding Capacity:

Magdoff, Fred, and Harold van Es. *Building Soils for Better Crops.* 3rd ed. Beltsville: Sustainable Agriculture Network, 2010, esp. 53–55, 92, 195. Available for free online at http://www.sare.org/Learning-Center/Books /Building-Soils-for-Better-Crops-3rd-Edition.

Merrill, S. D., D. L. Tanaka, J. M. Krupinsky, M. A. Liebig, and J. D. Hanson. "Soil Water Depletion and Recharge Under Ten Crop Species and Applications to the Principles of Dynamic Cropping Systems." *Agronomy Journal* 99 (2007): 931–38.

On Genetically Modified Organisms and the GMO Debate:

Benbrook, Charles M. "Impacts of Genetically Engineered Crops on Pesticide Use in the U.S.—The First Sixteen Years." *Environmental Sciences Europe* 24, no. 1 (2012): 1–13. http://www.enveurope.com/content/24/1/24.

Schurman, Rachel, and William Munro. *Fighting for the Future of Food.* Minneapolis: University of Minnesota Press, 2010.

Union of Concerned Scientists. "Genetic Engineering in Agriculture." http://www.ucsusa.org/food_and_agriculture/our-failing-food-system /genetic-engineering/.

On Crop Insurance and Access to Credit for Diversified and Organic Farmers:

O'Hara, Jeffrey K. *Ensuring the Harvest: Crop Insurance and Credit for a Healthy Farm and Food Future.* Washington, DC: Union of Concerned Scientists, 2012. http://www.ucsusa.org/assets/documents/food _and_agriculture/ensuring-the-harvest-full-report.pdf.

On Farmers and Health Insurance:

Brasch, Sam. "Why Don't Young Farmers Get Insured?" *Modern Farmer,* March 24, 2014. http://modernfarmer.com/2014/03/obamacare-imperfect -lifeline-new-farmers/.

Chang, Kuo-Liang, George L. Langelett, and Andrew W. Waugh. "Health, Health Insurance, and the Decision to Exit from Farming." *Journal of Family and Economic Issues* 32, no. 2 (2011): 356–72.

Zheng, Xiaoyong, and David Zimmer. "Farmers' Health Insurance and Access to Health Care." *American Journal of Agricultural Economics* 90, no. 1 (2008): 267–79.

CHAPTER 16

On Community Supported Agriculture:

Henderson, Elizabeth, and Robyn Van En. *Sharing the Harvest: A Citizen's Guide to Community Supported Agriculture.* Rev. and expanded ed. White River Junction, VT: Chelsea Green, 2009.

Hinrichs, C. C. "Embeddedness and Local Food Systems: Notes on Two Types of Direct Agricultural Markets." *Journal of Rural Studies* 16, no. 3 (2000): 295–303.

Local Harvest. "CSA Directory." http://www.localharvest.org/csa/.

On Conservation on Working Lands:

Charnley, Susan, Thomas Sheridan, and Gary P. Nabhan, eds. *Stitching the West Back Together: Conservation of Working Landscapes in the American West.* Chicago: University of Chicago Press, 2014.

Quivira Coalition. http://quiviracoalition.org/.

Sayre, Nathan F. *Working Wilderness: The Malpai Borderlands Group and the Future of the Western Range.* Tucson, AZ: Rio Nuevo Press, 2005.

CHAPTER 17

On Values-Based Supply Chains:

Food Hubs and Values-Based Supply Chains, University of California, Davis. http://asi.ucdavis.edu/sarep/sfs/VBSC.

Roep, Dirk, and Han Wiskerke. *Fourteen Lessons about Creating Sustainable Food Supply Chains.* Rural Sociology Group. Wageningen, Netherlands: Wageningen University, 2006.

Stevenson, G. W., and R. Pirog. "Values-Based Supply Chains: Strategies for Agrifood Enterprises of the Middle." In *Food and the Mid-Level Farm: Renewing an Agriculture of the Middle,* edited by Thomas A. Lyson, G. W. Stevenson, and Rick Welsh, 119–43. Cambridge, MA: MIT Press, 2008.

On Large-Scale and Policy Solutions for Transforming the Food System:

Institute for Agriculture and Trade Policy. http://www.iatp.org/.

La Via Campesina. http://viacampesina.org/en/.

National Sustainable Agriculture Coalition. http://sustainableagriculture .net/.

The characters in this book have their own ideas about how to change the food system, based on their considerable experience attempting to do it. Should you get the chance, I highly recommend asking them about it.

GLOSSARY

2,4-D. A common systemic herbicide used in the control of broadleaf weeds.

AGROECOLOGY. A scientific discipline and set of farming practices that seek to better understand and utilize ecological interactions within agricultural systems.

AGRONOMY. The science of producing and using plants for food, fuel, fiber, and land reclamation.

AG TASK FORCE. A subgroup of the Alternative Energy Resources Organization, founded in 1983 to develop programs, resources, and advocacy campaigns related to sustainable agriculture.

ALTERNATIVE ENERGY RESOURCES ORGANIZATION. Non-profit "citizens' renewable energy organization" founded in 1974 to promote alternatives to fossil fuel–based technologies. Headquartered in Helena, Montana.

AMMONIUM NITRATE. A chemical compound commonly used in agriculture as a high-nitrogen fertilizer; also used as an oxidizing agent in explosives. Although it can occur naturally, it is rare, and virtually all contemporary sources are synthetic.

BASE ACRES. A farm's crop-specific acreage eligible to participate in USDA commodity programs.

BLACK BELUGA LENTIL. Small, hard-seeded black lentil, first developed as a food crop by Timeless Seeds, which holds the trademark.

BLACK KABULI CHICKPEA. Trade name for a specialty chickpea variety of South Asian origin, distinguished by its black seed coat. Timeless Seeds holds the trademark.

BLACK MEDIC. A self-seeding annual legume that can be used as a semiperennial green manure or cover crop, particularly in dry areas, since it fixes relatively large amounts of nitrogen on low moisture. Also known as a lawn weed.

BROADLEAF. A flowering plant that is dicotyledonous, meaning its seed has two embryonic leaves, or cotyledons.

CHECKOFF. Program that collects funds from producers of a particular agricultural commodity and uses these funds to promote and do research on that particular commodity. In the United States, checkoff programs are overseen by the USDA, which can mandate participation, but are operated by industry trade groups.

CHEMICAL FALLOW. The use of herbicides to prevent vegetative growth on farmland that is not currently in production, for the purpose of weed control and soil moisture conservation.

COMBINE. A machine that harvests grain crops, so named because it combines three operations—reaping, threshing, and winnowing.

COMMUNITY SUPPORTED AGRICULTURE. A direct relationship between farmers and consumers, in which members typically pay in advance for a share or subscription and receive regular boxes of produce from the farm. By paying up front and accepting whatever products are seasonably available, members bear some of the risk typically absorbed solely by the farmer.

CONSERVATION RESERVE PROGRAM (CRP). A USDA land conservation program administered by the Farm Service Agency. In exchange for a yearly rental payment, farmers enrolled in the program agree to remove environmentally sensitive land from agricultural production and plant species intended to improve environmental health and quality.

COST-PRICE SQUEEZE. A period of increasing costs and simultaneous decreasing or stable prices. Within agriculture, a typical scenario involves commodity crop farmers facing increasing costs of fertilizer or other inputs and decreasing crop prices.

COVER CROP. A crop grown to protect the soil from erosion during the time of the year when it would otherwise be bare. Cover crops often function as green manures, and the terms may be used interchangeably.

COVER CROP COCKTAIL. A mixed cover crop that contains a diversity of plant species.

CROP ROTATION. The practice of growing a series of different types of crops in the same area in sequential seasons, typically to replenish nutrients and break pest and disease cycles.

CULTIVATION. The process of preparing land to raise crops, typically through plowing, or tillage. Also refers more generally to growing and caring for crops.

DEAD ZONES. Low-oxygen areas in the world's oceans and large lakes, caused by an increase in chemical nutrients, particularly nitrogen and phosphorous.

DIVERSITY-STABILITY HYPOTHESIS. Scientific hypothesis at the heart of conservation ecology, which holds that more biodiverse ecological communities are more stable and productive.

DRYLAND FARMING. The cultivation of crops without irrigation in regions with limited moisture.

DUST BOWL. A period of severe dust storms that greatly damaged the ecology and agriculture of the US and Canadian prairies during the 1930s, triggered by drought and erosion on improperly managed farmlands.

EARL BUTZ. US secretary of agriculture, 1971–76, best known for instructing farmers to plant "fencerow to fencerow" and "get big or get out."

ECOSYSTEM SERVICES. The benefits people obtain from ecosystems, including provisioning services such as food and water; regulating services such as flood and disease control; cultural services such as spiritual, recreational, and cultural benefits; and supporting services, such as nutrient cycling, that maintain the conditions for life on Earth.

EMMER. An ancient variety of wheat, often marketed as farro.

EROSION. The wearing away of soil by runoff water (water erosion), wind shear (wind erosion), or tillage.

FARM BILL. A comprehensive piece of legislation, reauthorized approximately every five years by Congress, that covers most federal government policies related to agriculture in the United States.

FARMERS UNION (officially the Farmers Educational Cooperative Union of America). The nation's second-largest farm organization, formed in 1902 to assist farmers in organizing cooperatives, fighting monopoly power, and advocating for farmer-friendly policies.

FARM IMPROVEMENT CLUB PROGRAM. Small grants program directed by the Alternative Energy Resources Organization from 1990 to 2000, to encourage groups of farmers to work together on common production and marketing challenges.

FARRO. Italian common name for emmer, sometimes also used to refer to two related species of ancient wheat, einkorn and spelt.

FOOD MILES. The distance food travels from where it is produced to where it is consumed.

GENETICALLY MODIFIED ORGANISMS (GMOS). Plants or animals that have been genetically engineered with DNA from bacteria, viruses, or other plants and animals. Typically, these are experimental combinations of genes from different species that do not occur in nature or in traditional crossbreeding.

GOLDEN TRIANGLE. An area of north-central Montana known for good wheat-growing conditions, located roughly between Conrad, Havre, and Great Falls.

GREEN MANURE. A crop grown for the main purpose of building up or maintaining soil fertility and organic matter, sometimes called a cover crop or plowdown.

HEIRLOOM VARIETIES. Varieties that have a history of being grown and shared within a family or community, in contrast to varieties developed for use in industrial agriculture. Sometimes called heritage varieties.

INCUBATOR FARM. A training farm that provides access to land, equipment, capital, and/or training for beginning farmers, who typically compensate their host farm by leasing a small parcel of land at reduced rates, paying tuition, or exchanging labor.

INDIANHEAD LENTIL. Lentil variety released by the University of Saskatchewan for use as a legume green manure crop. Now marketed as a food crop, under the trade name Black Beluga.

INOCULANTS. Microbial organisms used to promote plant health, typically by forming symbiotic relationships with the target crops, as with rhizobia bacteria and lentils.

INTERCROPPING. The agricultural practice of cultivating two or more crops in the same space at the same time, also known as polycropping.

KAMUT. Brand name of an ancient khorasan wheat variety, sold under a trademark that specifies organic production and prohibits hybridization or genetic engineering.

LAND SHARING. An approach to conservation ecology in which agricultural production and biodiversity conservation are integrated.

LAND SPARING. An approach to conservation ecology in which agricultural production and biodiversity conservation are separated, based on the theory that intensively farming certain parcels of land is the best way to spare remaining lands for habitat and ecosystem service provision.

LEGUMES. Plants—including lentils, beans, peas, clovers, and alfalfa—that form a symbiotic relationship with nitrogen-fixing bacteria living in their roots. These bacteria help supply the plants with nitrogen from the air that would otherwise be unavailable.

LOCAVORE. A person committed to eating locally produced food.

MILPA. An intercropping system prevalent throughout Latin America, typically centered on corn, beans, and squash, but often including several other crops. Also refers to a field managed according to this system.

MONOCULTURE/MONOCROPPING. Production of the same crop in the same field year after year.

NATURAL PRODUCTS EXPO WEST. The world's largest trade show for natural and organic products, hosted annually in Anaheim, California, since 1981.

NATURAL RESOURCES CONSERVATION SERVICE (NRCS). The primary federal agency that works with private landowners to help them conserve, maintain, and improve their natural resources, located within the US Department of Agriculture and formerly known as the Soil Conservation Service. The agency emphasizes voluntary, science-based conservation, technical assistance, partnerships, incentive-based programs, and cooperative problem solving at the community level.

NITROGEN FIXATION. The conversion of atmospheric nitrogen by bacteria to a form that plants can use. A small number of bacteria, including the rhizobia living in the roots of legumes, are able to make this conversion.

NODULES (or root nodules). Small growths on the roots of legumes, which house nitrogen-fixing rhizobia bacteria.

NORTHERN PLAINS RESOURCE COUNCIL. Nonprofit conservation and family agriculture organization founded in 1972 to protect working farm and ranch lands from the extractive industry. Headquartered in Billings, Montana.

NO-TILL. A system of planting crops without tilling the soil with a plow, disk, chisel, or other tillage implement. Also called zero tillage.

NUTRIENT DENSITY. Ratio of nutrient content to total energy content or calories.

OILSEED. A crop primarily grown for the oil in its seeds, such as sunflower or flax.

OPEN POLLINATED. Refers to plants pollinated by insects, birds, wind, humans, or other natural mechanisms. Because there are no restrictions on the flow of pollen between individuals, open-pollinated plants are more genetically diverse. This can cause a greater amount of variation within plant populations, which allows plants to slowly adapt to local growing conditions and climate from year to year. As long as pollen is not shared between different varieties within the same species, then the seed produced will remain true to type year after year, which means farmers and gardeners can save their own seed, rather than buying it each year, as they must do with hybrid varieties.

ORGANIC MATTER. The fraction of the soil composed of anything that once lived, including plants and animals in various states of decomposition, cells and tissues of soil organisms, and substances from plant roots and soil microbes. An important indicator of soil health and productivity.

PERENNIAL. Refers to plants and cropping systems with life cycles longer than two years.

POLLEN DRIFT. Accidental cross-pollination of different varieties of crops through natural dispersal methods, of particular concern to organic farmers located near growers of genetically modified organisms.

PULSE CROPS. Annual leguminous crops grown for their edible seed, such as lentils, peas, and dry beans.

QUONSET HUT. A lightweight prefabricated structure of corrugated galvanized steel, a semicircular cross section. Originally developed for military use and manufactured in large quantities during World War II, the Quonset hut is commonly used as a farm outbuilding.

RHIZOBIA BACTERIA. Bacteria that live in the roots of legumes and have a mutually beneficial relationship with the plant. These bacteria fix nitrogen, providing it to the plant in an available form, and in return receive energy-rich molecules that the plant produces.

ROCKY MOUNTAIN FRONT. The transition zone between the Rocky Mountains and the mixed-grass prairie.

SALINE SEEP. An expanse of salt crystals forming when underground salty water reaches the soil surface and evaporates.

SPELT. Ancient, hulled wheat variety with a lower gluten content than conventional wheat.

SPLIT PRODUCTION. Refers to farmers who grow a portion of their crop under organic certification but also farm noncertified land, sometimes using chemicals not allowed under organic regulations.

SUMMER FALLOW. The practice of allowing land to lie idle during the growing season. Also refers to the land under this form of management.

SUN TIMES. Periodical published by the Alternative Energy Resources Organization, from 1976 to the present.

SWATHER. A farm implement that cuts hay or small grain or pulse crops and forms them into a windrow.

TILLAGE. The mechanical manipulation of soil, generally for the purpose of loosening the soil, creating a seedbed, controlling weeds, or incorporating amendments.

TRANSGENIC. Containing one or more genes transferred from another species through genetic engineering.

TRIPLE BOTTOM LINE. Phrase coined by corporate responsibility advocate John Elkington to describe an accounting framework with three dimensions: social, financial, and environmental (or people, profit, and planet).

UNDERSOWING. Sowing one crop into a field in which another crop has already established, so that both crops develop at the same time.

VALUES-BASED SUPPLY CHAINS. Supply chains, or wholesale, non-direct-market channels where consumers receive information about the social, environmental, or community values incorporated into the production of a product, or the farm or ranch producing it.

ZERO TILLAGE. A system of planting crops without tilling the soil with a plow, disk, chisel, or other tillage implement.